TRUTHFULNESS, REALISM, HISTORICITY

In memory of my Grandmother

Barbara Ternent Hurst (1913–2009)

Truthfulness, Realism, Historicity

A Study in Late Antique Spiritual Literature

PETER TURNER

ASHGATE

Published by
Ashgate Publishing Limited
Wey Court East
Union Road
Farnham
Surrey, GU9 7PT
England

Ashgate Publishing Company
Suite 420
101 Cherry Street
Burlington
VT 05401–4405
USA

www.ashgate.com

British Library Cataloguing in Publication Data
Turner, Peter.
  Truthfulness, realism, historicity : a study in late antique spiritual literature.
  1. Religious literature – History and criticism. 2. Literature, Ancient – History and criticism. 3. Literature and society – History – To 1500. 4. Spiritual life – Early works to 1800. 5. Spiritual biography – Early works to 1800. 6. Hagiography – History – To 1500. 7. Realism in literature.
  I. Title
  809.9'3382'09015–dc23

Library of Congress Cataloging-in-Publication Data
Turner, Peter.
  Truthfulness, realism, historicity : a study in late antique spiritual literature / Peter Turner.
     p. cm.
  Includes bibliographical references (p.   ) and index.
  ISBN 978–0–7546–6954–8 (hardcover : alk. paper) – ISBN 978–0–7546–9715–2 (ebook) 1. Christian literature, Early – Greek authors – History and criticism.
  I. Title.
  BR67.T87 2012
  270.2–dc23   2011051253

ISBN 9780754669548 (hbk)
ISBN 9780754697152 (ebk)

MIX
Paper from
responsible sources
FSC® C018575
www.fsc.org

Printed and bound in Great Britain by the
MPG Books Group, UK

Contents

Abbreviations

AHB	Ancient History Bulletin
AR	Archivum Romanicum
ANRW	Aufstieg und Niedergang der römischen Welt
AS	Augustinian Studies
CS	Circerstian Studies
C&M	Classica and Mediaevalia
CQ	Classical Quarterly
COCR	Collecteana ordinis cistersiensium reformatorum
CSEL	Corpus Scriptorum Ecclesiasticorum Latinorum
ICS	Illinois Classical Studies
JECS	Journal of Early Christian Studies
JMEMS	Journal of Medieval and Early Modern Studies
JTS	Journal of Theological Studies
LCM	Liverpool Classical Monthly
MGH AA	Monumenta Germaniae Historica. Auctores Antiquissimi
MH	Museum Helveticum
NS	New Series
PG	Patrologia Graeca
PL	Patrologia Latina
PCPS	Proceedings of the Cambridge Philological Society
RA	Recherches augustiniennes
Repr.	Reprinted
RPLHA	Revue de philologie, de littérature et d'histoire ancienne
REA	Revue des études anciennes
REL	Revue des études latines
SP	Studia Patristica
SO	Symbolae Osloenses
TPAPA	Transactions and Proceedings of the American Philological Association
VC	Vigiliae Christianiae

Acknowledgements

This book had its origins in a DPhil thesis submitted in 2007 and subsequently much revised. As such, its debts to others are very considerable.

My DPhil supervisor Peter Heather has been a constant source of knowledge, shrewd judgement and generous encouragement for many a year and continues to be so. The same is true of my thesis examiners, Neil McLynn, and the late Robert Markus. It was a great privilege to make Prof. Markus's acquaintance before his sad death, and in the short time I knew him, his influence on me, and support for my work, were both invaluable.

I am very grateful to the various institutions who supported my doctoral research: the AHRC for two years of funding spent at UCL and Oxford respectively; the Alexander von Humboldt Stiftung which awarded me the Theodor Heuss Fellowship which made it possible to spend an excellent year in Jena in 2003-4; and finally Worcester College, Oxford, who awarded me the Martin Scholarship for the year 2004-5.

More recently, I am grateful to John Smedley and everyone at Ashgate Publishing for giving me this opportunity to get my work into print. I am particularly grateful to an anonymous reviewer whose suggestions have vastly improved the work, and refined some of its crasser claims.

The discussion of Theodoret's commitment to truthfulness and the notion of the 'Spontaneity Principle' in Chapter 1, and elements of the discussion of Augustine's spiritual lifestyle in Chapter 4, were published in my article in Philip Booth, Matthew J. Dal Santo, and Peter Sarris (eds), *An Age of Saints? Power, Conflict and Dissent in Early Medieval Christianity* (Leiden: Brill, 2011). I am grateful to be able to reproduce parts of them here. The basic concept of comparing hagiography and autobiography – discussed especially in Chapters 3 and 4 – was explored in my article 'Hagiography and Autobiography in the Late Antique West', in *Studies in Church History* 47 (Woodbridge: Boydell and Brewer, 2011).

Many thanks also go to the various people who have been generous enough to read, comment on, and correct my work over the years: (in no particular order) Philip Booth, Matthew J. Dal Santo, Luuk Huitink, Nell Aubrey, Jamie Buchanan, Margaret Snow, Henry Mead, Mark Edwards, Stefan Rebenich, Gillian Clark, Mark Vessey and Claudia Rapp (who very usefully asked 'are you arguing against the linguistic turn?'). A big thanks too to John Adams, Nigel

Greenhill, Malcolm Bracken, Jonathan Mitchell, Duncan Brett and Andrew Robinson, who have by turns encouraged, goaded, entertained, consoled and ignored – all necessary ingredients in successful scholarship.

A particular thanks go to three people who over the years have all in different ways served as midwives for my ideas: Chris Barrett, Damian Caluori and Gloria Ayob.

I am very grateful to my parents for all their support.

Introduction
Boethius in Exile

When I saw you weeping in your grief I knew at once that you were wretchedly banished; but how remote was that banishment I should not have known if your speech had not told me. But how far from your homeland have you strayed! Strayed, not driven, I say; or if you prefer to be thought of as driven, then how far have you driven yourself! For in your case it could never have rightly been possible for anyone else to do this. You must remember what your native country is: not one, like that of the old Athenians, governed by the rule of many, but 'There is one ruler, one king' (Homer, *Iliad*, ii.204–5) who delights in the great number of its citizens, not in their expulsion; to be guided by his hand and obey his justice is true freedom ... So I am more moved by the sight of you than of this place ... [1]

Thus Philosophy consoled Boethius as he sat, incarcerated and in exile, awaiting possible execution in the twilight days of Theoderic's reign in Italy. The passage cited above is the beginning of Philosophy's 'gentle remedies' for Boethius' soul; it represents a turning point in a text which, amongst other things, traces a journey from the pain of one type of exile, to the awareness, and resolution, of another. In time, Boethius would come to recognize his exile from God's heavenly kingdom as of immeasurably greater importance. Whilst earthly enemies had caused his earthly exile, Boethius had to acknowledge that he alone was responsible for his spiritual one, before – guided by Philosophy, and by obeying God – he could be liberated from it. To his earthly exile, however, Philosophy could provide no solution, not because the machinations of his enemies were necessarily inescapable, but because, in contrast to his real exile, earthly banishment constituted only an illusory problem.

This passage from Boethius' *Consolation of Philosophy* presents a problem of interpretation which will be very familiar to scholars of late antiquity. There is a natural intuition to imagine that many works from the period contain two really quite different types of information: on the one hand, a factual content at least purporting to relate to a world of events outside and prior to the text;

---

[1] Boethius, *Philosophiae Consolationis Libri Quinque* 1.5.4–25, ed. Rudolf Peiper (Leipzig, 1871), tr. S.J. Tester in S.J. Tester, Hugh Fraser Stewart and Edward Kennard Rand (trs.), *Boethius: The Theological Tractates and the Consolation of Philosophy* (London/New York, reprinted 1973), p. 163.

on the other, an intellectual content much less directly related to the former world, more self-enclosed, and detectable chiefly through a textual analysis of such things as rhetoric, genre, and ideology. Such a duality is often detected in many types of late antique literature, including hagiographies and religious autobiographical writings, forms which constitute the basis of the material discussed in this book.

Of course, this is a manifestation of a much broader, philosophical issue: can a text, even a purportedly 'historical' one, ever reflect the world outside itself, or is it ultimately an entity understandable only in its own terms? The latter half of the twentieth century witnessed a 'linguistic turn' across the humanities stemming from the rise of Structuralism: scholars of many different disciplines developed an enhanced awareness of the fundamental conceptual difference between text and world, questioned the ability of the former to represent the latter, and reconsidered the writer's status as the locus and the arbiter of meaning. However, though these concerns have had a very widespread impact, the nature of late antique society justifies them in a very particular and direct way. Throughout the Roman world, generations of the elite underwent a strict and conservative education overwhelmingly literary in its emphasis: its most systematic achievement was to beat into its charges – literally as well as metaphorically – common codes of reading, writing, speaking and interpretation. The values of this heritage, whose results appear by turns elegant and stifling, may seem the antithesis of straightforward truthfulness. The historian's natural suspicion of the texts produced by this society can be aggravated by the transcendental metaphysics accepted by nearly all late antique thinkers, both pagan and Christian. For them, the world of events constituted the lowest level of reality; permeated with illusion, it was only dimly reflective of the truth. Even if not consciously misleading, late antique writers may simply not have regarded the rich and detailed world of events as an object of profound interest, at least not in its own right, and not in the way that most modern historians do. Since so much narrative information about this period occurs in works of a highly ideological and stylized nature, scholars are therefore constantly confronted with the question of how, if at all, their content can be interpreted historically.

It is important to acknowledge, however, that a certain notion of historicity can be attributed to either type of information contained within the sort of text discussed above. To speak of a factual content is not necessarily to refer to a content which is simple or banal. Rather, it corresponds to an entire notion of historical reality in which events are seen as discrete, prominent, and causally related. For example, in the early parts of the *Consolation*, Boethius tells readers about his career, his enemies at court, his political fall and punishment. For a historian of late Ostrogothic Italy, such a factual account (whether or not he agrees with its details) is likely to be of great interest.[2] On the other hand, as a religious and philosophical meditation, the *Consolation* offers access to a different type of reality: namely the mental world of the author and his society. This second content would probably be of greater interest to an intellectual historian and may, for example, be seen as a valuable source for the problem of how late antique Christians integrated Platonic philosophy into their theology. An intellectual historian would not necessarily deny that real life events had affected Boethius' thought (for one thing he seems exemplary of the intuitive view that 'misery and mysticism are related facts')[3] but precise biographical details would be considered as of secondary importance compared to the rich intellectual life which gives him such a prominent place in a different kind of history – the history of ideas.[4]

For scholars of late antiquity in particular, then, the historical method often assumes a division between two broad types of information: a factual or literal content on the one hand, an intellectual, or (to be more specific to the concerns of much late antique literature) spiritual content on the other. The distinction is not just notional; the very act of interpretation often takes the form of an exercise in separation, an attempt to discover where one type of reality begins and the other ends. As we shall later see, this can be a very complex process, and the historian's entire response to a text as a source for either factual and/or intellectual reality, may hang on the interpretation of highly contestable details.

The central purpose of the current book is to question this duality and, in doing so, to articulate a different notion of historicity. It questions both its existence within late antique literature, and also the corresponding attempt to identify and exploit it which often constitutes the historical method. By questioning it, it does not claim this duality is wholly misplaced, for there are certain scholarly questions which rightly invite such a distinction; rather that, the habitual imposition of this distinction can project an incomplete view, and conceal certain notions of historicity, and certain types of historical reality into which scholars could profitably enquire. The distinction between the intellectual and the factual, akin to what R.G. Collingwood called the 'inside' and 'outside' of events, is certainly central to religiously-focused narrative writing, as the case

---

[2]   E.g. John Moorhead, *Theoderic in Italy* (Oxford, 1992), pp. 220–22.

[3]   'car misère et mysticisme sont des faits connexes': André-Jean Festugière, 'Cadre de la mystique hellénistique', *Aux sources de la tradition chrétienne: Mélanges Goguel* (Neuchâtel, 1950), p. 84.

[4]   E.g. Anna Crabbe, 'Literary Design in the *De Consolatione Philosophiae*', in M. Gibson (ed.), *Boethius: His Life, Thought and Influence* (Oxford, 1981), which has a major philosophical component.

of Boethius suffices to show.[5] But, runs the argument of the current book, it is equally central to human religious experience, and therefore to religious history more broadly. The duality extends, in other words, far beyond the written text, to a realm of experience in which there was a constant, complex, mutual interplay between the factual and the intellectual, between the attitudes of believers and the phenomenal world around them. Furthermore, the relationship was not simply oppositional, but could take many complex and complimentary forms; life could imitate art just as surely as art claimed to imitate life.

I have termed the sources on which this argument depends 'spiritual narratives'; that is, written works, or parts of written works which purport to relate to real events but whose principal focus are religious or philosophical truths. Indeed, the events in question are usually presented by their authors as evidence for, or consequences of, these truths. This means, in practice, two main types of text: hagiographies i.e. works dedicated to people whose lives were believed to be exemplary of higher truths, and 'spiritual autobiographies', a much more diverse group of writings in which authors lay out doctrinal positions, relate them to personal experiences, and consider the relation of their own lives to deeper realities. The passage from Boethius discussed above is a good example of this second category. Although each type of writing is treated in a separate section, the basic objective in each case is the same: to demonstrate a much greater continuity between the written texts and the lives they relate than is usually accepted.

The remainder of this introduction will attempt to explain in more detail the historical and philosophical issues at stake, the way in which previous scholars have responded to them, and the approach to them pursued throughout this book. A major reason for beginning with a discussion of Boethius' *Consolation* is because, on the face of it, the division between the factual and intellectual contents of the work appears so straightforward. Few other late antique authors seem to justify the conceptual separation so thoroughly and this is strongly attested in the existing literature on Boethius.[6] Indeed, the division

---

[5]   R.G. Collingwood, *The Idea of History* (Oxford, 1946), p. 213.

[6]   Crabbe, 'Literary Design in the *De Consolatione Philosophiae*'. Jo-Marie Claassen also studies the work from a purely intellectual perspective, and doubts whether much of the factual material contained within it is genuinely autobiographical: *Displaced Persons* (1999), p. 168. Henry Chadwick, *Boethius: The Consolations of Music, Logic, Theology and Philosophy* (Oxford, 1981) contains a very clear division between the two types of content: the first section deals with predominantly biographical issues, before the work moves onto intellectual concerns. Jon Marenbon's *Boethius* (Oxford, 2003) is similarly structured: an early biographical section (pp. 7–10) is fairly self-enclosed, and Chapter 8 ('Interpreting the *Consolation*') includes little analysis of the work's biographical information, tackling instead

between factual and intellectual seems to be reflected in the very structure of the *Consolation* itself: whilst the early sections detail earthly events, the spiritual process soon takes over almost completely; the passage cited is more or less at the turning point. Furthermore, the factual/intellectual border also appears to be signalled by a clear shift from literal to metaphorical language: the language of exile is first used in a political sense then given a philosophical meaning as a metaphor for man's earthly condition.

But is this transition between literal and metaphorical, between factual and intellectual, really so straightforward? And does it correspond neatly to our distinction between different notions of historical reality? As far as the latter question is concerned, there is one clear difference. For Boethius, the types of exile he describes do not represent interests which are merely alternative; rather, they exist in a strict hierarchy rooted in his Christian-Platonist world view. The central message of the *Consolation* is that the profound, eternal truths revealed by Philosophy are of vastly greater significance than earthly contingencies: the contemplation of the former inevitably involves a recognition of the latter's unimportance. Therefore, although it is entirely possible to treat one or other concern, there exists a type of information which only emerges if we examine the hierarchical relationship which connects them. An intellectual historian may, like Boethius himself, find Philosophy's message of greater significance but, if so, it is for different reasons. The danger for a factual historian is to imagine that the transition from literal to metaphorical language denotes a move from the real to the metaphorical or imaginary. Quite the contrary: Boethius, like other late antique thinkers, accorded to human language the same lowly ontological status possessed by the rest of the sensible world. Consequently, according to this view, language became more metaphorical the more real, i.e. ontologically superior, its referent.[7]

This may seem like a rather technical point whose only relevance to our discussion is to confirm the necessary distance between the text and the world beyond it. But this would be simplistic. What Philosophy encourages in her charge is not an abandonment of language, but its correct use in contemplation. She encourages Boethius to undertake a meditation on the aspects of likeness

---

what its author regards as the text's main interpretative problem: the relationship between Christianity and Philosophy (esp. p. 154).

    [7]   For this aspect of late antique thought, see Rein Ferwerda, *La signification des images et des métaphores dans la pensée de Plotin* (Groningen, 1965), pp. 1–5; Richard T. Wallis, *Neoplatonism* (London, 1972), pp. 42–4; Margaret Ferguson, 'St Augustine's Region of Unlikeness: The Crossing of Exile and Language', *The Georgia Review*, 29 (1975); Peter Crome, *Symbol und Unzulänglichkeit der Sprache: Jamblichos, Plotin, Porphyrios, Proklos* (München: W. Fink, 1970).

and unlikeness present in the relationship between the literal aspect of the world around him on the one hand, and its real meaning on the other. What seems like a purely literary device could, from another viewpoint, be treated as something more active and experiential: the exercise of a philosophical technique.

The personification of Philosophy could potentially be treated in a similar way. No-one, I think, would deny that this deserves to be called a 'device', any thorough analysis of which would include reference to the playful rules of Menippean satire, to the tradition in classical literature of personification, and to the status Christian authors accorded to philosophy. But might a purely inter-textual analysis overlook the possibility that the device in question not merely embellishes the text, but represents another aspect of Boethius' experience: namely the strange sense of exteriority often produced by rational introspection?[8]

And what about the chains around the author's neck?[9] In Henry Chadwick's words, 'this ... is primarily a symbol of his earth-bound condition. It may be literal as well as symbolic; one cannot be sure, for his physical prison is simultaneously the counterpoint of the Platonic prison of his soul from which he seeks liberation.'[10] Since the detail is unverifiable, Chadwick's reserve is entirely appropriate. Of significance to us, however, is the major difference implicit in each of the possibilities he mentions. An entirely fictive chain hints at a literary Boethius, decorating his account with pathetic and metaphorical detail. Imagined in this way, the text remains a text, and one implicitly contrasted with the extra-textual realities of the writer's world. A literal chain, by contrast, suggests a practice of spiritual-minded observation, an active interpretation of sensible reality as a realm replete with symbolic truths. An intellectual history which described Boethius purely in terms of his ultimate philosophical convictions might overlook the role of his environment and recent life in guiding his meditations. Similarly, a factual history which saw his captive musings only as a source for the events which preceded them would ignore a major sphere of the author's activity. The purpose of the interpretations so far advanced is not to provide conclusive answers to these questions but simply to demonstrate that by considering the interaction between the factual and intellectual aspects of the *Consolation*, rather than simply prising them apart, we may at least begin to consider a realm of religious experience which might otherwise go unnoticed.

Later in this introduction, we shall consider Boethius further. The immediate task, however, is to consider the wider relevance to late antique scholarship of the

---

[8]   'ait mihi subito sive ego ispe sive alius quis, extrinsecus sive intinsecus, nescio; nam hoc ipsum est quod magnopere scire molior' Augustine, *Soliloquia* 1.1, ed. H. Fuchs, *Selbstgespräche; Von der Unsterbichkeit der Seele* (Munich, 1986).

[9]   Boethius, *The Consolation of Philosophy* 1.2.25–7.

[10]   Chadwick, *Boethius*, p. 226.

problems which his case exemplifies. Nothing reveals it more clearly than saints' *lives*, or hagiographies, a type of writing as notorious as it is vital to the field. The general importance of hagiographies in our period lies not merely in their spectacular rise as a form; the very fact this type of writing came to prominence ensures that a relatively large proportion of our narrative information from late antiquity (not to mention the subsequent mediaeval period) is contained within works of this type. It should be understood from the outset that this book uses the term 'hagiography' in reference to a wide range of works, both Greek and Latin, pagan and Christian, collective and individual. This convenience mirrors a tradition of scholarship which, though recognizing the very specific circumstances in which each work was produced, has also emphasized the common culture and intellectual background on which they drew.[11]

Within the context of the present work, hagiographies have a more specific importance. Like Boethius' *Consolation*, they are often read in expectation of two different types of information: a factual content on the one hand, an intellectual content on the other. To be specific, they describe phenomena believed to be indicative, in various ways, of realities which transcend the lowly confines of the sensible world. The subjects of hagiographies – holy men and (less frequently) women – are perhaps best defined as those who grasp reality in a manner which vastly exceeds the abilities of ordinary people. As Michael Williams has recently argued, the main effect of the holy man's presence in hagiography is to expose to the reader, albeit in an incomplete and provisional way, the very nature of reality in a deep, spiritual sense.[12] As a result, works of this kind are characterized by many features alien to modern historical writing. Undoubtedly the most notorious of these are miracles – events claimed by the author to be historical facts, but causally explicable only as divine interventions.

---

[11] This tendency is clear from the juxtaposition of papers on pagan and Christian, of collective and single works in a collection such as Tomas Hägg and Philip Rousseau (eds), *Greek Biography and Panegyric in Late Antiquity* (Berkeley, 2000), and also from directly comparative work e.g. Patricia Cox (Miller), *Biography in Late Antiquity: a Quest for the Holy Man* (Berkeley, 1983). E.R. Dodds, *Pagan and Christian in an Age of Anxiety: Some Aspects of Religious Experience from Marcus Aurelius to Constantine* (Cambridge, 1965); Salvatore Pricoco, *Monaci, Filosofi, e Santi: Saggi di storia della cultura tardoantica* (Messina, 1992); John Dillon, 'Die Vita Pythagorica – ein "Evangelium"', in Michael von Albrecht (ed.) *Jamblich: Peri tou Pythagoreiou biou. Pythagoras: Legende – Lehre – Lebensgestaltung* (Darmstadt, 2002), pp. 295–302; Mark Edwards, *Neoplatonic Saints: the Lives of Plotinus and Proclus by their Students* (Liverpool, 2000).

[12] 'These lives perhaps functioned not in the imperative but rather in the *indicative*. They represented a proposition about the world in which their readers lived': Michael Williams, *Authorised Lives in Early Christian Biography* (Cambridge, 2008), p. 183.

This highly ideological content has won for hagiographies a reputation as difficult historical sources. We frequently encounter in late antique scholarship the claim that they are, to a greater or lesser extent, unhistorical; that they 'cannot bear too much reality',[13] that elements of them are disingenuous,[14] that a particular text is 'more hagiographic than historical',[15] that lives are not the same as *Lives*,[16] that verisimilitude was as important as strict historicity.[17] These views are sufficiently widespread to make extensive elaboration unnecessary. Sometimes, as in the cases just referenced, these positions are elaborated explicitly. But often, within the course of a particular analysis, the antithetical formula – historical v. hagiographical – serves almost as a basic principle of interpretation: self-evident and in need of little justification.[18]

Before commenting on the legitimacy of this intuition, let us reflect on the various historiographical approaches that spring from it. The sheer quantity of hagiographical writing from late antiquity means that even historians of non-religious history are often obliged to assess pieces of information contained within such works on an *ad hoc* basis; it would be foolish to deny that this is sometimes legitimate. A similar, but more extended, application of this technique can occur where a certain hagiography happens to be a rare or unique source for a particular region and/or period; this is especially relevant for social and political historians. When analysed in this way, the texts' ideological content can become, in a negative way, a tool for identifying genuine factuality:

---

[13] Stephanos Efthymiadis, 'Two Gregories and Three Genres: Autobiography, Autohagiography and Hagiography', in Jostein Børtnes and Tomas Hägg (eds), *Gregory of Nazianzus: Images and Reflections* (Copenhagen, 2006), p. 246.

[14] Averil Cameron, *Christianity and the Rhetoric of Empire: the Development of Christian Discourse* (Berkeley, 1991), p. 113. A more extreme expression of this view is Timothy D. Barnes, *Early Christian Hagiography and Roman History* (Tübingen, 2010), esp. pp. 151–233.

[15] Andrea Sterk, *Renouncing the World yet Leading the Church: the Monk-Bishop in Late Antiquity* (Cambridge MA, 2004), p. 106.

[16] Neil McLynn, 'A Self-Made Holy Man: The Case of Gregory Nazianzen', *Journal of Early Christian Studies* 6:3 (1998), p. 483.

[17] Claudia Rapp, 'Storytelling as Spiritual Communication in Early Greek Hagiography: the Use of *Diegesis*', *JECS* 6 (1998), p. 443; C.R. Ligota, '"This story is not true". Fact and Fiction in Antiquity', *Journal of the Warburg and Courtauld Institutes* 45 (1982), p. 3.

[18] The ubiquity of this assumption is noted by Thomas Pratsch, 'Exploring the Jungle: Hagiographical Literature between Fact and Fiction', in Averil Cameron (ed.), *Fifty Years of Prosopography: the Later Roman Empire, Byzantium and Beyond* (Oxford, 2003), p. 62.

information which, in Ferdinand Lotter's phrase, is *tendenzneutral*[19] i.e. most incidental to the hagiographer's explicit aim of praising a saint, is considered to be of the greatest reliability and interest. It is in this spirit, for example, that E.A. Thompson, following Lotter, praises Eugippius' 'magnificent biography' of Severinus for its wealth of information about the collapse of Roman Noricum.[20]

An inverse approach has been followed by scholars such as Patricia Cox Miller and Alison Goddard Elliot. Cox Miller adopts a 'mythical perspective' towards the pagan sage and Christian saint;[21] Elliot investigates the prevalence in hagiographies of folkloric themes. Whilst not denying that hagiographies may contain some factual truth, their approach is first and foremost textual in focus. If we can describe the object of their research as historical reality, it is a cultural and intellectual one in which the question of factual accuracy is indefinitely suspended. Indeed, as Goddard Elliot states, although hagiography as a genre includes a basic premise of truthfulness, fiction is actually more revealing than fact for a study of this type since it more directly exposes the mental worlds under consideration.[22] As James Howard-Johnston and Averil Cameron have observed, this sort of approach to hagiography and sanctity, which follows a literary and structuralist paradigm, has proved dominant in recent decades.[23]

Although these approaches aim at different kinds of reality, they clearly spring from the same scholarly intuition that the content of hagiographies is of a twofold nature, and that the historical method involves delineating them and privileging one type of content above the other. But where does the border between them lie? At one extreme, are saints and their activities basically idealized inventions of the hagiographer? Or, at the other, do they fundamentally attest to real lives in particular times and places? Of course, these questions have no simple answers. The sheer range of late antique hagiographies is such

---

[19]   Ferdinand Lotter, *Severinus von Noricum*: *Legende und historische Wirklichkeit* (Stuttgart, 1976), p. 179.

[20]   E.A. Thompson, *Romans and Barbarians* (Wisconsin, 1982), p. 115. Only the last and shortest section examines Severinus' saintly activities.

[21]   Cox (Miller), *Biography in Late Antiquity*, p. xii.

[22]   Alison Goddard Elliot, *Roads to Paradise: Reading the Lives of the Early Saints* (Hanover/London, 1987), pp. 10–11.

[23]   James Howard-Johnston, 'Introduction', in James Howard-Johnston and Paul Antony Hayward (eds), *The Cult of Saints in Late Antiquity and the Early Middle Ages: Essays on the Contribution of Peter Brown* (Oxford, 1999), p. 15; Averil Cameron, 'On Defining the Holy Man', in Howard-Johnston and Hayward (eds), *The Cult of Saints in Late Antiquity and the Early Middle Ages*, p. 36. A *tour de force* of this approach is Averil Cameron's own work, *Christianity and the Rhetoric of Empire* (Berkeley, 1991), esp. 1–14 for discussion of discourse theory.

that some works have a better reputation for factual accuracy than others;[24] a historian may be interested both in the factual and intellectual aspects of texts, and may recognize the complexity of their relationship. Nonetheless, the crucial point for us is not merely that the historical method tends towards separation, but that the relationship between the factual and intellectual aspects tends to be imagined as innately oppositional. A representative statement of this view is found in Clare Stancliffe's study of the *Life of Martin*: hagiographies, she claims, are always written more or less about a person, and, conversely, more or less about an ideal.[25] The methodology associated with this claim is extremely informative. Stancliffe argues that Sulpicius wrote about Saint Martin far more accurately than many earlier scholars recognized.[26] A major piece of evidence she advances in support of this claim is that many of his actions lack inter-textual models, thus suggesting that they really happened. For example, Martin tears his cloak in two on a cold night and gives half to a freezing beggar: for Stancliffe, the truthfulness of this action lies not only in its general plausibility but also in the absence of any direct biblical parallel.[27] More often in modern historiography, we encounter the logical flipside of this argument: namely that any detail with too strong a textual (often biblical) echo is likely to be ideologically motivated *ergo* factually suspect.[28]

The intention here is not to attack this distinction *per se*. We should, however, reflect on the consequences of invoking it. One major problem it raises is the question of whether late antique writers and readers themselves believed the contents of hagiography. In this regard, one widespread and defining characteristic of the genre has received much less attention than it deserves: namely the statements hagiographers make about their own works and more specifically their guarantees to write truthfully. Such statements, of course, pose many complex questions: firstly, what precisely did hagiographers agree to

---

[24]   John Dillon, 'Holy and not so Holy: On the Interpretation of late antique Biography', in Brian McGing and Judith Mossman (eds), *The Limits of Ancient Biography* (Swansea, 2006), p. 156; Barnes, *Early Christian Hagiography and Roman History*, pp. 323–4.

[25]   Clare Stancliffe, *St. Martin and his Hagiographer* (Oxford, 1983), p. 315. Note, likewise, the contrast between historical truth and intellectual content implicit in Averil Cameron's description of Christian saints' *lives*: 'The *lives* are far from bare records. They are full of meaning, signs by which Christians taught one another how to interpret the present and past and how to live in the future': *Christianity and the Rhetoric of Empire* (Berkeley, 1991), p. 146.

[26]   Her principal target is Ernest-Charles Babut, *Saint Martin de Tours* (Paris, 1912).

[27]   Stancliffe, *St. Martin and his Hagiographer*, p. 321.

[28]   E.g. René Nouailhat on the miracles of Honoratus: 'les "bêtes venimeuses" et les "serpents innombrables" qui peuplent le "désert redoutable" sortent de la Bible plus que de la rocaille de *Lerina*', *Saints et Patrons* (Paris, 1988), p. 115.

and how did their audiences understand it? To what extent did their notion of truthfulness correspond to that of a modern historian? How distant from the audience's own experience of the world was the world of hagiography supposed to be? Whatever the ultimate answers to these questions, the purportedly truthful stance of hagiographers should be regarded as an important *explanandum*. For unless we consider the intellectual context in which the texts were produced and the assumptions underpinning them, then we risk leaving something out of the picture. A factual historian can admire a hagiography precisely because its religious function, i.e. the very quality that makes it a hagiography as opposed to something else, does not predominate. (The *Life of Severinus* is indeed a fascinating source for the end of Roman Noricum, but Eugippius would surely not have been flattered by Thompson's description of it as a 'magnificent hagiography' for this reason alone.) By contrast, an intellectual historian can describe the ideal of sanctity without recognizing that a crucial part of that ideal was its instantiation in earthly events through real practitioners.

The work of Peter Brown has not yet been mentioned, partly because the importance of his contribution to late antique scholarship requires special attention, and partly because his work could be regarded as an attempt to address the distinction just described. Following Evelyne Patlagean in France,[29] Brown in his classic essay of 1971, 'The Rise and Function of the Holy Man in Late Antiquity',[30] applied the tools of sociology and anthropology to the study of late antique religious practice. Taking Syria as a case study, Brown depicted the holy man as a village patron in a world where mundane social, economic, and judicial responsibilities constituted the main sphere of his activity.[31] Brown's quotidian emphasis in no way denies the strong ideological content of our sources: holy men certainly embodied a Christian conception of God,[32] and since the hagiographical form existed to capture this, there was an extent to which its narrative content was artificial, in particular in stressing dramatic moments to the detriment of more mundane processes.[33] What Brown rightly rejected, however, is a methodological consequence which commonly flows from this recognition, namely the crude attempt to distinguish fictional elements of the text from hard facts on the basis that late antique people were too gullible to

---

[29] Evelyne Patlagean, 'Ancienne hagiographie byzantine et histoire sociale', *Annales: Economies, Sociétés, Civilisations* 23.1 (1968), pp. 106–26.

[30] Peter Brown, 'The Rise and Function of the Holy Man in Late Antiquity', *Journal of Roman Studies* 61 (1971), pp. 80–101.

[31] Ibid., pp. 85–7.

[32] Ibid., p. 90.

[33] Ibid., p. 81.

do so themselves.[34] Instead, the text should be taken as a whole and treated as a source both for intellectual attitudes and for patterns of social behaviour.

Brown's model proved highly effective: it eschewed the simplistic explanatory dichotomies of earlier scholarship and succeeded in offering what Clifford Geertz called a 'thick description' of late antique holy men, in which the practicalities of specific environments could sit alongside the beliefs of their inhabitants. Thus the two aspects of the holy man, as historical agents and as religious symbols, both found a place in his analysis. Nonetheless, we must read Brown's 'Holy Man' carefully to see how this is achieved. Although he does not treat the intellectual and factual elements of hagiography as inherently oppositional, the claims he makes about each are, in fact, advanced separately; on a structural level, the essay switches, as it were paratactically, between quite different modes of explanation, and the relationship between them is never entirely clarified.[35] This leaves important questions unanswered: when holy men instantiated an ideal of God, to what extent was this a textual by-product of their work, and to what extent was it inherent in their actions? In the latter case, did the same actions that made them socially useful project the idea of God or did they constitute two different classes of action? The problem becomes particularly acute in the case of miracles. On this issue, one of Brown's most distinctive techniques is the artfully naïve register he uses to describe them, implying continuity with other kinds of event.[36] The effect is powerful: by describing such events in a vocabulary which does nothing to contest the beliefs of the authors who first reported them, Brown brings great colour to their motives and imagination.[37] But in doing so,

---

[34]   Ibid., p. 96.

[35]   Ibid., p. 91 for a summary of these roles: 'We can never simply reduce the holy man to the role of a charismatic *Ombudsman* in a tension-ridden countryside. There were elements in his power that stretched far beyond a village setting: he played a role that was applicable to urban conditions; his person summed up widespread ideals, common to Byzantine culture as a whole in town and country alike; he could be approached, therefore, to minister to needs both more intimate and more universal than arbitration on the loans and boundaries of farmers.' A similar ambiguity also lingers in Brown's later essay, 'The Christian Holy Man in Late Antiquity', in *Authority and the Sacred* (Cambridge, 1995). The essay begins by discussing the role of holy persons in the late antique Christian imagination (p. 58) before moving onto their practices (p. 60). But how the imaginative and historical aspects related to one another is never made entirely clear.

[36]   E.g., 'The emperor's power ... was made intelligible by miracle ... An abundance of miraculous happenings and of wonder-working persons ... was the surest sign of that blessing', Peter Brown, *Power and Persuasion in Late Antiquity: Towards a Christian Empire* (Madison, Wisconsin, 1992), p. 134.

[37]   Perhaps Peter Brown's most explicit statement of this policy is in *Society and the Holy in Late Antiquity*, pp. 17–19.

he is often content to leave the question of factuality indefinitely suspended. When Brown claims that 'the occasional *coup de théâtre* ... (was) rather like the cashing of a big cheque on a reputation'[38] are we supposed to imagine such events as the closing episodes of long social processes, or rather as purely textual episodes which somehow encapsulate those processes only symbolically and metaphorically? Were they, in other words, *coups* worthy of theatre, or nothing more than theatre?

The notion of historical reality Brown offers is an intoxicating mixture. On the one hand, we are made aware that hagiographies are relevant to both the intellectual and factual realms. On the other, what is not clear in every instance is the extent to which the realities he depicts are intellectual or factual. What Brown achieves in his famous essay of 1971 is a historicity of an unconventional type, a sort of socially vivid verisimilitude whose ingredients, which include both religious attitudes and behavioural patterns, are blended in uncertain measure as in a secret recipe. Human experience in late antiquity is given a strong and distinctive flavour, but what becomes mysterious in its creation is the idea of events as discrete, specific, immediately experienced phenomena.

Does this matter? In one way, no: most events contained in hagiographies are impossible to verify, and, as Brown warns, a systematic attempt to do so can encourage a judgemental attitude in which 'the unique and individual character of an age'[39] is lost. But in another way, his model of historicity fails to capture one crucial aspect of late antique religious sensibility. By blurring rather than confronting the distinction between the factual and the intellectual, Brown allows the impression to form that this frontier was only vaguely delineated at the time. This is misleading: it was vigorously policed, and for good reasons. Especially in religious terms, late antiquity was a highly competitive society; to believe claims about the extraordinary status of one's own holy man was the direct flipside to the cynicism and ridicule with which an opponent's was dismissed. Since extraordinary spiritual claims often rested on the allegorical interpretation of minutiae, the otherworldliness for which late antique society is so famous was often matched by a pedantic insistence on the literal truth (or untruth) of events. It is for this reason that hagiographers much more commonly voice concern that their stories will be disbelieved than that their religious significance will be missed.

An adequate interpretation of late antique hagiography must make a place for the role of factuality, on both the textual and experiential level: Brown's original 'Holy Man' falls some way short of this. Nonetheless, in the course of four decades of prolific research since 1971, Brown himself has highlighted a number

---

[38] Brown, 'Rise and Function of the Holy Man', p. 81.

[39] Ibid., p. 96.

of weaknesses in his original essay which should be redressed. These include the overwhelmingly social and collective emphasis he gave to holy men which left little room for the first person perspective on their own activities and beliefs.[40] This desideratum is entirely legitimate: as Charles Taylor has observed in his discussion of William James's *Varieties of Religious Experience*, in any study of religion, there is always a tension between a perspective which stresses corporate and collective aspects on the one hand, and individual experience on the other.[41]

But in the context of the present study, this balance has an additional relevance since it examines not just third person hagiographies, but first person spiritual narratives. Although, by general consensus, late antiquity lacked what we might term a genre of autobiography, it did produce a considerable body of spiritually-minded material written in the first person, some of it more or less self-standing (the most famous example being Augustine's *Confessions*) some scattered throughout hagiographies and often describing the author's relationship with his subject. As suggested in the earlier analysis of Boethius, first person documents can yield insight into immediate and specific events, explain how these sustained and were shaped by beliefs, and describe how the relationship between them affected religious experience. In this sense, it may appear to help address the concerns about factuality described above. Furthermore, a new perspective on hagiographies emerges when read in conjunction with spiritual autobiographies: the often remarkable concurrence of concerns suggests a genre not divorced from the wider patterns of religious life, but one which reflected certain essential aspects of it, albeit from a different viewpoint.

By claiming this, we must avoid the naïve assumption that autobiography can be taken as a straightforward record of personal experience. The last century has seen many prominent thinkers challenge the natural intuition that humans enjoy a direct and reliable access to their own past; some have even depicted autobiography as an impossible activity, incapable of referring to reality and inevitably prone to the distortions of hindsight and idealization.[42] Another consequence of the 'linguistic turn', such arguments have reverberated widely, including in late antique scholarship. For example, as we shall explore in Chapter 3, a long-standing debate has raged around Augustine's famous conversion scene in the *Confessions*, and the extent to which it was retrospectively contrived;

---

[40]   Peter Brown, 'The Rise and Function of the Holy Man, 1971–1997', p. 368.

[41]   Charles Taylor, *Varieties of Religion Today: William James Revisited* (Cambridge MA/London, 2002), pp. 4–7.

[42]   Michel Schramm, 'Augustinus' *Confessiones* und die (Un)-Möglichkeit der Autobiographie', *Antike und Abendland*, 54 (2008), pp. 173–5.

similar doubts have been raised about the autobiographical testimonies of Jerome[43] and Gregory of Nazianzus.[44]

Again, an analysis of Boethius helps illustrate the complexity of first person testimony. Earlier in this introduction, his claims were analysed in such a way as to suggest that certain aspects of his text which appear purely metaphorical, and therefore explicable only in intellectual rather than factual terms, may have represented concrete aspects of his experience. However, a contrasting argument could be made about his apparently literal use of the term 'exile' whose strangeness in this context appears to have gone unnoticed.[45] Imprisoned, awaiting execution, still near the centre of royal power – for all his Ovidian allusions,[46] 'exile' seems an unconventional term for this particular form of punishment. Of course, in antiquity no less than in the modern period, the idea had romantic connotations; there is a hint, perhaps, that, as part of the text's satirical agenda, Philosophy mocks these connotations in raising her patient's mind above the here and now: 'If you prefer to be thought of as driven ... ' (*si te pulsum existimari mavis ...*). But regardless of the register in which Boethius intends it, his apparently literal use of the term, rather than giving rise to a metaphorical usage, in fact seems to have been determined by it. Indeed, the metaphorical and philosophical use of exilic language was so common in late antiquity that at least in religious writing it practically came to constitute its primary meaning.[47] In other words, spiritual exile seems to have preceded literal exile in Boethius' description and to have infused it with significance. One could, of course, argue that this metaphorical usage simply reinforces the distance between the text's factual and intellectual content. But it is also possible that it indicates another way in which the world as Boethius experienced it was open to textual influence: he did not merely draw an extended spiritual interpretation from a set of literal circumstances to which he had been exposed; rather, his perception and experience of those circumstances was spiritually pregnant from the outset. The existence of both a factual and an

---

[43]   Stefan Rebenich, *Jerome* (London, 2002), p. 20.

[44]   E.g. Efthymiadis, 'Two Gregories and Three Genres', pp. 246–56.

[45]   Crabbe notices the metaphor without commenting on its apparent oddness: 'Literary Design in the *De Consolatione Philosophiae*', p. 241. The same is true of Joachim Gruber, *Kommentar zu Boethius* de Consolatione Philosophiae (Berlin/New York, 1978), pp. 141–3; and Chadwick, *Boethius*, p. 227. I am grateful to Neil McLynn for observing the unusualness of this usage.

[46]   For these allusions see Seth Lerer, *Boethius and Dialogue: Literary Method in the Consolation of Philosophy* (Princeton, 1985), p. 7; Chadwick, *Boethius*, p. 225.

[47]   For an overview of this usage see Claudio Moreschini, 'Il motivo dell'esilio dell'anima', in Fabio Rosa and Francesco Zambon (eds), *Pothos: Il viaggio, la nostalgia* (Trento, 1995): 97–105.

intellectual content, the complex questions of where they meet and how they interact, are therefore considerations as relevant to spiritual autobiography as they are to hagiography.

If, as stated earlier, the aim of this book is to demonstrate continuity between life and text, then it is clear that this continuity will be complex, and that the various forms it takes will need to be explained differently in the case of specific texts. Very broadly, however, these various forms are covered by the three terms of our title: truthfulness, realism and historicity. 'Truthfulness' means the basic desire of authors to give an accurate account, and the audience's expectation that they will do so. An important source for this idea are the statements made by authors about their own writings, the guarantees they offer, and the ethical obligations they claim to feel. For example, many Christian authors claim that, because the Bible was a truthful account of sacred history, this constituted a precedent they were obliged to follow.

Truthfulness, however, is not necessarily a self-evident value; it can been argued that what constitutes truthfulness for a particular author reflects their deeper notions of reality as well as their experience of the world. This explains the role of the term 'realism': by being truthful, what notion of reality were authors claiming to respect? In particular, did the very spiritually-minded authors of late antiquity feel themselves obliged to relate literal details accurately, or did their form of realism aim only at the higher, hidden truth? An analysis of realism in this sense focuses not only on the overt guarantees of authors, but also on the literary techniques they exploit in order to achieve and sustain a reader's belief in the truthfulness of their account. What picture of the world is represented by, and in turn emerges from, the use of these techniques?

'Historicity', the third term in the title, relates more to us as modern readers of the texts. It denotes what we can learn about the late antique period, especially its religious life, from the texts under discussion. In part, it draws on the other two concepts: if authors were sincere in their guarantees of truthfulness then this clearly constitutes a reason at least to give the contents of their works a serious hearing, although such contents must be seen as functions of a realism rooted in a certain world view. But the notion of historicity advanced here involves more than an assessment of the texts as representations of reality; rather, it also includes the idea that much of what is commonly termed 'textuality' should not be treated exclusively as a phenomenon of writing set in opposition to real life, but recognized as a dynamic and ordering principle within it.

This point can best be explained by considering it in relation to the assumptions of the 'linguistic turn'. Throughout the many contexts to which the insights of Structuralism have been applied, two main debates stand out. The better known is probably the extent of determinacy within any given structure – a debate which, amongst other things, gave rise to post-Structuralism. Of greater interest to us is the breadth of the phenomena to which Structuralist principles can be usefully applied or, to put it another way, the question 'what counts as a "text?"' Staying relatively close to the Saussurean origins of Structuralist thought, many scholars emphasize the arbitrary, inadequate and (in both senses) partial ability of written documents to represent the phenomena they purport to describe. By contrast, others extend the scope and type of phenomena which participate in the system of signs far beyond linguistic parameters narrowly defined. In the abstract, these trends may represent only a difference of extent. But within the framework of a given analysis, the difference can be fundamental. An example of the first tendency is Edward Said's *Orientalism*, one of the founding texts of post-Colonial theory, which contrasts the 'textual attitude' of scholars with 'the swarming, unpredictable, and problematic mess in which human beings live.'[48] By contrast, as a Structural anthropologist, Claude Levi-Strauss applies the notion of the text far more broadly, and shows how the system of signs extends into a vast number of human practices.[49] Nowhere is this basic dichotomy more apparent than in the ongoing debate about the nature of narrative: should it be seen primarily as an artificial and retrospective imposition of order onto the disorder of life, or, alternatively, as an inescapable mode of human existence and understanding?[50]

Very broadly, the present study can be associated with these latter tendencies, although its principal arguments are rooted much more in the philosophical beliefs of the late antique period than in modern theory. The argument for the historicity of the texts rests on several pillars: on their genuine attempt to represent the world truthfully; on the likelihood that religiously-minded people would, to use Ernst Kris's expression, 'enact biographies' they had encountered textually;[51] on the claim that the same narrative expectations prevailed amongst the followers of a holy man as amongst the audience of a hagiography. To put it in the language of Semiotics, it may indeed be legitimate to regard hagiographies and other religious texts as merely the *paroles* of the *langue* which was the period's

---

[48]   Edward Said, *Orientalism* (London, 1978), pp. 92–3.

[49]   The central question is 'whether different aspects of social life (including even art and religion) cannot only be studied by the methods of, and with the help of concepts similar to those employed in linguistics, but also whether they do not constitute phenomena whose inmost nature is the same as that of language', Claude Levi-Strauss, *Structural Anthropology* (London, 1972), p. 353. For an excellent introduction to these problems see Terence Hawkes, *Semiotics and Structuralism* (London, 1977), pp. 32–5, and Elizabeth A. Clark, *History, Theory, Text: Historians and the Linguistic Turn* (Cambridge MA/London, 2004), pp. 145–55.

[50]   Ibid., pp. 86–105. A classic pro-narrative argument is given by Alisdair MacIntyre, *After Virtue* (London, 1984), pp. 211, 214.

[51]   Ernst Kris, *Psychoanalytical Explorations in Art* (London, 1953), p. 83.

religious beliefs. But, this book argues, it is also important to recognize that the lives themselves could function as *paroles* of precisely the same *langue*. It is in this sense that the third term in our title, 'historicity', should be interpreted: as the proximity of text and life *within* the system of signs.

This book is divided into two parts of two chapters each. The first part deals mainly with third person hagiographies; the second with spiritual autobiographical writings. The first part progresses systematically through the three main concepts of truthfulness, realism and historicity; it attempts to demonstrate how hagiographies could be said to fulfil these criteria, and to show how each of these concepts relate to one another. The focus of Chapter 1 is essentially literary, and deals with the first two of these concepts: in other words, it examines what a wide range of hagiographers from the third to sixth centuries said about their works, considers the world view these texts contain and the techniques used to represent it. The second chapter concentrates on the third term by judging the historicity of particular hagiographical claims. In doing so, it focuses on a somewhat narrower range of texts which, for various reasons, provide sufficient evidence to legitimize historical judgements, such as Eugippius' *Life of Severinus*, Hilarius' *Life of Honoratus* and the closely associated *In Praise of the Desert* by Eucherius of Lyons.

The same principal issues of truthfulness, realism and historicity also apply in Part II. Nonetheless, a different structure was needed because of the much greater diversity of this form of writing and, in particular, by the extreme importance of one particular text: Augustine's *Confessions*. After an initial description of the problems posed by first person writing, much of the first chapter is dedicated to an analysis of the *Confessions* using the same types of question that in the first part were applied to hagiography. A second chapter extends conclusions drawn about the *Confessions* to other first person writings both by Augustine and other authors in order to make a more general statement about late antique religious sensibilities. Although the book's main themes are common to both parts, the aim of juxtaposing these two types of writing is not simply to repeat the same arguments. Rather, an important concern is the differences between them, and what they tell us in combination which might remain invisible in isolation. This applies especially to an issue introduced at the end of the first part and revisited in the general conclusion: namely the historical identity of holy men, who seem to have been such a prominent feature on the late antique landscape, and who consequently feature heavily in modern literature on the period.

This introduction is best completed by considering the scope, origins and the limitations of the present study. The theories outlined above and explored in the course of this book are intended to be a number of things: a solution to certain specific problems in the religious history of late antiquity, a new explanatory tool more generally applicable within that field and even, potentially, a theory about religious life and experience extendable to other historical contexts.

To achieve these objectives, there were basic choices to be made about how the book should be written. One question was how comprehensive the work should attempt to be both in terms of its temporal and geographical boundaries, and also the quantity of texts that should be included. As the need for limits grew clearer, I decided to focus on texts written between the third and sixth centuries and only in the Greek and Latin languages, although even within these boundaries it was not possible to cover all potentially relevant material. Rather than attempt a definitive statement about the religious life of late antique people, or even about the miniscule proportion who wrote or about whom texts were written, the decision was made to focus on a few particularly productive texts and follow the existing debates which have grown up around them. In so far as a general statement about the period does emerge, it is because the book is written in a comparative spirit, and attempts to forge links between debates which have often been treated in isolation: for example, between hagiography and spiritual autobiography, between Christian and pagan holy men, between Augustine's *Confessions* and other first person writings.

Another question was how the theories developed in this book could best be expressed. One possibility was to balance them against others, and to attempt to establish precisely how far they do or do not apply in any particular case. Another possibility was to give these theories their maximal expression, and to focus on cases which best lent themselves to such an interpretation. The approach chosen comes closer to the latter than to the former option. This is partly a practical question: within the limited constraints of space, it allows a fuller exploration of the theory's potential. But it is also intended as a corrective to tendencies which, as we saw above, have been expressed many times before and become orthodox. That such interpretations are consistently challenged throughout this book, therefore, should not be seen as a dogmatic rejection of them as always and entirely misled. Rather, it should be seen as a strategic opposition, designed to reveal them as incomplete, and in doing so to make room for useful and new ideas.

By calling these ideas new, I do not claim that they are entirely unprecedented either within late antique scholarship or other fields. In the case of Augustine, Robert Markus has persuasively shown how and why a late antique Christian might observe sensible reality with expectations and techniques derived from, and continuous with, textual culture.[52] The same insight is central to *Authorised Lives*, an excellent recent work by Michael Williams. Williams is particularly

---

[52] 'Habits of reading the biblical text had profound repercussions on the way Augustine read his world', Robert Markus, *Signs and Meanings* (Liverpool, 1996), p. 29.

effective in emphasizing the centrality not only of allegory to late antique Christians, but also of typology: the belief that spiritually significant patterns were present not merely in texts but also in historical events.[53] Williams does more than outline the theory; he applies these attitudes as explanatory tools to a series of late antique (auto)biographical works including Augustine's *Confessions*. The substantial concurrence between our views, as well as the occasional disagreement, will become clear, especially during the discussion of Augustine. But the most important difference is not a disagreement *per se*, but merely concerns the scope of the material covered. Williams offers close, detailed readings of a number of Christian works on the peripheries of biography which, with the exception of the *Confessions*, do not receive substantial treatment here. The present work, by contrast, draws conclusions from a somewhat greater number of different works, including pagan ones. As stated earlier, the idea of comparing works from both sides of this religious divide follows the lead of scholars such as E.R. Dodds, Salvatore Pricoco and Mark Edwards.[54]

Other late antique scholars have made statements compatible with the central message of this book within the context of specific debates more or less closely related to the authors discussed here. In a celebrated article James Goehring observed that the practice of desert asceticism by some late antique Christians was not merely recorded in hagiographical writings; rather, the growth of the literary genre itself encouraged the physical, self-perpetuating instantiation of the idea.[55] In their analysis of the Jura fathers, Tim Vivian et al. argue that certain aspects of practice attributed to the saints by their hagiographer but found suspicious by modern historians become more plausible once they are recognized as conscious imitations of their Egyptian predecessors.[56] A comparable point is made by Goulven Madec about the supposedly stylized setting and arrangements of the intellectual retreat recorded by Augustine in his Cassiciacum dialogues.[57] Discussing Christian conversion narratives, Pierre Hadot shrewdly suggests that famous examples are likely to result not merely in accounts of conversion which conform to type, but in analogous experiences too.[58]

---

[53]　Williams, *Authorised Lives*, pp. 11–15.

[54]　See footnote 11 above.

[55]　James E. Goehring, 'The Encroaching Desert: Literary Production and Ascetic Space in Early Christian Egypt' in *Ascetics, Society and the Desert: Studies in Early Egyptian Monasticism* (Harrisburg PA, 1999), p. 88.

[56]　Tim Vivian, Kim Vivian and Jeffrey Burton Russell, 'Introduction', in idem (tr.), *The Lives of the Jura Fathers* (Kalamazoo, 1999), p. 62.

[57]　Goulven Madec, 'L'historicité des *Dialogues* de Cassiciacum', *REA* 32 (1986), p. 230.

[58]　'Il y a en effect un <stéréotype> de conversion ... Ce stéréotype risque d'influencer non seulement la manière dont on fait le récit de la conversion, mais la manière dont on

Other examples could no doubt be found. What is most striking about such statements, however, is not merely their relative infrequency, but the fact that they are generally advanced sporadically within the context of very specific debates, and then often by way of an aside. With the partial exception of Williams, what has so far been lacking in the late antique context is a consistent and systematic attempt to apply the theories in question to the religious life of late antiquity generally. Indeed, some of the closest parallels to the arguments advanced here come from other fields of late antique scholarship, or from other historical periods altogether. In an ongoing debate about the authenticity or artifice of Ammianus Marcellinus, John Matthews developed the suggestion, originally made by Erich Auerbach,[59] that the famous style of this historian was not necessarily a distortion of a late antique reality, but rather a representation of an already distorted environment; after all, social relations are themselves a language.[60] There is no opportunity here to treat this complex debate about Ammianus in depth, and in any case, Matthews's contribution to it has been contested,[61] but there is an obvious structural parallel between his arguments and those applied here to the period's religious life.

Similarly, in a discussion of Golden Age Latin love poetry, Jasper Griffin argued that its formal qualities were not mere literary artifice as often claimed by Structuralists, but reflected recognizable, real life practices.[62] Gábor Klaniczay argues that in the thirteenth century, legends formed the basis of life strategies for courtly women aspiring to sanctity.[63] The argument is similar to that made long ago by Ernst Kris in his case studies of Renaissance artists: namely that, once biographical patterns became known, a phenomenon of 'enacted biography' sprang up, as younger artists imitated their forebears, and understood their lives according to the precedents they had set.[64] In other words, formulae could apply as much to life as to the text; indeed, the more it applied to the text, the more deeply it would eventually impact on life.

---

l'éprouve', Pierre Hadot, *Exercises spirituels et philosophie antique* (Paris, 1981), p. 179.

[59]   Erich Auerbach, *Mimesis: the Representation of Reality in Western Literature*, tr. William R. Trask (Princeton, 1953), pp. 52–60.

[60]   John Matthews, 'Peter Valvomeres, Re-arrested' in Michael Whitby, Philip Hardie and Mary Whitby (eds), *Homo Viator: Classical Essays for John Bramble*, Bristol Classical Press (Bristol, 1987), esp. pp. 281–4.

[61]   E.g. by Timothy D. Barnes, *Ammianus Marcellinus and Representation of Historical Reality*, Cornell University Press (Ithaca/London, 1998), p. 13.

[62]   Jasper Griffin, 'Genre and Real Life in Latin Poetry', in *JRS* 71 (1981).

[63]   Gábor Klaniczay, 'Legends as Life Strategies for Aspirant Saints in the Later Middle Ages', *Journal of Folklore Research* 26 (1989), pp. 151–72.

[64]   Kris, *Psychoanalytical Explorations in Art*, p. 83.

Of course, like any approach, that adopted here, which focuses on broad patterns and on general theoretical principles, implies certain limitations. One problem is that the wide range of texts on which such a study must draw can never be wide enough; limits, however necessary, are usually ultimately arbitrary, and since they more closely reflect the limits of the author's knowledge and ability rather than the intrinsic relevance of the subject matter, they are on some level unsatisfactory. Another risk is that in a wide-focused study of this kind, conclusions drawn about specific texts will seem inadequate to specialists. The best that can be hoped is that any such failings are outweighed by the new possibilities generated by comparing texts usually treated in isolation, and by the applicability of the book's arguments to contexts beyond those under immediate consideration.

As one prominent historian has recently observed, as a field of scholarship, late antiquity has in recent decades leant itself to specificity and fragmentation.[65] Against this background, there remains a need for works of synthesis, and I make no apology for attempting to produce such a work. How far I have succeeded is for others to judge.

---

[65] Peter Heather, *The Fall of the Roman Empire: a New History* (London, 2005), p. xiii.

PART I

Chapter 1
Hagiography – A Truth-telling Genre?

Defining Truthfulness

In 440 A.D., Theodoret of Cyrus wrote a *Religious History* dedicated to the most prominent monks that had lived in his homeland of northern Syria over the preceding century.[1] Like many late antique authors, he prefaced his work with a substantial prologue which introduced his subject matter, himself as author, his motivation for writing and his literary strategy. The central message of the prologue was that an absolute commitment to truthfulness pervaded the entire work.

This bold assertion contained several subtle strands. At its heart was the extraordinary nature of his inspiration – 'excellent men, the athletes of virtue' (ἀρίστων ἀνδρῶν καὶ τῆς ἀρετῆς ἀθλητῶν).[2] Such spiritual excellence demanded to be recorded for posterity, even if 'mere narration' could only be a substitute for the lives themselves. Theodoret also sought to win the reader's trust by explaining his meticulous research methods. He had recorded only events to which he was eye-witness, or which he had heard about from trustworthy associates of the monks themselves. He could maintain with confidence, therefore, that the events he recorded demanded belief no less urgently than those of the Bible. For a reader to doubt them would be the equivalent of doubting 'the truth of what took place through Moses, Joshua, Elijah and Elisha ... the working of miracles that took place through the sacred Apostles'.[3]

As we shall shortly see, such assurances of truthfulness are a common and characteristic feature of late antique hagiography. They have, however, been subjected to little systematic, comparative analysis. It is not hard to see why this should be the case for those historians who approach the texts in the search for hard data. A good example of such an approach is a recently published lecture series by T.D. Barnes. Beginning by contesting very specific claims within hagiographies, for example points of chronology, Barnes moves to a

---

[1]   Here I follow R.M. Price's calculation in his introduction to Theodoret of Cyrrhus, *History of the Monks of the Syria* (London, 1985), p. xv.

[2]   Theodoret, *Philotheos Historia* Prologue 1, eds Pierre Canivet and Alice Leroy-Molinghen, *Histoire des moines de Syrie : Histoire Philothée,* Sources Chrétiennes 234, 257 (2 vols, Paris 1977–79).

[3]   Ibid., Prologue 10.

more general statement about the genre by arguing that many texts contain far more fabrication than has often been acknowledged.[4] Whilst Barnes does not ignore assurances of truthfulness entirely, he exploits them principally as further evidence of authorial disingenuousness by juxtaposing them with information he holds to be fallacious.[5] Seen from this positivistic perspective, hagiographical guarantees of truthfulness can appear incongruous and indeed hollow, or at very least peripheral to the main interest of the text.

Since very few people would claim that all information contained within hagiographies is either entirely true or entirely false, the positivist project of assessing and separating both types of content is legitimate. However, the present chapter neither discredits nor pursues this approach; its aims are simply different. Rather than moving from points of detail to general evaluations of the works as historical documents, it begins with a systematic and comparative analysis of the various guarantees of truthfulness offered by hagiographers. This is partly because the consistency and sophistication of these statements demands our attention; it is also because they are usually the first part of a work encountered by a reader, located as they often are within prologues, and thus the nearest thing they contain to a literary definition. By beginning our examination here, the present study attempts to reflect on the way that truthfulness was professed and presented within the hagiographical genre, on the role of truthfulness in defining these texts as a genre and, subsequently, on the way in which this value was reflected throughout the work. By adopting this approach, the aim, at least initially, is to shift attention away from the relationship between the hagiographer and the information he relates, and onto the complex and mutual set of attitudes that connected him to his audience. As Averil Cameron rightly observes, the question how audiences read hagiographies and what they expected remains an area of great uncertainty.[6]

Theodoret's purportedly truth-telling stance was quite typical of late antique Christian hagiography. By definition, hagiographers located their inspiration and justification in the extraordinary nature of their subjects. For the sixth-century Palestinian author Cyril of Scythopolis, for example, to record the lives of local monks could be regarded as an act of faith whose omission would be sinful, though by its very nature, any record was bound to fall short of the

---

[4]   Barnes, *Early Christian Hagiography and Roman History*, p. 324.

[5]   Indeed, in the case of Sulpicius, he sees these guarantees as ironic: ibid., p. 221.

[6]   'It is not clear to what extent these Christian texts were thought of by contemporaries as historical narratives', Averil Cameron, *Christianity and the Rhetoric of Empire*, p. 118. The current work also addresses analogous issues amongst pagans.

truth.[7] Such a task demanded scrupulousness: like a bee gathering pollen he had travelled through the desert, interviewing the oldest living monks about the lives of their predecessors. Similar attitudes prevail in hagiography dedicated to more contemporaneous figures. For example, Sulpicius Severus, the first Latin Christian hagiographer, saw in Martin a Gallic hero every bit as significant as his Egyptian counterparts, and promised to record only events to which he had been eyewitness or which had been related to him by the saint himself.[8]

Comparable guarantees are offered in many hagiographical texts including the *History of the Monks of Egypt*,[9] Palladius' *Lausiac History*,[10] and Ferrandus' *Life of Fulgentius of Ruspae*.[11] That the author himself was an eyewitnesses to the events he recorded, or a recipient of information from trustworthy sources, were common claims. There is no simple correlation between the intensity of these claims and either the extent of their miraculous content or the reputation for accuracy they have enjoyed in modern times; indeed, precisely because their details are challenging, miracles are often an occasion to remind readers of the hagiographer's factual integrity. The first story in Paulinus' *Life of Ambrose*, for example, is the mysterious visitation to the saint's cradle of a swarm of bees symbolic of future literary achievements.[12] But this anecdote immediately follows a specific plea by the author 'to believe that what we say is true. And let no one think that I have put down anything which lacks truth, through the bias of love; since it is indeed better to say nothing at all than to set forth something false'.[13] Similarly, although the historicity of Jerome's *Lives* has been vigorously contested by modern scholars, not least because of their exaggerated

---

   [7]   Cyril of Scythopolis, *Lives* 6.10–15, ed. E. Schwartz, *Kyrillos von Skythopolis* (Leipzig, 1939).

   [8]   Sulpicius originally claims to record only tested information, since things to which Martin alone was witness are unknowable: Sulpicius Severus, *Vita Martini* 1.7–9, ed. and tr. Jacques Fontaine, *Sulpice Sévère: Vie de Saint Martin*, Sources Chrétiennes 133–5 (3 vols, Paris, 1967–69). Nonetheless, Martin's own testimony is later used as proof: ibid. 24.8.

   [9]   *Historia Monachorum in Aegypto*, Prologue 1–2, ed. André-Jean Festugière (Brussels, 1961).

   [10]   Palladius, *Historia Lausiaca* 2, ed. G.J.M. Bartelink, *La storia lausiaca* (Milan, 1974).

   [11]   Ferrandus felt able to rebut any charge of falsification by recording either what Fulgentius had told him, or what he and his correspondent Felicianus had witnessed: *Vita Fulgentii* 3, ed. Jacques-Paul Migne, *S. Fulgentii Episcopi Ruspensis Opera Omnia*, PL 65 (Paris, 1847).

   [12]   Paulinus, *Life of Ambrose* 3, ed. and tr. Mary Simplicia Kaniecka, *Vita sancti Ambrosii, mediolanensis episcopi, a Paulino eius notario ad beatum Augustinum conscripta* (Washington D.C., 1928).

   [13]   Ibid. 2 (tr. Kaniecka, p. 41).

and sometimes fantastical content,[14] we must remember that few authors were more vigorous and explicit in defending their own works' truthfulness.[15] That these guarantees were more than introductory conventions is suggested by the fact that a number of authors, such as Cyril of Scythopolis and the author of the *Lives of the Jura Fathers*, intermittently reminded readers of their commitment to truthfulness during the course of the narrative.[16] They might offer general assurances or defences of specific information. In a way which could be said to anticipate the *isnad* system of early Islamic tradition, Cyril details the chain of informants from whom he has learnt about a particular miracle.[17] Such assurances are also offered by authors of miracle collections such as that of Thecla:[18] works which detail the lives and achievements of saints after their physical death.

Another extremely common feature of Christian hagiography was the recognition of the limitations of the literary work. This could take several forms. Often it was very personal: many authors professed either their unworthiness to write about such great men or their inability to do so.[19] For Theodoret, the sheer quantity of saints made a complete account impossible and necessitated a regional perspective;[20] for Constantius, the immeasurable number of Germanus' spiritual achievements caused a similar problem.[21] These limitations too are not just mentioned at the outset, but reiterated later in the narrative.

---

[14] For a review of this debate surrounding the work's historicity, see A.A.R. Bastiaensen, 'Jérôme hagiographe', in Guy Philippart (ed.), *Hagiographies* vol. 1 (Turnhout, 1994), pp. 110–19.

[15] Jerome condemns earlier accounts of the hermit Paul as untruthful: *Vita Pauli* 1; attacks the *maledicorum voces* who have doubted Paul's existence, and will probably doubt Hilarion's: *Vita Hilarionis* 1.6, and stresses that he heard about the story of Malchus from the saint himself: *Vita Malchi* 1, ed. and tr. Pierre Leclerc and Edgardo Martín Morales, *Jérôme: Trois Vies de Moines (Paul, Malchus, Hilarion)*, Sources Chrétiennes (Paris, 2007). See E. Coleiro, 'St. Jerome's Lives of the Hermits', *Vigiliae Christianae* 11 (1957), pp. 177–8.

[16] *Vitae Patrum Jurensium* 4; 78; 86; 96, ed. François Martine, *Vie des Pères du Jura*, Sources Chrétiennes 142 (Paris, 1988); Cyril, *Lives* 71.10, 82.12–19, 86.1–5, 164.25–7; 237.25–9.

[17] Cyril, *Lives* 45.5–25.

[18] *Life of Thecla*, Prologue, 1.20–28; *Miracles of Thecla* Prologue 16–21, 94–102, ed. and tr. Gilbert Dagron, *Vie et Miracles de Sainte Thècle* (Brussels, 1978). Similar guarantees occur in the early seventh century *Miracles of Demetrius*, esp. Prologue 8, ed. and tr. Paul Lemerle, *Les plus anciens recueils des miracles de Saint Démétrius* (2 vols, Paris, 1979).

[19] E.g. Hilarius Arelatensis, *Vita Honorati*, Prologue 3, ed. Samuel Cavallin, *Vita Hilarii* in *Vitae Sanctorum Honorati et Hilarii, Episcoporum Arelatensium* (Lund, 1952); Paulinus, *Life of Ambrose*, Preface 1.

[20] Theoderet, *Lives*, Prologue 9.

[21] Ibid., Prologue, 7; Constantius of Lyons, *Vita Germani*, Praefatio, ed. and tr. René Borius, *Constance de Lyons: Vie de Saint Germain d'Auxerre*, Sources Chrétiennes, 112 (Paris, 1965).

We should not think of the admission of these limitations as merely accompaniments to the insistence on truthfulness; rather, they are a crucial aspect of it. This is shown by the many authors who in various ways point to language itself as inadequate to the task in hand: far from exaggerating the truth, they simply lack the tools to represent such great truths adequately. Within the limits of the possible, hagiography claimed to be a direct representation of the extraordinary reality of saints' lives, or at least the external lives they had led on earth. Such a claim had major implications in terms of authorial self-perception. For Theodoret, it meant writing, or at least claiming to write, like the Evangelists whose plain style was no obstacle to recording the historical truth of Christ's life.[22] Conversely, writing in a way suitable to hagiography meant declining to write according to the established rules of poetry, history, tragedy, comedy and panegyric[23] – secular genres dedicated to far lesser themes. With more or less justification, hagiographers regularly excused their own styles as rustic, whilst simultaneously portraying this as a legitimate rejection of secular culture.[24] Such attitudes had deep roots in the Christian community of a classical world whose education system had for centuries been overwhelmingly literary and rhetorical in emphasis. Against this background, the truthfulness of much of the Bible had sometimes been associated precisely with its lack of literary pretensions. One might almost say that for Theodoret and others, to write about the saints required, in a very real sense, not to follow a *literary* tradition at all; rather, it involved claiming to commit oneself – however imperfectly – to the truth itself.[25]

This literary positioning of hagiographers, which might include associating their work with biblical tradition and dissociating it from secular writing, has a third, less well known aspect. At least in their explanatory prologues, hagiographers rarely mention other examples of their own genre. Usually, the saints in question are not described as part of an ongoing tradition, but as comparable only to distant biblical figures or, less frequently, superior to classical ones;[26] consequently, the obligation to write is one of an unprecedented urgency.

---

[22]   Theoderet, *Lives*, Prologue 11.

[23]   Ibid., Prologue 3;11.

[24]   Paulinus, *Life of Ambrose*, Preface 1; Constantius, *Life of Germanus*, Prologue; Hilarius, *Life of Honoratus* 1.4.

[25]   For a good discussion of the literary attitudes of Theodoret and other related authors, see Derek Krueger, *Writing and Holiness: The Practice of Authorship in the Early Christian East* (Philadelphia, 2004), pp. 94–109.

[26]   An excellent example is the preface to Sulpicius' *Life of Martin* (1.1–9) in which a direct rejection of Homeric legend and Platonic philosophy is woven into a discussion which subtly and respectfully refutes a notion of history outlined by Sallust in the preface to the *Catiline Conspiracy*. See Jacques Fontaine, *Commentaire. Sulpice Sévère: Vie de Saint Martin*

We might be tempted, on the basis of this silence, to question the very idea that hagiography was a genuine literary genre in late antiquity. Certainly, as Felice Lifshitz[27] and Claudia Rapp usefully remind us, we must not underestimate its variety.[28] Such works might be individual or collective, written in Greek, Latin, Syriac and other languages; they might overlap with various other genres such as funeral oratory, travel writing, and miracle collections. But none of this makes 'genre' an entirely misleading term as Lifschitz argues it is in relation to Carolingian and early Capetian works.[29] At least in the late antique context, such a view would fail to account for the fact that some authors positively conceptualize 'lives' as a group when describing the reading matter of their own subjects, thus implying that such works could be thought of collectively.[30] And within the main body of the text, some hagiographers do allude to works of the same genre. For example, Cyril of Scythopolis uses another hagiography when describing the spiritual life of his own hero Sabas: 'He (*the Devil*) who had formerly appeared to the great Abba Antony appeared also to him'.[31] At least part of the reason why hagiographers omit such references in their explanatory prologues is surely to establish the idea that they are simply telling the truth, rather than operating within the confines of literary tradition, with all its compromises and vanities. Cyril, after all, does not explicitly refer to Athanasius' *Life of Antony*, but to an event in what he believed that work to concern: the life of the real saint Antony. In so far as its participants presented hagiography as a way of writing, they treated it as a tradition of truth-telling rather than as a literary genre.

(Tome 2), pp. 394–8. In a related vein, Cyril's work is partly a response to the unfortunate fact that whilst the impious get written about, the lives of pious men too often go unreported: *Lives* 50.50–19.

27   Felice Lifshitz, 'Beyond Positivism and Genre: "Hagiographical" Texts as Historical Narrative' in *Viator* 25 (1994), esp. 102.

28   Claudia Rapp, '"For next to God, you are my salvation": reflections on the rise of the holy man in late antiquity', in James Howard-Johnston and Paul Anthony Hayward (eds), *The Cult of Saints in Late Antiquity and the Early Middle Ages* (Oxford, 1999), p. 63.

29   Lifshitz, 'Beyond Positivism and Genre', esp. 108–13. More generally, modern literary theory has tended to emphasize the impurity and flexibility of all generic categorizations. See John Frow, *Genre* (Abingdon, 2006), esp. pp. 51–5.

30   E.g. Ferrandus, *Life of Fulgentius* 23; Gerontius, *Vita Melaniae Iunioris* 26, ed. and tr. Denys Gorce, *Vie de* Sainte Mélanie, Sources Chrétiennes, 90 (Paris: Editions du Cerf, 1962); *Regula Benedicti* 42.3, ed. and tr. H. Rochais, *La Règle de Saint Benoît* (Paris: Desclée De Brouwer, 1980).

31   Cyril, *Lives* 110.15–19, tr. Richard Price, *Cyril of Scythopolis: Lives of the Monks of Palestine* (Kalamazoo, 1991), p. 119; echoing Athanasius, *Vita Antonii* 6, ed. G.J.M. Bartelink, *Athanasius: Vie d'Antoine*, Sources Chrétiennes 400 (Paris, 1994).

It hardly needs to be said that, for Christians, the Bible had a major role to play in these literary sensibilities. It was regarded not only as a source of ultimate spiritual truth but also as a record of real events. Amongst late antique thinkers, this literalist stance is usually associated with Augustine who, as we shall later see, engaged in an unusually thorough discussion of it. It seems very likely, however, that Augustine was giving a sophisticated expression to intuitions which were widespread and this picture tends to be supported by hagiography. For example, when comparing his own holy men to their biblical predecessors, Theoderet clearly felt he could simply assume that readers already believed stories contained within Scripture.[32]

Nonetheless, a consideration of pagan philosophical biographies from late antiquity shows that such attitudes were not inevitably and directly dependent on the Bible. These works, from Porphyry's *Life of Plotinus* at the turn of the third century to Damascius' *Philosophical History* in the first half of the sixth will form a major part of our discussion in this chapter and beyond. As we saw in the introduction, there has been fruitful comparative study between Christian and pagan *lives*, and terms like 'saint' and 'hagiography' have begun to be applied to works of this latter category (see p. 7). Some scholars have even detected in pagan hagiographies a conscious, anti-Christian agenda which included polemical allusions to, and imitations of Scripture;[33] others have played down this aspect.[34] Parallels with such an application are certainly interesting, but the terms of the debate can obscure the vital point that, whilst pagan hagiography may have had a real anti-Christian function, it only very rarely took a specific inter-textual form. There are good reasons for this: rather than attack the faith directly, pagan biographers preferred to allude to it euphemistically as a typically deceptive aspect of our unstable world, and one serenely anticipated by their own metaphysics.[35] For such biographies to be at all effective in an anti-Christian

---

[32]   This logic is not restricted to Theodoret's prologue, e.g. *History* 6.11.

[33]   E.g. Lucien Jerphagnon, 'Les sous-entendus anti-chrétiens de la Vita Plotini ou l'Evangile de Plotin selon Porphyre', in *Museum Helveticum* 47 (1990), pp. 41–52.

[34]   Gillian Clark, 'Philosophical Lives and the Philosophical Life', in Hägg and Rousseau (eds), *Greek Biography and Panegyric*, pp. 30–31; Robert J. Penella, *Greek Philosophers and Sophists in the Fourth Century A.D* (New York, 1990), pp. 141–5. For a similar argument about Lucian's *Peregrinus*, see Jason König, 'The Cynic and Christian Lives of Lucian's *Peregrinus*', in B. McGing and J. Mossman (eds), *The Limits of Ancient Biography* (Swansea, 2006), pp. 227–54.

[35]   When we encounter statements like 'he alone remained unshaken by the storm' (Eunapius, *Vitae Philosophorum ac Sophistarum*, 504, ed. with tr. Wilmer Cave Wright, *Philostratus and Eunapius: Lives of the Sophists*, Loeb Classical Library (London/New York: Harvard University Press, 1921; reprinted 1968), p. 561, or 'he carried on a sober and undaunted existence even amid the perils' (Marinus, *Vita Procli* 15, ed. Rita Masullo, *Marino*

role, they first had to promote a superior, alternative world view. In other words, any competitive connotations had to be possible, but not necessary.

The inclusion of pagan biographies in our discussion, then, follows the lead of a number of modern scholars who locate parallels with Christian works in the common cultural and intellectual atmosphere of late antiquity. This was, after all, a world in which Christians such as Theodoret could describe their faith as the ultimate philosophy[36] and in which pagan Neoplatonism took on an increasingly religious aspect. (This is why in most cases throughout this book the terms 'philosophical' and 'theological' are used synonymously.) A recognition of these religious similarities should not downplay many important and heartfelt differences, some of which went beyond the most obvious doctrinal level. To name just one example, pagan biographers generally had a less ambiguous relationship with secular forms of writing than did their Christian counterparts, and were more content to see their works as contributions to what were for them ultimately worthy literary traditions. Eunapius, for example, regarded himself as the reviver of a sadly neglected genre of collective philosophical biography.[37] But for all their differences, authors on both sides of this great religious divide shared certain basic philosophical assumptions, of which the most important was a transcendental metaphysics which viewed the sensible world as the lowest level of reality.

This fundamental similarity is manifested not least in the pagan hagiographers' insistence on truthfulness and in the form this insistence took. The realism of Porphyry's portrait is perhaps only implicit in his contemporaneous emphasis (Plotinus was 'the philosopher who lived in our time'[38]). But Iamblichus, whose subject was the long-deceased founder of philosophy Pythagoras, insisted on the

---

di Neapoli, Vita di Proclo (Naples, 1985); tr. Mark Edwards in *Neoplatonic Saints: the Lives of Plotinus and Proclus by their Students* (Liverpool, 2000), p. 79, we may assume that resistance to the threats and lures of the Christian state is being indicated. See Richard Goulet, *Etudes sur les vies des philosophes* (Paris, 2001), p. 20.

[36]   For Christian definition of Philosophy, see Theoderet, *Lives*, Epilogue, 15.

[37]   Eunapius, *Lives* 454. This fitted into a more general pagan attitude about the moral value of traditional *paideia* e.g. Julian, *Against the Galilaeans* 229E, ed. Friedrich Karl Gottlob Hertlein, *Iuliani imperatoris quae supersunt praeter reliquias apud Cyrillum omnia* (2 vols, Leipzig, 1875–76).

[38]   Porphyry, *Life of Plotinus* 1, ed. and tr. A.H. Armstrong, *De Vita Plotini et Ordine Librorum Eius*, in idem, *Plotinus* vol. 1, Loeb Classical Library (London/New York, 1966; repr. 1995), tr. Mark Edwards, *On the Life of Plotinus and the Arrangement of his Works* in *Neoplatonic Saints: the Lives of Plotinus and Proclus by their Students* (Liverpool: Liverpool University Press, 2000), p. 1.

caution with which he had composed his work[39] and portrayed it as a divinely guided activity.[40] For Eunapius and Marinus, telling the truth was an act of piety imposed by their deceased masters.[41] As we shall later discuss in more depth, some pagan writers felt it necessary at crucial points to guarantee the literal precision of particular narrative details. Most significantly of all, Neoplatonists, like Christians, invariably went out of their way to confess the incompleteness of their accounts compared to the brilliance of their subjects' lives. By having Plotinus describe a planned portrait of him as 'the shadow of a shadow' (εἰδώλου εἴδωλον) at the beginning of his biography, Porphyry was, amongst other things, conceding the limitations of his own literary efforts, however truthful in intent.[42] As Iamblichus said, 'when people cannot look at the sun directly we find ways to show them some kind of eclipse'.[43] For Eunapius, writing was like being so in love that one cannot bear to look at the target of desire, but only at her 'sandal or chain or ear-ring'.[44] Marinus agreed with Porphyry that no portrait could capture the original.[45] Damascius stressed how the inherent imprecision of his task meant his work inevitably fell short of legalistic proof; he would not strive 'for absolute accuracy of argument' (πρὸς τὸ ἀκριβέστατον ἀμιλλωμένης) but would write 'according to the rules of biography' (ἀλλ' οἶα μέτρα βιογραφίας), i.e. piecemeal and patiently from fragments of narrative evidence.[46]

Guarantees of truthfulness were widespread features of late antique hagiography, both pagan and Christian. The sophistication of these claims, as well as their consistency across a very diverse range of texts, are highly noteworthy, and form the basis for our comparative study. Of course, in an ultimately historical enquiry, they can be no more than a basis: in isolation, an ancient hagiographer's insistence will not, and should not, oblige a modern historian to accept all his claims at face value. Indeed, the very existence of such guarantees was a recognition that, even at the time, belief was sometimes difficult and, as the juxtaposition of pagan and Christian works reminds us, far from universally effective in a religiously competitive society. What we can say, however, is that truthfulness is very frequently asserted as a value when hagiographers mention,

---

[39] Iamblichus, *De Vita Pythagorica Liber* 1(1), ed. Ludwig Deubner (Leipzig: B.G. Teubner, 1937), revised Ulrich Klein (Stuttgart, 1975).

[40] Ibid. 1(2).

[41] Eunapius, *Lives* 500; Marinus, *Life of Proclus* 1; 38.

[42] As argued by Mark Edwards, 'A Portrait of Plotinus', in *CQ* 43 (1993), pp. 480–81.

[43] Iamblichus, *On the Pythagorean Life* 15(67), tr. Gillian Clark, (Liverpool, 1989), p. 28.

[44] Eunapius, *Lives* 455 (tr. Wright, p. 351).

[45] Marinus, *Life of Proclus* 3.

[46] Damascius, *Vitae Isidori Reliquiae* 6, ed. and tr. Polymnia Athanassiadi, *Damascius: the Philosophical History* (Athens, 1999).

, or define their own writing. However sincerely or insincerely we believe aims were made, whatever precise meaning we give to these notions of ulness, in one form or another they can hardly avoid featuring in any definition of hagiography as a literary genre.

Defining Realism

To most people most of the time the notion of reality, and ideas related to the representation of it, such as truthfulness, realism, and accuracy etc., seem like intuitive notions which require little explanation. But modern theorists have tended to emphasize the profound subjectivity inherent in any attempt to communicate reality in a written form (or, for that matter, other forms).[47] One proof of this, observed by F.R. Ankersmit, is the myriad meanings acquired by the term 'realism' across the centuries.[48] In this vein, literary critics such as Erich Auerbach[49] and Roland Barthes famously analysed realism in terms of the artistic techniques employed by authors to represent human experience. Barthes in particular saw no essential difference between the style of writing employed in a realist novel and that used in purportedly factual historical writing.[50] It is perfectly possible, in other words, to treat realism as a linguistic technique whose employment bears no necessary relationship (or at least not a straightforward and direct one) to factually accurate information.

In any examination of the veracity of hagiographical texts, these considerations are potentially more challenging than the sort of arguments which contest individual details but at least assume the notion of truthfulness to be self-evident. The more subjective we concede the notion of reality to be, and therefore truthful ways of representing it, the less straightforward hagiographical guarantees become. What is required is not just a judgement about the extent to which such guarantees were respected, but an enquiry into what they meant in the first place. What, precisely, was guaranteed by hagiographers and what was not? If truthfulness is the intention to record reality, to what sort of reality did it apply?

---

[47]   Nelson Goodmann, *Languages of Art* (Indianapolis, 1976), pp. 34–9.

[48]   F.R. Ankersmit, *The Reality Effect in the Writing of History; the Dynamics of Historiographical Topology* (Amsterdam, 1989), p. 14.

[49]   Erich Auerbach, *Mimesis: the Representation of Reality in Western Literature*, tr. William R. Trask (Princeton, 1953).

[50]   For an excellent discussion of this view, see F.R. Ankersmit, *The Reality Effect in the Writing of History; the Dynamics of Historiographical Topology* (Amsterdam, 1989), esp. pp. 19–21.

The question is important, because, as Darío Villenueva observes, notions of realism are not just questions of technique; rather, different philosophical world views can profoundly affect the way authors represent even their immediate reality. In the context of modern literary scholarship, the term most commonly refers to the bourgeois realism of the post-Enlightenment novel, a stance with its closest philosophical parallels in Aristotelianism; a realism rooted in Platonism, Villenueva argues, would be of an entirely different character, and geared towards the eternal truths believed to transcend the distortions of the sensible world.[51]

This latter point is, of course, not merely hypothetical in the late antique context since Platonism was, amongst both pagans and Christians, the dominant philosophical influence. As discussed in the introduction, hagiographies contain a factual and an intellectual content: they purport to record real lives exemplary of particular philosophical/theological truths. But this book's objective – namely to show that these things are not necessarily opposed – is only meaningful if the original authors themselves regarded their agreement as necessary to a stance of truthfulness, to their own project of writing realistically.

The deepest notions of reality held by people in late antiquity might appear to cast this into doubt. By definition, their radically transcendental world views presupposed that the literal, factual details of human life such as were recorded in hagiography had only a subordinate value in revealing higher truths. For pagan philosophers, the sensible world was a mere mirror of an invisible reality; Sallustius memorably accorded it the status of a myth,[52] and the sense that it lacked reality was, for Dodds, a crucial aspect of the late antique psychological condition generally.[53] For Christians too, themselves heavily influenced by Platonism, hidden patterns could be read into events throughout history; the significance of saints' miracles, for example, often lay less in their constituent details than in their echoing of biblical precedents. By definition then, the truths with which hagiographers were concerned lay beyond immediate events. It is not hard to imagine how, to those informed by such a world view, accuracy and precision of detail might seem like inessential values. The modern historian's

---

[51] 'An artist steeped in Platonism will be a realist through the stylized forms, purified from the world of the senses, liberating this world from its imperfections and bringing it closer to the archetypes; whereas an Aristotelian artist will present the visible in an integrative manner, in order to discover an authentic reality in it': Darío Villenueva, *Theories of Literary Realism* (Madrid, 1992), tr. Mihai I. Spariosu and Santiago García-Castanón (New York, 1997), p. 8.

[52] Sallustius, *De Diis et Mundo* 3, ed. and tr. Arthur Darby Nock, *Sallustius: Concerning the Gods and the Universe* (Cambridge, 1926).

[53] Dodds, *Pagan and Christian in an Age of Anxiety*, pp. 7–36.

suspicion of a conflict between a text's factual and intellectual content may therefore appear to find support in the period's metaphysical assumptions.

Another aspect of the period's intellectual culture may appear to point in the same direction: namely the significance attributed to literal accuracy within the ancient rhetorical tradition. This tradition, of course, incorporated historical writing, and the extent to which classical historians felt themselves restrained by factual accuracy is an issue which has stimulated significant modern discussion. As Michael Wood has observed, whilst the opposition between the concept of 'truth' and 'falsehood' seem to be fairly constant across human cultures, 'fiction' is a far more ambiguous and variable notion.[54] As far as Graeco-Roman antiquity is concerned, a general view has emerged that truthfulness was not a precise or self-evident value, and historians used certain rhetorical techniques to enhance their material, often to the detriment of factual accuracy.[55] Christopher R. Ligota warns that, just as history had no separate identity as a discipline, nor was the notion of 'historical reality' comparable to the modern sense either.[56] In a similar vein, Christopher Pelling, in his discussion of Plutarch, observes that 'the boundary between truth and falsehood was less important than that between acceptable and unacceptable fabrication, between things which were "true enough" and things which were not. Truth ... can sometimes be bent a little'.[57]

How far we should transfer these lessons from classical historiography to late antique hagiography is, of course, another question. The central reason for believing that the same attitudes might prevail is the extraordinary conservatism of the classical education system. One approach to early hagiography, therefore, has been to consider which classical rhetorical categories it most closely resembles. To this question Claudia Rapp provides a fascinating response: hagiography was a Christianized form of writing which drew, amongst other things, on this classical rhetorical tradition.[58] Specifically, it was a form of *diegesis*, that is to say a form of reportage which demanded an unadorned style, but also,

[54]   Michael Wood, 'Prologue', in Christopher Gill and T.P. Wiseman (eds), *Lies and Fiction in the Ancient World* (Exeter, 1993), p. xvi.

[55]   T.P. Wiseman, 'Lying Historians: Seven Types of Mendacity' in Gill and Wiseman (eds), *Lies and Fiction*, pp. 122–46.

[56]   Christopher R. Ligota, '"This story is not true". Fact and Fiction in Antiquity', pp. 1–3.

[57]   C.B.R Pelling, 'Truth and Fiction in Plutarch's *Lives*', in D.A. Russell (ed.), *Antonine Literature* (Oxford, 1990), p. 43.

[58]   Claudia Rapp, 'Storytelling as Spiritual Communication in Early Greek Hagiography: the Use of *Diegesis*', JECS 6 (1998), p. 443.

crucially, an emphasis on plausibility.[59] In Rapp's reading, therefore, hagiography followed literary conventions to which the representation of familiar reality was central. This position, of course, leaves somewhat ambiguous the precise point at which the border between truthfulness and verisimilitude was supposed to lie. Was the importance of plausibility felt to carry with it any kind of obligation towards literal, factual detail? Or was it more akin to Barthes' *effet de réel*,[60] an aesthetic commitment towards the familiar created by certain techniques of language? Rapp's ambiguity is reflected by other scholars. Averil Cameron associates hagiographies with a realm of 'intended truth' (and in this sense they differed from the ancient novel).[61] Michael Williams argues that hagiographies 'could incorporate a certain amount of unreality, as long as they took place in a recognizable conteporary world and were at least seemingly historical'.[62]

These are, of course, extremely difficult issues, which the present work will not pretend to resolve definitively; it will seek simply to bring some fresh considerations to the problem. On the philosophical side, it is vital to recognize that the problems were not new; indeed, they were inherent in the transcendental metaphysics dominant in the period. Plato's *Republic* had already observed the inevitable loss of reality resulting from any artistic attempt to copy an original object.[63] Discussing the issue as raised by Plato, W.J. Verdenius convincingly argued that any philosophically satisfying solution to the problem of mimesis required a number of elements on the artist's part: divine inspiration to create, an acceptance of limitations, a focus on the original object's most essential features and, not least, a commitment to render the original truthfully. This notion of truthfulness was complex: it aimed at the object's inner essence. But in doing so, it did not abandon or deform, but used and respected its external appearance.[64] Within a transcendental system, we might almost say that these attitudes constitute a theory of realism. Although the artist was extending the mimetic chain still further, he could, by signalling this fact, draw attention to

---

[59]   Ibid., pp. 437–8. For the uses of hagiography in teaching contexts, see also Claudia Rapp, 'The Origins of Hagiography and the Literature of Early Monasticism: Purpose and Genre between Tradition and Innovation' in Christopher Kelly, Richard Flower and Michael Williams (eds), *Unclassical Traditions: Alternatives to the Classical Past in Late Antiquity* vol. 1 (Cambridge, 2010), pp. 119–38.

[60]   Ibid., pp. 442–4. Roland Barthes, 'L'Effet de réel', *Communications* 11 (1968), pp. 84–9.

[61]   Averil Cameron, *Christianity and the Rhetoric of Empire*, p. 118.

[62]   Michael Williams, *Authorised Lives*, p. 183.

[63]   Plato, *Respublica*, 10. 596–9, ed. and tr. P. Shorey: *Plato* vols 5 and 6 (London/New York, 1930; repr. 1994).

[64]   W.J. Verdenius, *Mimesis: Plato's Doctrine of Artistic Imitation and its Meaning to Us* (Leiden, 1949), pp. 18–20.

the sensible world's own status as an imperfect representation of the invisible truths which transcended it. In this sense, art might indeed offer a preliminary access to reality rather than representing merely a further dilution of it; it might become less an act of creation than one of interpretation: 'Only that artist who is convinced of the smallness of his art will create great art'.[65]

The intellectual theory Verdenius draws out from Plato seems very close to that applied by the Christian and Platonic hagiographers of late antiquity. As we have seen, they too consistently emphasized the inspired nature of their literary calling, the need to select only a few crucial stories from a possible mass. Above all – and this is especially true of pagan hagiographers – they admitted the limitations implicit in their task; they recognized, in other words, that literal accuracy was only one kind of truthfulness and had to be balanced against other considerations (see p. 29). There was a philosophical value in this recognition: for example, as mentioned above, the story about Plotinus' refusal to sit for a portrait can be read both as a self-reflective acknowledgement on Porphyry's part of the limits of mimetic art as well as a statement about the sensible world itself.[66] However, although the texts' literal contents were certainly subordinate to their ideological aims, it does not follow that they could be thoroughly subsumed by them; or, to put it another way, that factual accuracy was not itself at least one sincere objective of truthfulness. Indeed, if anything, the overtly religious nature of hagiography made this obligation more not less urgent. The sensible world may have been only a sign, but it was also the sign through which the divine communicated the truth, the only sign where contemplation of the truth could begin. There was every reason to regard its precise details as extremely important.

Let us now consider the importance accorded to literal truthfulness within the classical rhetorical tradition. It is certainly valid to recognize the possibility of continuity between this tradition and hagiography; it is also important to recognize that there is not necessarily a straightforward opposition between the constraints of a literary tradition and an ethic of truthfulness: as Rapp rightly observes, the *diegesis* carried with it a certain expectation of realism. Nonetheless, whilst this general literary heritage must be acknowledged, we must surely remain circumspect when applying it to any given late antique author. The conservatism of classical education notwithstanding, we must recognize that, at least directly, classical rhetorical authorities like Hermogenes and Quintillian are only very weakly attested in late antique sources, and not at all in hagiography. Furthermore, since our period saw a decline in the classical education system, especially in the West, we must expect the impact of these

---

[65]   Ibid., p. 37.
[66]   Edwards, 'A Portrait of Plotinus', pp. 482–3.

rhetorical categories to have varied from author to author, and generally to have diminished over time (compare, for example, Sulpicius and Eugippius). Most importantly, assertions of truthfulness by hagiographers often involve the author drawing a more or less explicit contrast between their own project and the literary traditions of the past. Pagan authors sometimes contrasted their own well-researched accounts from the vagaries of oral tradition;[67] similarly, as we have seen, Christian ones sometimes explicitly distinguished their works with classical forms of writing (see p. 29). Literary heritage could be presented as contrast as well as continuity.

In general then, hagiographical guarantees of truthfulness appear to include an important and continued sensitivity towards the idea of literal truthfulness; their philosophical commitments and literary heritage may complicate this idea but they do not abolish it. However, what such statements reveal about the inner intentions of hagiographers and the way in which they approached their work is limited. By its nature, literary genre is a contract between the author and the audience and, as Averil Cameron observes (see p. 26), the expectations of the latter towards hagiography remain very unclear. Were authorial guarantees taken seriously or were they, at the limit, merely a rhetorical adornment and accepted as such? In any case, we can expect the same ethic towards truthfulness to have been shared by both author and audience since knowledge of the genre could only have circulated amongst (or at least with the aid of) literate people who, to a greater or lesser extent, would have shared with hagiographers a common educational background.

Unfortunately, we have only very meagre evidence from late antiquity for how hagiographies were read. The little there is, however, very strongly suggests that readers expected from hagiographers a literal truthfulness as well as a spiritual message. We mentioned above the trusting way in which hagiographers appear to have accepted the claims of their predecessors: thus when the author of the *Lives of the Jura Fathers* claims of Eugendus that 'the deeds of blessed Antony and Martin and their way of life never slipped away from his spirit' (*Non illi beatorum Antonii atque Martini gesta aut mores unquam labebantur ex animo*),[68] there is no mention of the works of Athanasius and Sulpicius; not the slightest suggestion that they may be anything other than literal and trustworthy accounts. Cyril and Palladius seem to have been similarly accepting of the *Life of Antony* as a true record of the saint's life.[69] As for Jerome's notoriously unhistorical *Life of Paul*, as Stefan Rebenich has pointed out, belief in the hero

---

[67] See especially Iamblichus, *Life of Pythagoras* 18(86).

[68] *Lives of the Jura Fathers* 168 (tr. Vivian et al., p. 178).

[69] Palladius, *Lausiac History* 8.6; Cyril, *Lives* 110.15–19.

in late antiquity was sufficiently widespread and enthusiastic to give rise to a major popular cult.[70]

A further very unusual and very direct example of hagiographical readership occurs in Augustine's *Confessions* where the author describes in some depth his inspirational discovery of the Antony story. The evidence is especially important because Augustine claims to have encountered the work not in the course of regular Christian reading but accidentally when he was still in a state of religious uncertainty. As Williams has rightly stressed,[71] the most immediate and striking aspect of this intellectual encounter is Augustine's emphasis on Antony's historicity:

> Ponticianus told us about Antony, the Egyptian monk, whose name was well known among your servants but unknown among us until that hour. When Ponticianus discovered this fact, he persisted on that topic of conversation, giving us to understand what a great man Antony was, and amazed at our ignorance. We were dumbfounded to hear of your mighty works (Ps. 145.5 [Ps. 144.5]), which you had wrought through the orthodox faith of the Catholic Church. There was the strongest attestation (*testatissima*) for them; they had occurred within living memory, and almost, indeed, within our own lifetimes (*tam recenti memoria et proper nostris temporibus*). We were all amazed: Alypius and I at the greatness of these wonders, Ponticianus at our ignorance of them.[72]

Before the precise spiritual significance of Antony's life occurred to him in the Milan garden, then, Augustine had been struck by the literal truthfulness of the great saint's life (a truthfulness lacking in much of the classical literature he had studied at school.)[73] Although it is difficult to generalize from one example, it is highly significant that a thinker of Augustine's sophistication should respond to hagiography in a way entirely consistent with the sort of guarantees of literal truthfulness offered by hagiographers themselves.

Everything suggests, then, that when hagiographers promised to write truthfully, this guarantee had two aspects: firstly, that the events selected were spiritually significant in that they pointed to higher truths beyond the sensible world; secondly, that these same stories were literal and factual accounts of events

---

[70]   Stefan Rebenich, 'Inventing an Ascetic Hero', pp. 13–14.

[71]   Williams, *Authorised Lives*, p. 166.

[72]   Augustine, *Confessiones* 8.6.14, ed. with commentary, John J. O'Donnell (Oxford, 1992), tr. Philip Burton, *Augustine: Confessions* (London, 2001), p. 171.

[73]   'If I ask them whether it is true, as the poets say, that Aeneas once upon a time came to Carthage, the less educated will say they do not know, but the more educated will admit that it is false.' Augustine, *Confessions* 1.13.22 (tr. Burton, p. 20).

that had occurred within the sensible world. Not only did hagiographers promise this; their readers expected it. These were not easy aims and hagiographers admitted their inadequacies; a certain balance no doubt needed to be struck between literal truthfulness and other considerations. It is often very difficult to say where the border of acceptability lay in the mind of any given author, but there were clearly those, like Jerome, who played fast and loose with it.

Generally speaking, however, one of the principal dangers facing the modern interpreter is to underestimate the sensitivity of religiously minded people in late antiquity towards the literal. To say that the task of the hagiographer was to balance the spiritual and literal aspects of the truth does not go far enough; it was to reveal spiritual truths already present in literal events. The modern interpreter must thus avoid formulating on behalf of hagiographers a literary ethic which permanently and tranquilly resolves the competing pressures of different categories of information, for hagiographers recognized the potential for conflict between their various aims, as well as their readers' capacity to suspect it. Occasionally, the risk was that the details of a saint's life might seem too prosaic and therefore of insufficient spiritual significance. Hilarius, for example, had explicitly to justify the fact that his hero Honoratus did not produce the tally of miracles expected from a saint: 'what could be greater manifestation of spiritual power than to shun manifestations and hide the powers?'[74] he pleaded somewhat feebly. Normally, however, hagiographers were not worried that the significance of events might be overlooked, but rather that they were too extraordinary to be believed. Hence, as we saw above, hagiographical prologues often give much space to specific assurances about an author's research methods and sources. It is also, as we shall discuss later in the case of miracles, why the possibility of doubt in the amazing literal truth of events was sometimes anticipated and directly addressed at crucial moments in the narrative. Just as the hagiographer had the ability to distort the truth in the face of his audience's expectations, the audience had the capacity to doubt despite his protestations of truthfulness.[75] For example, not everyone believed the *Life of Paul*; it was against contemporary sceptics that Jerome felt obliged to defend it so rigorously.[76] The point, however, is that these

---

[74] Hilarius, *Life of Honoratus* 8.37 (tr. Hoare, p. 278). Theodoret makes a similar point about Marcianus: 'Eager to hide the grace given to him, he worked miracles reluctantly', *History* 3.9 (tr. Price, p. 40).

[75] The possibility of scepticism towards the cult of saints in the Byzantine period is explored by Gilbert Dagron, 'L'ombre d'un doute: l'hagiographie en question VIe–XIe siècle', *Dumbarton Oaks Papers* 46 (1992), pp. 59–68; and over a longer period in a recent essay collection by Philip Booth, Matthew J. Dal Santo and Peter Sarris (eds), *An Age of Saints? Power, Conflict and Dissent in Early Medieval Christianity* (Leiden, 2011).

[76] See footnote 15, p. 28.

people, in not believing its literal truthfulness, simply disbelieved it and accused Jerome accordingly. What contemporary audiences do not appear to have conceptualized are forms of appreciation divorced from literal, factual belief.

The result of this may seem somewhat paradoxical: in a form of literature dedicated to higher truths which transcended mere events, it was literal belief which was felt to be especially difficult and was therefore most extensively discussed. The reason for this has partly to do with the genre's intellectual scope. Hagiography was not the place to discuss complex doctrines; indeed some pagan works, such as Porphyry's *Life of Plotinus* and Iamblichus' *On the Pythagorean Life* were intentionally written as introductions to longer philosophical volumes.[77] More fundamentally, we must assume that the vast majority of readers of hagiography were intellectual partisans more interested in finding further support for what they already believed than in exploring alternative world views. Amongst such readers, therefore, ultimate truths were less controversial than the extent to which stories about particular saints genuinely instantiated and supported these truths. As Stancliffe has observed, Sulpicius did not have to prove to readers that holy men existed, but (no less demandingly) that the controversial figure of Martin was a genuine example of one.[78] Similarly, the scepticism Damascius anticipates towards his claims about Isidore ('how can you prove, my friend, that your philosopher descended from that (*Hermaic*) order of souls?'[79]), never questions the existence of the deity Hermes, but the specific status of his hero.

Gilbert Dagron has argued that 'des doutes, des réticences, des résistances'[80] towards the cult of saints did not have to be those of total unbelievers, but of people with more specific and subtle concerns about the 'tricheries et excès de l'imagination' of hagiographers.[81] Although Dagron is referring to the subsequent Byzantine period, the basic patterns he observes seem equally applicable to the more religiously diverse late antique period. Consider, for example, Theodoret: when he argued for the historicity of his subjects' lives by comparing them to biblical characters, he could simply assume that his readers would already believe in the latter; it was the difficulty of believing the former that he recognized and addressed. His defence of the facts thus rests on a strongly hierarchical structure of belief based on various appeals to authority. The possibility of narrative

---

[77]   Gillian Clark, 'Philosophic Lives and the Philosophic Life', in Hägg and Rousseau (eds), *Greek Biography and Panegyric*, pp. 33–5.

[78]   Stancliffe, *Saint Martin and his Hagiographer*, p. 261.

[79]   Damascius, *Philosophical History* 6A (tr. Athanassiadi, p. 83).

[80]   Gilbert Dagron, 'L'ombre d'un doute: l'hagiographie en question VIe–XIe siècle', *Dumbarton Oaks Papers* 46 (1992), p. 59.

[81]   Ibid., p. 60.

exaggeration is answered by showing the holy man himself to be the source of the stories about him; the Bible is invoked as evidence of the reality of human sanctity and of the miracles that result from it. Theodoret clearly felt able to take for granted his audience's most basic religious commitments, which include the absolute truthfulness and authority of Scripture; lesser objections are not contested piecemeal but by exposing their incompatibility to the belief system *in toto*: to doubt the miracle would be to doubt the holy man; to doubt the holy man would be to doubt the Bible.

This book derives two principal lessons from the continued importance of the literal in late antique hagiography. One, mentioned in the introduction and to be explored at the end of this chapter and beyond, is the need for a different approach towards the historicity of information contained within hagiographies, an approach which both recognizes the profoundly ideological and subjective nature of these texts, but also takes seriously their sensitivity towards literal information and the general ethical pressure to relate reality truthfully. The second, more immediate need, is of a literary nature: to examine how authors, beyond their ostensive declarations of truthfulness, continued to fulfil the dual need of relating information which the audience could believe to be at once literally true and spiritually significant. To do so, we must thus consider the literary techniques by which the sensible world was represented, the type of phenomena which are repeated and emphasized, as well as the particular philosophical significance that attaches to them. We must, in other words, describe the nature of hagiographical realism. And in the course of such an exercise, it may be useful to reflect that hagiography perhaps has more in common with more familiar notions of literary realism than its ultimate metaphysical transcendentalism might initially lead us to assume. Many hagiographies depicted environments which were local, recent, and therefore tangible to the reader; in this respect at least, they had something in common with the modern realist novel.[82] Within the context of the present project, this is not a statement about literary history

---

[82] This 'tangible' aspect is stressed by Peter Brown in relation to the cult of saints generally: 'throughout the Christian world of the fifth and sixth centuries, average Christian believers ... were encouraged to draw comfort from the expectation that, somewhere, in their own times, even maybe in their own region, and so directly accessible to their own distress, a chosen few of their fellows ... had achieved, usually through prolonged ascetic labour, an exceptional degree of closeness to God': *Authority and the Sacred: Aspects of the Christianisation of the Roman World* (Cambridge, 1995), pp. 57–8. He makes a related point in 'Rise and Function of the Holy Man', p. 81: 'In studying the most and most detested figures in any society, we can see ... the nature of the average man's expectations and hopes for himself'.

per se; rather, it is designed to highlight the possibility of learning lessons from modern discussions about literary realism.

The remainder of this chapter, therefore, is a discussion of three aspects of late antique hagiography, aspects so fundamental that they constitute not so much discrete themes within the genre as its defining characteristics. These are: the physical appearance and movements of holy men, miracles and 'supernatural' phenomena generally, and the precise spiritual status and identity of holy men. Each aspect highlights the problem, faced by all late antique hagiographers, of presenting a picture of a higher reality which remained compatible with the audience's notions of plausibility.

The Holy Man's Appearance and Movements

As an impeccable Platonist, Porphyry understood very well the reasons why Plotinus felt shame at his physical existence and therefore refused to sit for a painting. But this did not diminish his own fascination with the philosopher's body. On the contrary, the great man's medical history and death are introduced as early as the second chapter of Porphyry's biography. His vile appearance and rich pathology were spectacularly enhanced by a total avoidance of treatment. He refused an enema for his bad bowels, he never bathed, he gave up massage and 'succumbed to intense diphteria'. His voice was 'destroyed by hoarseness, his vision was blurred and his hands and feet were ulcerated'. Friends avoided his kiss of greeting. To the very end, he identified only with his soul and died 'trying to raise the divine in himself to the divine in the all'.[83]

Although extreme, Porphyry's emphasis on his subject's infirmity and ugliness is not entirely unique. Plato had made much of Socrates' snub nose and protruding eyes and the *Symposium* ends by contrasting the old man's true, inner beauty, with the sham of Alcibiades' good looks.[84] Later pagan biographers included comparable descriptions: Eunapius, for example, saw in Alypius' diminutive physical stature evidence of his great soul and intellect.[85] The philosophical message is clear: soul is more real than body; the philosopher's indifference to physical imperfection demonstrates to the reader how deeply he understood this truth. But the relationship between a philosopher's soul and body was not always presented as one of contrast. Applying the ancient science of physiognomy which regarded the body's state as analogous to that of the

---

[83]   Porphyry, *Life of Plotinus* 2.

[84]   Plato, *Symposium* 218D–E, ed. W.R.M. Lamb in Plato vol. 3 [*Lysis, Symposium, Gorgias*] (London/New York, 1925; repr. 1983).

[85]   Eunapius, *Lives* 460.

soul, Marinus detected in Proclus' physical health and beauty a reflection of his spiritual condition.[86] In Damascius' *Philosophical History*, Isidore's appearance is that of a 'sensible old man, dignified and resolute'; his nearly square face is said to reflect his divine model Logios Hermes[87] and his eyes revealed the presence of Aphrodite and Athena.[88] According to their respective biographers, a trace of the spiritual brilliance of the female philosophers Sosipatra and Hypatia could be found in their extraordinary physical beauty.[89]

A second aspect of the philosopher's appearance, namely the use of language in speech or writing, also constituted an important theme in pagan biography. The treatment it receives is closely analogous to that of visual appearance. Plotinus habitually made linguistic errors,[90] refused to revise work, wrote inelegantly without dividing syllables, and had little concern for spelling.[91] Eunapius' teacher Chrysanthius 'neither knew the art of writing verse nor was trained in the science of grammar'.[92] Damascius emphasizes the point still more explicitly: his hero Isidore detested rhetoric and had only minimal sympathy for poetry;[93] like his distant predecessor Plotinus, he was verbally clumsy in lectures.[94] But as in the case of visual appearance, the implied philosophical contrast – this time between thoughts and mere words – is not the only way language could be treated. Elsewhere biographers praise their subjects' linguistic skill and the charm of their speech as indications of spiritual brilliance.[95]

What is striking about these conventions is not just their consistency over a range of texts but also their tendency to take two opposing forms: physical phenomena may variously reflect, or contrast with the spiritual world. It is not the case that individual authors necessarily chose one or other possibility. Porphyry, who gave such prominence to Plotinus' physical decay, elsewhere

---

[86]   Marinus, *Life of Proclus* 3.

[87]   Damascius, *Philosophical History* 13 (tr. Athanassiadi, p. 89).

[88]   Ibid. See also Eunapius' description of Prohaeresius' beauty, *Lives* 486–7.

[89]   Sosipatra had, from infancy, 'exceeding beauty and charm', Eunapius, *Lives* 467 (tr. Wright, p. 401). See also Damascius on Hypatia's beauty: *Philosophical History* 43.

[90]   Porphyry, *Life of Plotinus* 13.

[91]   Ibid. 8 (tr. Edwards, p. 17).

[92]   'For him the god took the place of all else': Eunapius, *Lives* 504 (tr. Wright, p. 579).

[93]   Damascius, *Philosophical History* 48. For Socrates' ban on poetry see Plato, *Republic* 606E–607B.

[94]   Damascius, *Philosophical History* 37D.

[95]   Further examples of this tendency are Eunapius' descriptions of Aedesius and Iamblichus: *Lives* 460; 461; Eustathius: ibid. 465 (pp. 393–4); Maximus: ibid. 473 (p. 427); Chrysanthius: ibid. 501 (p. 549); Olympos: Damascius, *Philosophical History* 42B. In the case of Sosipatra, a more positive view of language found expression in the breadth of her literary interests: Eunapius, *Lives* 469.

praised Pythagoras for inventing the science of physiognomy.[96] Despite his afflictions and verbal clumsiness, when Plotinus taught his 'mind was manifest even in his countenance, which radiated light'.[97] In a similar vein, Eunapius claims that Chrysanthius seemed unintelligent until, when discussing philosophy, his hair stood on end and revealed his soul 'leaping and dancing'.[98] In both these passages, the conventions concerning a philosopher's appearance are used in a particularly complex way. Changes in mental state somehow become visible in the philosopher's face: the sensible world which had contrasted with the spiritual now comes to reflect it. And the two types of appearance – visual and verbal – are intertwined: the former is introduced as a counterweight to the perceived limitations of the latter.

Doubtless these conventions included a tactical function: however good or bad a philosopher looked or sounded, his appearance could be turned to his advantage.[99] But the philosophical coherence of these conventions also needs to be considered not least because they appear vulnerable to a charge of inconsistency. The sophisticated treatments of Eunapius and Porphyry would not escape such criticism; they merely increase the number of forms the conventions could take. The philosophical problem that underlines these portraits, and determines their dual nature, is neatly described by John Fielder:

> For Plotinus, and for Platonists generally, the sensible world is not the only reality. A philosophical examination of this world reveals higher realities of which this world is said to be an 'image'. Thus the problem of chorismos is not simply that the higher realities are ontologically 'separate' from the sensible world, but that this separation must be consistent with a very close connection between them. Whatever unity, structure, and value sensibles have is provided by the higher realities despite their ontological separation. The philosophical account of this relationship must, as it were, bring the higher realities into the world without sacrificing their ontologically distinct status. Too sharp a separation tends to

---

[96]　Porphyry, *De Vita Pythagorae* 13, ed. and tr. E. des Places, *De Vita Pythagorae; Ad Marcellam* (Paris, 1982).

[97]　Porphyry, *Life of Plotinus* 13 (tr. Edwards, p. 23).

[98]　'Many of those ... who had not sounded the depths of his soul, accused him of lack of intelligence ... but when they heard him maintaining a philosophical theme ... they decided that this was a very different person from the man they thought they knew. So transformed did he seem by the excitement of dialectic debate, with his hair standing on end, and his eyes testifying that the soul within him was leaping and dancing around the opinions that he expressed': Eunapius, *Lives* 502 (tr. Wright, pp. 549–51).

[99]　Health, beauty, and size were qualities expected of a philosopher, 'dont l'absence doit être justifiée et ne peut l'être que par la présence de qualités d'ordre supérieur'. Goulet, *Etudes sur les vies des philosophes*, pp. 21–2.

preclude any influence, while too close an association tends to eliminate the separation.[100]

Although Fielder is not referring to hagiography, his words can certainly be applied to one of the deepest problems confronted by the genre. The sensible images of relevance to our authors were, of course, the human body and the words it produced; the philosopher's soul the entity to which these things were ontologically subordinate. And the truth of this basic hierarchy could variously be expressed through either opposition or analogy.

Although conventions dealing with physical appearance are particularly prominent in pagan hagiography, the problem did not apply uniquely to the self-styled heirs of Plato. Similar, if less pronounced patterns existed in Christian hagiography. For example, Theodoret draws an analogy between the nature of Publius' soul and the beauty of his physique.[101] For the author of the *History of the Monks of Egypt*, either a beautiful or a terrible appearance could be an indication of sanctity.[102] Some saints, like Martin, were marked by the simple purity of their speech;[103] others, like Severinus, for their eloquence.[104] This was not a mutually exclusive contrast: the discourse of the uneducated Antony, for example, was unadorned, but he could speak with great beauty and skill when necessary.[105]

In the present context, the conventions surrounding physical appearance are chiefly of interest for what they reveal about the form of realism hagiography entailed. As argued above, the particular challenge for hagiographers was to present information which was both spiritually significant and factually credible. One way this need was met was by revealing the spiritual significance of even quite mundane categories of human experience. Though they might emphasize the extraordinary nature of the appearance of certain philosophers, the basic categories they depicted – beauty and ugliness, eloquence and verbal clumsiness – are universally familiar. From one viewpoint, this greatly enhanced hagiography's scope for literal truthfulness since every type of detail carried with it the possibility of a greater significance beyond itself. Conversely, because this

---

[100] John H. Fielder, '*Chorismos* and Emanation in the Philosophy of Plotinus', in *The Significance of Neoplatonism*, (Norfolk, Virginia, 1976), p. 101.

[101] Theodoret, *History* 5.1.

[102] Compare the lovely appearance of Abba Or with the terrible appearance of Abba Elijah: *History of the Monks of Egypt* 2.1–2 v. 7.2.

[103] Sulpicius, *Life of Martin*, 25.6.

[104] Eugippius, *Letter to Paschasius* 10, ed. and tr. Philippe Régérat, *Eugippe: Vie de Saint Séverin*, Sources Chrétiennes 374 (Paris, 1991).

[105] Athanasius depicts Antony as illiterate: *Life of Antony* 1.2 but easily able to out-argue professional philosophers: ibid., pp. 72–3.

philosophical world view could account for all diversity by the greater unity which transcended it, no piece of information could challenge the basic hierarchy it espoused; indeed every detail proved it. Thus hagiography demonstrated practically what philosophers argued theoretically, that 'all things are full of signs, and it is a wise man who can learn about one thing from another'.[106] A realism linking the spiritual to the physical was achieved by infusing the entire realm of the latter with an inexhaustible potential significance.

The holy man's physical appearance was not the only convention which manifests this point. Something similar can be said about another major field of interest in hagiography: a saint's location, movements, and relationship with space in general. As we shall see, both pagan and Christian hagiographies reflect this problem in a similar way, but for the sake of clarity, each tradition will be dealt with in turn. In the transcendental metaphysics of late antiquity, space belonged to the sensible world and not to the worlds beyond it; necessary to the sensible world's status as an image, it lacked any independent reality. The consequences of this were extremely significant. As Plotinus repeatedly emphasized, in the quest for understanding, the spatial confines of the sensible world could provide metaphors for transcendental realities, but these could never be more than provisional.[107] In a celebrated passage, Plotinus compares man's spiritual life to an exile in the Homeric sense. However, his metaphor exploits not only similarities between these two concepts, but defines the spiritual sense of exile by systematically negating the spatial aspects of the physical sense:

> 'Let us fly to our dear country' (Iliad 2.140). What then is our way of escape, and how are we to find it? We shall put out to sea, as Odysseus did, from the witch Circe or Calypso – as the poet says (I think with a hidden meaning) – and was not content to stay though he had delights of the eyes and lived among much beauty of senses. Our country from which we came is there, our Father is there. How shall we travel to it, where is our way of escape? We cannot get there on foot; for our feet only carry us everywhere in this world, from one country to another. You must not get ready a carriage, either, or a boat. Let all these things go, and do

---

[106]   Plotinus, *Enneades* 2.3.7, ed. and tr. A.H. Armstrong, Loeb Classical Library (7 vols, London/New York, 1966–85; repr. 1995), vol. 2, p. 69.

[107]   This is shown not least by Plotinus' instructions about grasping the Forms, which involves picturing objects in the phenomenal world and then removing from the mind all spatial restrictions: Plotinus, *Enneads* 5.8.9 (tr. Armstrong, vol. 5, pp. 265–7). Consider, for example, Augustine's difficulty in imagining God without reference to spatial imagery: *Confessions*, 1.3.3; 7.1.1. For discussion see, Ferwerda, *La signification des images et des métaphores dans la pensée de Plotin*, pp. 1–5.

not look. Shut your eyes, and change to and wake another way of seeing, which everyone has, but few use.[108]

The lowly ontological status of space had long been expressed in the lifestyles of philosophers and continued to be so in late antiquity. The ancient philosophical tradition of Cosmianism dated back at least as far as Plato (and was attributed to the even more ancient Pythagoras by Iamblichus):[109] it stated that the true sage, being spiritually stable, was equally content wherever he lived. We might imagine that this made hagiography a genre insensitive to geography. But this is far from the case. For one thing, the problem for hagiographers was more than purely doctrinal for they had to find ways of representing these metaphysical truths in narrative form through the life stories of the holy men who understood them. The most obvious way was for the sage to deny any attachment to homeland and background, as Plotinus is famously reported to have done at the beginning of Porphyry's biography. But this passage is not unparalleled. In both Porphyry's and Iamblichus' biographies of Pythagoras, the great sage's mystique is undoubtedly enhanced by conflicting rumours surrounding his birthplace, an omission both authors are content to pass on unresolved.[110] In other cases, the philosopher's non-attachment to place is represented by a radical flight from civilization of a type which Iamblichus reports the Pythagoreans to have undertaken after their expulsion from Southern Italy.[111] Like the body which enclosed it, harsh or alien places could provide a useful point of contrast against which to measure the philosopher's superior soul. Crossing the seas to Egypt, Pythagoras remained 'secure and undisturbed', his stability reflected in the boat's 'straight, continuous and direct' passage, 'as though some god were present'.[112] On the freezing borderlands of Gaul, Eunapius' teacher Prohaeresius remained 'passionless and made of iron',[113] treating the local winters as 'the height of luxury'. Exiled among barbarians, the virtuous Oribasius revealed his 'stability and constancy' like 'numbers and mathematical truths'.[114]

---

[108]   Plotinus, *Enneads* 1.6.8.17–28 (tr. Armstrong, vol. 1, pp. 257–9).

[109]   Iamblichus, *On the Pythagorean Life*, 33(237). For a history of the idea, see M-O. Goulet-Cazé, 'Kosmopolitismus' in *Der Neue Pauly*, vol. 6, pp. 778–9.

[110]   Porphyry, *The Life of Pythagoras* 1–2; Iamblichus, *On the Pythagorean Life*, 2(3)–(8).

[111]   Ibid., 35(253). An idea also inherited by Porphyry, *De Abstinentia* 1.36, ed. and tr. Jean Bouffartigue, Alain-Philippe Segonds, Michel Patillon *De Abstinentia, Porphyre: de l'abstinence* (3 vols, Paris, 1977–95).

[112]   Iamblichus, *On the Pythagorean Life*, 3(16), (tr. Clark, p. 7).

[113]   Eunapius, *Lives* 492 (tr. Wright, p. 507).

[114]   Ibid. 498 (p. 535).

The representation of any attitude towards space, however indifferent, inevitably bestowed on the genre a rich geographical aspect. But even a technical indifference towards space as a metaphysical entity failed to abolish the idea of a sacred geography which for pagans was undoubtedly enhanced by the encroachments of a militant Christianity.[115] For example, Eunapius' Athens is clearly a sacred city, just as both it and Byzantium are for Proclus.[116] But although these two treatments of space are conceptually opposed, when we consider them in combination we recognize how inevitably they became intertwined, and how many variations they produced. For Marinus, Byzantium is sacred because the city's tutelary goddess Rhea is Proclus' true nurse and midwife. But this claim involves the rejection of his human background in a manner reminiscent of the *Life of Plotinus*: Proclus' mother Marcella was merely 'the human mother who gave birth to him'.[117] Pythagoras abandons his home town, feeling no loyalty towards its ignorant inhabitants, but is also celebrated for his subsequent travels to lands like Syria and Egypt famed for their ancient cults.[118] Plotinus, so dismissive of his own earthly origins, dreams of visiting distant, sacred India.[119] Travel could indicate indifference to space as a metaphysical entity, but it could just as well represent an embrace of sacred geography. Damascius reports that Isidore was 'devoted to travel' of a very erudite kind;[120] another of his philosophical heroes, Sarapio, may have dwelt in the heart of the sacred city of Alexandria, but he lived like a hermit, owning almost nothing and avoiding almost all human contact.[121]

Perhaps nothing encapsulates the paradoxical nature of geographical space more neatly than India's exotic reputation in late antiquity as a land of religious and spiritual purity.[122] This reputation is summarized in *De gentibus*

---

[115]   This is clear, for example, in pagan accounts of the destruction of the Serapeum in Alexandria: ibid. 472 (tr. W.C. Wright, p. 421); Damascius, *Philosophical History* 42H.

[116]   For the state of the city and Proclus' relation to it, Garth Fowden, 'The Pagan Holy Man in Late Antique Society', *JHS* 102 (1982), p. 39ff. For Julian's view of Athens, Polymnia Athanassiadi, *Julian: An Intellectual Biography* (1992), p. 46.

[117]   Marinus, *Life of Proclus* 6 (tr. Edwards, pp. 65–6).

[118]   Iamblichus, *On the Pythagorean Life* 3(14).

[119]   Porphyry, *Life of Plotinus* 3.

[120]   Damascius, *Philosophical History* 21 (tr. Athanassiadi, p. 99).

[121]   Ibid., p. 111.

[122]   In Philostratus' *De Vita Apollonii Tyanei* 3.19–20 (ed. and tr. C.P. Jones, Loeb Classical Library 3 vols, London/New York, 2005–2006), the Indians are declared the oldest and purest philosophical culture, from which Egyptian, and ultimately Greek doctrines, derived. This view is consistently reflected in praise for the Indians' philosophical lifestyle. The message is repeated by Eunapius at *Lives* 481 where Indian methods of prophecy are said to predate Greek and Chaldean ones. By contrast, Diogenes Laertius vigorously rejects the (apparently quite common) view that philosophy had its origins amongst barbarians:

Indiae et Bragmanibus (*On the people of India and on the Brahmans*), a short work attributed to the fifth-century bishop Palladius which was compiled from a number of earlier accounts and reflects cultural attitudes common to both pagans and Christians.[123] The second part of the work imagines a meeting in a sacred grove in India between Alexander the Great and the ascetic sage Dandamis. On the one hand, Dandamis promotes a Cosmian vision: indifferent to human background, he lives outdoors and treats the whole natural world as his home.[124] On the other hand, the grove itself, as the location of his spiritual retreat, can hardly fail to become a sacred space. In a sense, the same point is underlined on a deeper level by the work's entire premise. Although Dandamis preaches geographical neutrality, his own appeal derives largely from the image of India as a land of Brahmanic wisdom (an idea cheerfully reinforced by extended comparison of its peaceable ways with those of worldly, warlike Greece).[125] The stereotype's inherent paradox appears again in Damascius' tale of a visit paid by a Brahmanic delegation to the pious nobleman Severus in Alexandria. Disinterested in 'all external things',[126] the Brahmans remain indoors and decline to visit the city's famous sites. But from the viewpoint of Severus and his companions, the very wisdom displayed by this attitude can only have enhanced the sacred connotations of the Brahmans' geographical homeland.[127]

Vitae Philosophorum 1.1, ed. and tr. Robert Drew Hicks, *Diogenes Laertius: Lives of Eminent Philosophers*, Loeb Classical Library (Cambridge MA: 1925; repr. 1970). Damascius asserts the immense antiquity of Egyptian rites, and their seniority *vis-à-vis* Greek ones: *Philosophical History* 1–4A. There is no direct comparison with Indian ones, although the Brahmans' spiritual excellence is discussed at ibid. 51D (tr. Athanassiadi, p. 147). Porphyry maintains the moral and philosophical excellence of the Indian spiritual classes (Brahman and Samanean) without speculating about the relative antiquity of their traditions: *De Abstinentia* 4.17–18. According to Augustine at *De Civitate Dei* 10.32, eds Bernhard Dombart and Alfons Kalb (5th edition, 2 vols, Stuttgart, 1981), Porphyry studied the morals and practices of the Indians and ranked them alongside the Chaldeans. See also John Dillon, in '"Orthodoxy" and "Eclecticism": Middle Platonists and Neopythagoreans', in idem; A.A. Long (eds), *The Question of 'Eclecticism'* (Berkeley, 1988), p. 124.

[123] Beverly Berg, 'Dandamis: An Early Christian Portrait of Indian Asceticism', in *C&M* 31 (1970), pp. 270–71.

[124] 'Οὐρανός μοι στέγη, γῆ μοι πᾶσα στρωμνή, ὕλαι τράπεζα, καρποὶ τροφῆς ἀπόλαυσις, ποταμοὶ διάκονοι δίψης'. Παλλαδίου περὶ τῶν τῆς Ἰνδίας ἐθνῶν καὶ τῶν βραχμάνων. *Palladius de gentibus Indiae et Bragmanibus* 2.24 in 'Palladius on the Races of India and the Brahmans' (ed. J.D.M. Derret) *C&M* 21 (1960), p. 122.

[125] 'Palladius on the Races of India and the Brahmans', 2.41–57 (ed. J.D.M. Derret) *C&M* 21 (1960), pp. 128–35.

[126] Damascius, *Philosophical History* 51D (tr. Athanassiadi, p. 147).

[127] Sarapio poses a similar problem: his hermit-like existence could be seen as a rejection of human categories of belonging; his pursuit of this lifestyle in Alexandria enhances the

Similarly paradoxical attitudes to space are reflected in Christian hagiography. Christians in the pre-Constantinian empire, which was variously hostile or indifferent towards their faith, sometimes expressed a radically otherworldly notion of identity which involved the complete rejection of earthly categories of belonging.[128] However, one rapid consequence of the Roman Empire's conversion was that the locations of biblical stories could now be visited and treated as a sacred landscape. As Jerome recognized, a possible conceptual conflict existed between the holy sites as special locations, and the idea of an omnipresent God: the subject of his *Life of Hilarion* could be praised for finding the right balance between these two considerations.[129]

But as in pagan hagiography, an acknowledgement of space as a mere physical entity could become entwined in complex ways with a metaphorical potential. Physical travel could come to symbolize identification with a spiritual homeland, as it does in the early fifth century *Life of Honoratus* in which the saint's abandonment of his Gallic birthplace with his brother is seen by his hagiographer Hilarius as proof that they were 'pilgrims thirsting for their heavenly fatherland'.[130] Another manifestation of this attitude was a very paradoxical and long-lasting geographical concept in Christian hagiography: namely the desert. Much has been written about the development of desert asceticism from the early fourth century and it is a topic to which we shall return elsewhere in this book. What is significant in the immediate context is its innately paradoxical character as an expression of space: even more so than its equivalents in pagan literature, the harshness and remoteness of the desert was the forum in which the holy man's geographical indifference could best be demonstrated. However, the demonstration of holiness by desert monks in turn transformed their environment into a sacred landscape in its own right. When the pilgrim Egeria travelled to the Eastern Mediterranean in the 380's her interests included both monks and biblical sites: the deserts of Egypt and the biblical sites of Palestine had blended into a 'single devotional landscape'.[131] (Some contemporary bishops, such as Gregory of Nyssa, were concerned about

city's sacred status: Damascius, *Philosophical History* 111.

[128]   Duncan Fisher, 'Liminality: the Vocation of the Church (I); the Desert Image in Early Christian Tradition', in *Cistercian Studies* 24 (1989), p. 187.

[129]   Jerome, *Letter* 58.3, ed. Isidore Hilberg, CSEL 54 (Vienna, repr. 1996). A similar attitude is displayed by Peter the Galatian: Theodoret, *History* 9.2. For the ambivalence of Christian notions of sacred space, see Robert Markus, *The End of Ancient Christianity* (Cambridge, 1990), pp. 153–5.

[130]   Hilarius, *Life of Honoratus* 2.12 (tr. Hoare, pp. 257–8).

[131]   E.D. Hunt, 'The Itinerary of Egeria: Reliving the Bible in Fourth-Century Palestine', in *The Holy Land, Holy Lands and Christian History* (Woodbridge, 2000), p. 38.

the social effects of such spiritual tourism.)[132] Another aspect of this process, observed by numerous modern scholars, is how terms for 'desert', increasingly laden with Christian ascetic values and correspondingly vaguer as a geographical notion, came to denote in the early mediaeval West any remote spot suitable for the contemplative life.[133] But in a sense the philosophical seeds of this linguistic transformation were present from the outset. Although the desert became a measure of holiness only by providing a physical environment whose harshness contrasted with the holy man's soul, its very role in doing so led to its reification as a forum and shorthand for holiness.

The use of space in hagiography is an extremely complex issue and can be analysed in many different ways. But despite its greater complexity, it reflects the same underlying philosophical problem that we saw in the case of the philosopher's appearance. Like fine words and beautiful bodies or clumsy words and ugly bodies, places – whether desolate or sacred – could be infused with meanings which ultimately confirmed the same spiritual truths. Philosophically, the status of space was one of indifference, a feature only of our sensible world. But in the pages of hagiography this status could be expressed in two opposing ways: either through the negation of the human concepts intuitively associated with it – belonging, comfort etc. – and an implied contrast with the spiritual realities which transcended it; or, alternatively, particular places could acquire a provisional, symbolic value as pointers to those same spiritual realities in their current state of concealment. As in the case of physical appearance, these two tendencies could interact in complex ways: a place of flight, like the Christian desert, could in turn acquire a positive symbolism.

By highlighting the symbolic potential of all phenomena, the analysis so far presented may suggest a very open system of signification. It is possible to imagine that there was a certain indeterminacy, even arbitrariness, in the way that hagiographers connected factual details to spiritual meanings: for example, Patricia Cox Miller makes much of the 'free play of the biographical imagination', of the 'supremely indirect' voice of myth, of a relationship between the mundane and the ideal which 'is not that of brilliant sunlight, but rather of shadows,

---

[132] See E.D. Hunt, *Holy Land Pilgrimage in the Later Roman Empire: AD 312–460* (Oxford, 1984), pp. 70, 91–2.

[133] For the earlier, Eastern aspect of this process, see Goehring, 'The Encroaching Desert', pp. 73–88; for later, Western developments, see Uwe Lindemann, '"Passende Wüste für Fata Morgana gesucht" Zur Etymologie und Begriffsgeschichte der fünf lateinischen Wörter für *Wüste*', in Uwe Lindemann and Monika Schmitz-Emans (eds), *Was ist eine Wüste?: Interdisziplinäre Annäherungen an einen interkulturellen Topos* (Würzburg, 2000), pp. 87–100.

shadings, and reflections'.[134] Such an observation, of course, echoes a broader post-modernist mood which has stressed the arbitrary and subjective quality of meaning and the legitimacy of multiple readings. In one sense, this parallel is valid. As we have seen, hagiographers continually stressed the provisionality of their conclusions; indeterminacy was not so much one theme within hagiography as the mode through which the genre's entire contents were delivered. However, indeterminacy in hagiography was of a specifically late antique character which must be understood on its own terms. In keeping with the world views which underpinned them, hagiographies were vigorously doctrinaire. The narrative details they drew upon may have been highly variable, indeed sometimes, as in the cases we have observed above, contradictory. But this was possible because the world views in question were capable of bestowing on any narrative details if not a precise meaning, then at least a confirmation of their basic philosophical assumptions. To put it in Saussurean terms, the signifiers themselves were radically variable, but what they signified was, ultimately, always the same core of philosophical truth. Authors felt obliged only to explain, not to explore. Their version of indeterminacy carried with it an ethic of humility, but it was not the sort of humility which was open to alternative readings; rather, it recognized only extents of understanding whilst confessing the limitations of the author's own.

The symbolic potential of all phenomena, the indeterminacy of meaning, an associated ethic of humility – if these things did not result in doctrinal open-mindedness nor did they equate to a sensible world so replete with significance that it became merely monotonous. As we have seen in the cases of the holy man's appearance and movements, conventional associations between types of phenomena and certain spiritual ideas certainly emerged in hagiography. In a sense, this occurred not despite the permanently ambiguous status which transcendental philosophy bestowed on the sensible world, but as a consequence of it. As we have seen, its ambiguity consisted partly in reflecting, partly in distorting higher realities; either aspect could be represented, but not both simultaneously. The clearest demonstration of this, perhaps, is the fact that, although we might consider it philosophically coherent to have done so, hagiographers did not refer to sages as *fairly* handsome or *fairly* eloquent. In a complex case like that of Plotinus, a sage might appear physically hideous (a relationship of contrast) until teaching philosophy and appearing beautiful (a relationship of analogy). Similarly, the deserts of Antony and his successors could either be thought of as places of desolation or as sacred places: although these two ideas could be juxtaposed, it was hard to apply them simultaneously to the same object. The desert had to *become* a city through at least a notional

---

[134]   Cox (Miller), *Biography in Late Antiquity*, pp. xii–xiii.

process of transformation, and the specific, appropriate symbols had to be found for each state.

It has been argued that, precisely because realism is relative, subjective, and culturally specific it depends on a certain process of stereotyping.[135] This was no less true of hagiography simply because the phenomena it recorded had a purely subordinate value as pointers to eternal truths: stereotyping occurred in the very process of unfolding this potential. In one sense, this was the result of exaggeration, of a tendency to bestow on extreme examples of relatively mundane phenomena a greater spiritual significance than on mere mediocrity; to apply to the holy man's appearance and travels superlatives such as 'amazing', or 'beyond expectation'. In another sense, it was the product of a conceptual exchange between phenomena and spiritual concepts. By being employed in a spiritual sense even only provisionally and metaphorically, terms like 'exile' entered a relationship whose connotations flowed in both directions. Rather than simply a tool by which people might reflect on their spiritual condition, the more familiar, literal notions of exile (physical, political etc.) now acquired a symbolic potential capable of repetition. The spiritual stance towards the sensible world taken by hagiographers did not, therefore, deprive it of texture, but gave it a texture specific to its most effective symbols. In this way too the literal content of hagiography was preserved.

The Problem of Miracles

The issue of miracles and other extraordinary phenomena with a spiritual significance raises a number of connected problems. These problems are not necessarily new; the entire issue was already highly contentious in antiquity. For one thing, what was the difference between a true miracle and mere sorcery? It was, of course, a highly subjective judgement. As Roland Smith suggests, this was a distinction particularly hard to draw in the case of pagan theurgical practices.[136] Conversely, there was a tradition amongst pagan polemicists such as Celsus of deriding Christ's miracles as mere sorcery.[137] Amongst Christian thinkers themselves, debate focused on whether and how God continued to intervene

---

[135]   This is argued by Nelson Goodman in respect to visual art: *Languages of Art* (Indianapolis, 1976), pp. 36–7, 39. See also Ankersmit, *The Reality Effect*, pp. 23–4.

[136]   Rowland Smith, *Julian's Gods: Religion and Philosophy in the Thought and Action of Julian the Apostate* (London, 1995), p. 101.

[137]   Jeffrey W. Hargis, *Against the Christians* (New York, 2001), pp. 6, 34–5.

directly in human affairs in a post-biblical age.[138] In one sense, hagiographies can be seen as an answer to this question: miracles are a sufficiently common theme within them to have become iconic of the genre; even a work like the *Life of Honoratus*, which fell short of the expected share of miracles did not deny their existence but simply explained why they were not necessary for the saint in question.[139] Some specific hagiographies, such as the *History of the Monks of Egypt*,[140] and the respective works of Theodoret[141] and Cyril[142] directly assert in the face of doubters that God continues to work miracles through the saints just as he did in biblical times.

That the Divine was capable of such action was, for pagans and Christians alike, a theological truth which must feature in any account of their view of reality and the way they represented it through hagiography. We must therefore work on the assumption that the basic hagiographical requirement for truthful and significant information applied in the case of miracles no less than elsewhere. Indeed, as we shall see, miracles were sometimes an occasion to reiterate this stance. For John Binns, the hagiographer's belief in the miracle is both crucial for the historian to recognize and also as far as his analysis can go: 'the events themselves are concealed from us'.[143]

Binns' statement really touches on two different issues which, in a sense, are extreme cases of the general problem of hagiographical realism. One problem is the historicity of miracles as they would be acceptable to us: should we treat them simply as fictions, as exaggerated accounts of more banal events, or should we remain entirely agnostic? More optimistically than Binns, this work will later offer an account of how at least some events came to be thought of as miraculous. The question of how miracles were presented and regarded by their original authors and audience, and of how they fitted into the general agenda of hagiographical realism, presents a slightly different problem. To say

---

[138]   See G.W.H. Lampe, 'Miracles and Early Christian Apologetic', in C.F.D. Moule (ed.), *Miracles* (London, 1965), pp. 203–18; Williams, *Authorised Lives*, p. 142; Paul M. Blowers, 'The Bible and Spiritual Doctrine: some Controversies within the Early Eastern Christian Ascetic Tradition', in Paul M. Blowers (ed.), *The Bible in Greek Christian Antiquity* (Notre Dame, 1997), pp. 230–33.

[139]   Hilarius, *Life of Honoratus* 8.37–8.

[140]   *History of the Monks of Egypt*, Prologue 13.

[141]   Theodoret, *History* 9.15.

[142]   Cyril, *Lives* 71.1–10; 228.1–5.

[143]   John Binns, *Ascetics and Ambassadors of Christ: The Monasteries of Palestine 314–631* (Oxford, 1994), p. 219: 'The only answer to the question of whether the miracles really happened is that the writers believed they did. There are no grounds for imputing fraud, deception or invention to the Palestinian hagiographers. We are offered a record of an event, shaped by the understandings and beliefs of the time. The events themselves are concealed from us.'

that hagiographers asked their audience to accept the miraculous as an aspect of reality, and particular miracles as true events, is part of the answer. The question, however, is whether the presentation of the miraculous bore any relation to other types of information in the sense that it also appealed not only to the reader's ultimate religious beliefs, but also to his or her familiar experience of the world and notions of plausibility. To some extent, at least, the miraculous had to exceed, defy and challenge these categories; in the words of Augustine who provides perhaps the most complete definition amongst late antique authors, a miracle was an event which appeared 'difficult or unusual, beyond the hope and power of those who wonder'.[144] Was it then an entirely separate category of information and one which demanded a separate kind of belief, or was there an extent to which it resembled other tendencies within hagiographical realism?

In many cases, especially where miracles are utterly extraordinary and entirely defy natural laws, it indeed seems to have been a separate kind of information. The centaur and faun in Jerome's *Life of Paul* are good examples of this.[145] Belief in these passages was hugely challenging and deeply subjective: it is hard to see how they were anything other than questions of faith, both in the author's reportage and in the God who created the world in which they were said to exist. But the role of subjectivity may precede the moment of judging a given account and interpretation of a particular miracle as true or false. We can show this by reflecting on the relationship and the differences between miracles and other phenomena, and by considering the question: what constitutes a miracle? In cases like that of Jerome mentioned above, this border seems extremely easy to define. But what about in other cases? As we have seen, many hagiographers tended towards extreme descriptions of familiar phenomena such as the way that holy men appeared physically. Was Plotinus' extraordinary and lucid appearance when teaching miraculous and, if not, how much more light or beauty would have made it so? Or, for that matter, the 'incredible' distances traversed by, for example, the monks of the Egyptian desert or the Jura mountains? The precise nature of the amazement expected from readers, the extent to which it corresponded to the excellence of the holy man on the one hand, or to the direct intervention of God through him on the other, is in most cases simply left ambiguous.

---

[144] 'I call a miracle any event, which appears difficult or unusual beyond the hope and power of those who wonder' (my translation): Augustine, *On the Profit of Believing* 34. *De Utilitate Credendi* 34, ed. Andreas Hoffmann, (Freiburg am Breisgau, 1992).

[145] Jerome, *Life of Paul* 7.4, ed. and tr. Pierre Leclerc and Edgardo Martín Morales, *Jérôme: Trois Vies de Moines (Paul, Malchus, Hilarion)*, Sources Chrétiennes 508 (Paris: Editions du Cerf, 2007).

Conversely, many incidents more or less explicitly declared miraculous by hagiographers in fact reveal a certain continuity with more mundane events. For example, for Theodoret, the subtle way in which the monk Aphrahat turns down the gift of a Persian tunic from a well-meaning visitor can be declared a 'miracle of shrewdness'.[146] For Cyril, the timely arrival at a monastery of a stranger with food supplies is miraculous;[147] as Binns observes, this differs from a non-miraculous story in the *Life of Antony* only in the respect that it was apparently unplanned.[148] An observation made by Bernard Flusin about Cyril's *Lives* could be applied to much Christian hagiography: namely that miracles had to echo a biblical precedent.[149] The very centrality of this criterion sometimes allows writers to treat as miraculous incidents which from a different perspective might appear merely fortuitous. It would surely have been possible, for example, to describe the discovery of fresh water on Lérins by Honoratus' followers in this way, rather than as a repetition of the incident in Exodus in which Moses struck a rock with his staff and produced water.[150] Although the category of the miraculous presupposes a distinction from other types of event, the more closely we examine and compare miracles, the more subtle and ambiguous the border often appears. On the one hand, as Dagron observes in the case of Thecla, the miraculous can imply a relatively minor effect in the narrative;[151] on the other, hagiographers often seem to encourage wonderment towards phenomena whose miraculous nature might escape immediate notice. For Pachomius, for example, simply to see God at work in a pure and humble man can and should be treated in this way.[152]

By observing the potential for a certain continuity between miracles and other types of event, the aim is not to abolish the category of the miraculous since this was an extremely important part of the late antique understanding of reality.

---

[146]   Theoderet, *Lives* 8.4.

[147]   Cyril, *Lives* 211.1–4.

[148]   Athanasius, *Life of Antony* 8; John Binns, 'Introduction', tr. R.M. Price, Cyril of Scythopolis, *Lives of the Monks of Palestine* (Kalamazoo, 1991), p. xxxiii, footnote 39.

[149]   'Il n'y a pas de miracle sans un précédent biblique': Bernard Flusin, *Miracle et histoire dans l'oeuvre de Cyrille de Scythopolis* (Paris, 1983), p. 157.

[150]   Exodus 17.5–7; Hilarius, *Life of Honoratus* 3.17: 'Water, unknown there for ages, began to flow copiously, repeating, in its origin, two miracles of the Old Testament.'

[151]   Dagron places Thecla's miracles 'dans une zone assez précise entre le normal et le merveilleux, dans la zone du savoir vacillant et de l'esperance incertaine ... il suffira qu'on invente ou qu'on trouve une rupture dans le fil du récit', in ed. and tr. Gilbert Dagron, *Vie et Miracles de Sainte Thècle* (Brussels, 1978), p. 108.

[152]   *Vita Pachomii* 48, ed. François Halkin, *Les vies grecques de S. Pachome* (Brussels, 1929). Reprinted with translation by Apostolos Athanassakis, *The Life of Pachomius (Vita Prima Graeca)*, (Missoula, Montana, 1975), p. 71.

Nor is it simply to lower the ontological threshold at which miracles were felt to occur; rather, it is to bring attention to the crucial epistemic foundations of any such judgement. This, after all, is already made clear in Augustine's definition in which the expectation of a witness is the ultimate yardstick of significance. To recognize events as miraculous, to detect in them a typological significance, to accept the invitation to treat them with wonderment – these things rely partly on what Auerbach called an *Interpretationswille*.[153] In a related vein, Sergio Franzese outlines a Jamesian view that religious experience does not ultimately equate to a specific object e.g. a set of doctrines, but constitutes a particular experiential stance, a special mood (*Stimmung*); this does not necessarily change the appearance of the world, but rather the relationship of its contents both mutually and to the believer.[154] In the case of hagiography, the reader may not have been required to adopt this stance directly and to test its full consequences against other possibilities; but by trusting the hagiographer's judgement he was accepting the legitimacy of such an approach. The same, of course, is true of the hagiographer's relationship to any sources on which he was dependent.

That the reader's acceptance of miracles included a certain subjectivity does not mean that their stance was entirely arbitrary or that it consisted of nothing more than mere wishful thinking. To demonstrate this, let us consider Marinus' account of Proclus' arrival in the sacred city of Athens:

> He set off for Athens, escorted as it were by all the gods and good daemons who are custodians of the oracles of philosophy ... This was proved conspicuously even by the events prior to his residence, and the truly god-sent omens ... For when he arrived at the Piraeus and those in the city were informed of this, Nicolaus ... went down to the harbour as though to an acquaintance. He led him therefore toward the city, but Proclus, feeling fatigue on the road because of the walk, and being close to the Socrateum – though he had not yet learned of nor heard that honours were being paid to Socrates anywhere (οὕτω εἰδὼς οὐδὲ ἀκηκοὼς ὅτι Σωκράτους αὐτοῦ που ἐγίγνοντο τιμαί) – begged Nicolaus to stop there awhile and sit, and at the same time also, if he could obtain water from anywhere, to bring it to him. For he was possessed, as he said, by a great thirst ... Nicolaus noted the omen, which he now perceived for the first time, that he was sitting in the Socrateum, and first drank the Attic water from this place. Proclus for his part rose, made a sign of obeisance, and went on to the city. And as he was climbing to the top, he was met

153 Erich Auerbach, 'Figura' in *AR* 22 (1938), p. 451.

154 Sergio Franzese, 'Is Religious Experience the Experience of Something? "Truth", Belief, and "Overbelief" in The Varieties of Religious Experience', in Sergio Franzese and Felicitas Kraemer (eds), *Fringes of Religious Experience: Cross-perspectives on William James' The Varieties of Religious Experience* (Frankfurt, 2007), pp. 153–5.

at the entrance by the doorman, who was already about to insert the keys – so much so that he said to him (I shall repeat the fellow's very words – ἐπ'αὐτῶν δὲ ἐρῶ τῶν τοῦ ἀνθρώπου ῥημάτων), 'Honestly, if you had not come, I was about to close up.' What omen, now, could have been more clear that this ... ?[155]

As an account of a miraculous event, this passage strongly exemplifies many of the issues highlighted above. The closing rhetorical question leaves the reader in no doubt as to the nature and grade of spiritual significance he should accord it: Proclus' god-given destiny is nothing less than to defend the sacred tradition of philosophy. The symbols it employs are quite precise: Proclus' physical thirst near Socrates' statue reveals the authenticity of his thirst for truth; the gate, which is about to close, represents philosophy's beleaguered condition in a Christian empire – a common theme in pagan biography.[156]

Most significantly, the passage is a good example of how an episode could come to qualify as miraculous, and also be accepted as plausible by the audience. On the one hand, there is a clear continuity with more ordinary events: none of the incident's constituent details – Proclus' tiredness, the water break, the gatekeeper's irreverence – in any way challenge natural laws; indeed they are quite compatible with a realism rooted in the mundane and familiar. On the other hand, a clear criterion establishes their extraordinary spiritual significance and thus difference from other events: only because Marinus can declare their occurrence absolutely spontaneous and unaffected can the events acquire the status of omens; conversely, any suspicion of human interference would be legitimate grounds for doubt and must therefore be refuted. Indeed, the relevant type of human interference in this case is not only the suspicion of retrospective exaggeration, but that of affectation on the holy man's part. One could easily imagine how a man as religious as Proclus might desire signs and seek them out, might deliberately take a route to the city which led past a spiritually significant spot and, displaying the appropriate reaction, might arrive at the city gates at an ostentatiously symbolic time. Marinus defends his interpretation using a criterion posited as objective – namely Proclus' own ignorance of the event's significance and the fact that at the time only his companion Nicolaus is (also entirely unexpectedly) struck by it. Similarly, Marinus clearly recognizes how the words of the doorman might be misremembered to fit the desired interpretation, and the reader is therefore assured that they are quoted *verbatim*. By referring to the doorman with the familiar term *anthropos*, Marinus also underlines the

---

155   Marinus, *Life of Proclus* 10 (tr. Edwards, pp. 70–72).

156   Goulet, *Etudes sur les vies des philosophes*, p. 20.

incident's spontaneous, unaffected quality: here was an ordinary man just doing a regular job, and therefore completely ignorant of his words' deeper meaning.

In its precision, plausibility, and assurances of literal reportage, the reader is asked to believe that, had he been present at the events described, he too would have noticed precisely the same details. But he is no less directly assured that, having observed these things, he would have attributed to them the same significance, namely that of an omen: in this sense, the two forms of truthfulness mentioned above are respected. This insistence on the incident's *petits faits vrais* surely brings us very close to *l'effet de réel* of Barthes. But in combination, they constitute much more than this: not just an effect of reality, but what we might term a 'principle of spontaneity',[157] a criterion of sacred significance apparently capable of falsification and established only once all human factors – desire, forethought, and affectation – have been discounted.

The spontaneity principle is a common element in many hagiographical miracle stories. On a visit to another cell, Pachomius mentions five figs hidden in a jar and, although he believes he is speaking only allegorically, its resident brother Elijah interprets it literally as a reference to the five physical figs he had secretly purloined, causing him immediately to repent.[158] Cyril reports how an accidental wrong turn taken by 400 Armenians brought them to Euthymius' laura and was followed by a miraculous surfeit of bread capable of feeding the vast crowd.[159] Elsewhere in his *Lives*, mysterious strangers appear with gifts; that they are 'totally unknown' implies the hand of providence.[160] Franzese's observations about the nature of the religious stance seem particularly pertinent with reference to the spontaneity principle: it is not necessarily in the things themselves that significance lies but in their mutual relationship – a relationship explicable only by recognizing them as elements of a communication from elsewhere – and in our relationship to them as fit receivers of that communication. To equate miracles with a principle of spontaneity is, ultimately, a statement of psychology. It describes a state of human ignorance, as well as an optimistic stance towards this ignorance: an authentic wonder at certain types of phenomenon, as well as an understanding of what category of significance to accord them. This interpretation will not explain every miracle in hagiography, but it may go some way to explaining how readers could acquire and sustain an understanding of the world in which the miraculous was only in a certain sense antithetical to the literal and the familiar; from another perspective, it was detectable within it.

---

[157]   I am grateful to Matthew dal Santo for suggesting this expression.

[158]   *Life of Pachomius* 97.

[159]   Cyril, *Lives* 27–8.

[160]   Ibid., Cyril, *Lives* 116.17, 211.

The Holy Man's Identity

If it is true that late antique hagiographies need to be understood within the context of a certain notion of reality, it is equally true that this form of realism required a specifically hagiographical form. There are two reasons for this. On the one hand, the existence of holy men as a category of human being can be seen as a feature of the world view in question. On the other hand, holy men could be regarded as necessary interpreters of transcendental reality in this deep sense. Although these claims differ philosophically, they are of course mutually supportive: just as a holy man's identity was often proved by his mysterious understanding of things, his pronouncements achieved their force partly in virtue of his identity. But in both cases, the hagiographer had to persuade readers that his subject was extraordinary.

The problem with the holy man's special insight was that it could be demonstrated only indirectly: neither the hagiographer nor the reader had the privilege to share it. But this limitation was also an opportunity. As we saw above, a holy man's special insight could be represented symbolically through certain aspects of the sensible world. For example, pagan hagiographers could describe a philosopher's extraordinary appearance during his contemplation; in one sense, this relieved them of the need to speculate about its precise content. Furthermore, a holy man's knowledge could also be meaningfully reported without necessarily understanding its precise nature or the way it was acquired. Plotinus' students were left baffled by his enigmatic claim about the gods that 'it is they who should come to me, not I to them',[161] but Porphyry recorded this story nonetheless. When the insight of a saint was in some sense miraculous (e.g. Severinus' foreknowledge of disaster) the very fact that it could not be explained became, using the spontaneity principle, a criterion of its spiritual significance. Hagiography therefore vigorously posited in the holy man a special mode of understanding whilst renouncing any possibility of explaining it, and therefore obligation to explain it. Cyril could claim that 'when God wishes to reveal something to his saints they are prophets, but when he wishes to conceal something they see no more than everyone else'.[162] Eunapius remarked that 'so great a difference does it make whether one beholds a thing with the intelligence (τῷ νῷ) or with the deceitful eyes of the flesh'.[163]

---

[161] Porphyry, *Life of Plotinus* 10 (tr. Edwards, p. 21).

[162] Cyril, *Lives* 205.9–11.

[163] Eunapius, *Lives* 473 (tr. Wright, p. 425). In a related vein, Julian claims that 'it is in knowledge that the gods surpass ourselves', *To the Uneducated Cynics* 184C (tr. Wright, vol. 2, p. 15).

Since he could not share it directly, the reader's belief in the holy man's insight, and therefore in the validity of his utterances and behaviour, depended on a certain preconception of his identity. We might expect this latter element, therefore, to constitute the firm theological core of hagiography, the point at which authors were at their most precise. As an example of how identity claims were formulated, let us consider Hilarius' *Life of Honoratus*, an early fifth-century text from Southern Gaul initially delivered as an oration on the first anniversary of the saint's death. Consciously avoiding a standard introduction, Hilarius frankly informs his readers that the nature of Honoratus' life renders formulae traditionally applied to men of God meaningless: his recent departure to a heavenly dwelling was really no departure at all; God had always counted him amongst the stars when he was alive and, even on earth, he had stood in Christ's presence. These formulae naturally recall the deaths of martyrs and it was only the lack of persecutors that had prevented Honoratus from joining their ranks directly. A self-taught Christian from childhood despite coming from an aristocratic pagan family, Honoratus gave all his wealth to the poor and left home with his brother in imitation of the Patriarch Abraham. It is for this reason that Hilarius omits to reveal Honoratus' precise homeland and family for 'none is more glorious in the heavenly places than are those who have ignored their pedigrees and chosen to be reckoned as fatherless except in Christ'.[164] After long travels, during which he persistently fled company, but found himself increasing loved and famous as a result, he ended up on the remote island of Lérins off the Provençale coast in search of solitude. But this waterless, snake-infested wilderness sprang to life on his arrival; the snakes disappeared and, as for Moses in the desert, a fresh spring miraculously opened, allowing habitation and the establishment of a monastery. Honoratus finally overcame his reluctance for office and humbly accepted his divine calling as abbot.

When considered closely, it becomes clear that Hilarius' portrait of Honoratus contains several classes of information. Many general statements, which simply assure readers of the extraordinary depths of his subjects' Christian faith, are hard to categorize. Sometimes contrasts and comparisons with other groups of people are drawn. These can be negative in intent. Honoratus' spiritual identity is stressed partly by the radical suppression of information about his earthly identity, implying his superiority to family, friends, and other members of his social class. They may also be positive: Honoratus was not, only because he could not, be a martyr – he was, for this reason, their equal. Finally, there are moments where a saint seems to acquire a quite specific identity by fulfilling a biblical precept or mirroring the actions of a particular biblical character. Honoratus' arrival at

---

[164]   Hilarius, *Life of Honoratus* 1.4 (tr. Hoare, p. 250).

Lérins fulfils Christ's promise to his followers that they will 'trample on snakes and scorpions';[165] by abandoning home he mirrors Abraham, by opening the spring, Moses. Marking the episodes which most define him as a holy man, these biblical comparisons appear to be the keystones of his religious identity.

All these forms of identification are representative of the various means by which Christian hagiographers accorded their subjects a religious identity. A certain distance from, and superiority to, secular society was innate to the whole idea of monasticism and could be stressed in various ways, often by showing this separation to be already present in childhood i.e. before a formal renunciation had been made.[166] Similarly, the need to achieve equivalence with the martyrs was one of the stimuli behind the monastic movement and was sometimes explicitly underlined by hagiographers.[167] As the ascetic movement developed and became celebrated, a similar equivalence was sometimes drawn by a hagiographer between their subject and earlier monks, especially the great Antony.[168]

The most interesting type of comparison from our viewpoint are biblical typologies which are a widespread and characteristic feature of Christian hagiography. Some hagiographers, such as Hilarius, are relatively sparing in their use; others, like Theodoret, deploy them frequently. There is not necessarily a one on one correspondence: it is important to Honoratus' status that he comes to reflect both Abraham and Moses.[169] Ambitious typologies are also strongly attested in pagan hagiography. Some sages are given a religious identity: Proclus' guardian divinity is the goddess Rhea according to Marinus;[170] according to Damascius, Isidore's is Logios Hermes;[171] Plotinus' spiritual guardian is not a regular daemon but a unnamed god;[172] Sosipatra's god forbids her to reveal her spiritual origins;[173] Damascius sees in Sarapio's ascetic lifestyle a divinely intended model of the myth of the Age of Kronos.[174] Historical analogies were also drawn: for many pagan thinkers living in a post-Constantinian empire such as Eunapius

---

[165]   Ibid. 3.15 (tr. Hoare, p. 260) citing Luke 10.19.

[166]   Hilarius, *Life of Honoratus* 1.5; Paulinus, *Life of Ambrose* 4.

[167]   Several Christian saints were said to have desired martyrdom despite its unavailablity: Athanasius, *Life of Antony* 46.2; Hilarius, *Life of Honoratus* 8.37–8; Ferrandus, *Life of Fulgentius* 49–50.

[168]   E.g. Cyril compares Sabas' life to Antony's at *Lives* 110.15–19. For the influence of Antony and Martin on Eugendus, see *Lives of the Jura Fathers* 168.

[169]   Hilarius, *Life of Honoratus* 2.12, 3.17.

[170]   Marinus, *Life of Proclus* 6.

[171]   Damascius, *Philosophical History* 13.

[172]   Porphyry, *Life of Plotinus* 10. For discussion see Jaap Mansfeld, 'Plotinian Ancestry' in *Illinois Classical Studies* 20 (1995), pp. 149–56.

[173]   Eunapius, *Lives* 469.

[174]   Damascius, *Philosophical History* 111.

and Damascius, Socrates could be invoked as a paradigm of heroic intellectual independence in the face of tyranny.[175] Eunapius even speculated that his teacher Chrysanthius may have been Socrates' contemporary reincarnation.[176] Porphyry places his deceased master in a canon with 'Plato, Pythagoras, and all the others who have "set going the dance of immortal love"'.[177]

As Brown rightly observed, the man of God necessarily revived other men of God from the past.[178] But as is clear even from the *Life of Honoratus* and the other cases mentioned above, there were many complex ways in which this process could be accomplished. Most straightforwardly, the human institutions with which holy men are associated – Christian monastic communities, pagan philosophical schools – included at their heart an ethic stressing imitation of and obedience to spiritual masters: hence the importance placed by collective hagiographers on these quasi-familial connections.[179] For pagans, there was also the exciting idea, exploited by Iamblichus, of an underground Pythagorean cult through which fragments of the great man's wisdom had been passed down across countless generations.[180] More broadly, these intellectual traditions provided a range of more distant, illustrious figures suitable for imitation: figures from a mythical or heroic past for pagan philosophers; martyrs, earlier saints and biblical characters for Christians. As shown in the case of Honoratus and Abraham, a typological analogy could quite legitimately be drawn on the basis of successful imitation.

Of course, many typological comparisons appear far more esoteric than this, such as that between Honoratus and Moses. Rather than the result of conscious imitation, it is conferred spontaneously, and through a miraculous event. Understandably, modern historians tend to treat such comparisons with a certain suspicion, especially since the concrete basis of many typologies can appear, in Auerbach's phrase, *schattenhaft* (shadowy).[181] Nonetheless, an observation by Williams helps explain why this is not necessarily the case:

---

[175]   Eunapius, *Lives* 462, 498; Damascius, *Philosophical History* 116E; Julian, *Fragment of a Letter to a Priest* 295B.

[176]   Eunapius, *Lives* 501.

[177]   Porphyry, *Life of Plotinus* 23 (tr. Edwards, p. 46).

[178]   Peter Brown, 'The Saint as Exemplar in Late Antiquity', *Representations* 2 (1983), p. 17.

[179]   For these bonds within the pagan schools, see Edward J. Watts, 'Orality and Communal Identity in Eunapius' *Lives of the Sophists and Philosophers*', *Byzantion* 75 (2005), pp. 334–61; for monastic bonds in Christian desert asceticism, see Graham Gould, *The Desert Fathers on Monastic Community* (Oxford, 1993).

[180]   Iamblichus, *On the Pythagorean Life* 1(1–2), 18(86–7), 35(252–3).

[181]   Auerbach, 'Figura', p. 451.

through their biblical reading, and in particular through the way in which the New Testament fulfilled events prefigured in the Old, Christians acquired a basic intuition about the tendency of history to repeat itself, to echo its own sacred symbols, and for connections to exist between characters throughout space and time: hagiographers merely extended these tendencies to their own, or at least much more recent, times. However, given the depth of the mysteries involved and the imperfection of the sensible world, this echoing process was usually imprecise and uncertain.[182] From this perspective, typologies, far from being a cause of suspicion, could serve as a principal of hagiographical realism by indicating both spiritual significance and factual plausibility.[183] The crucial importance of typology for Christian thinkers is illustrated in a highly ingenious passage by Theodoret. He defends Symeon Stylites' controversial and iconic style of pillar-based asceticism by arguing that it did have a precedent: the complete uniqueness and originality of its physical details followed in the footsteps of many unusual biblical behaviours which, though ordained by God, necessarily lacked a precedent on their first occurrence.[184]

Typologies in pagan hagiographies may seem more straightforward since pagans had theological options not available to Christians: there was the possibility of associating a holy man with a specific deity, or arguing that he was the reincarnation of an earlier holy man. But given these alternative possibilities, one is struck by the similarities with the Christian position. Despite lacking a model as definitive as Christian Scripture, the instinct that history repeats itself mysteriously and symbolically is not entirely alien to pagan hagiographers. For example, in his *Histories*, Eunapius comments on the extraordinary significance of the number seven throughout the ages.[185] The idea that holy men belong in a sacred tradition whose representatives, though separated by centuries, co-exist in some essential but invisible way is reflected in Porphyry's description of Plotinus' death which sees him enrolled beside 'Plato, Pythagoras, and all the others who have "set going the dance of immortal love"':[186] a claim with parallels not only in Christian hagiography, but also, perhaps, in Christ's

---

182   Williams, *Authorised Lives*, p. 15.

183   As argued by Vivian et al., *Lives of the Jura Fathers*, p. 59.

184   Theodoret, *History* 26.12.

185   'It ... seems that as time passes, over long periods the same phenomena recur. Thus, those who conspired with Darius against the Magi numbered seven, and, at a much later time, those who rebelled against the Macedonians were the same in number', Eunapius, *Fragmenta Historiarum*, Fragment 21.3 ed. with tr. R.C. Blockley in *The Fragmentary Classicising Historians of the Later Roman Empire: Eunapius, Olympiodorus, Priscus and Malchus* (2 vols, Liverpool, 1981–83), p. 33.

186   Porphyry, *Life of Plotinus* 23 (tr. Edwards), p. 46.

Transfiguration.[187] Furthermore, pagan typology was also prone to attract the language of uncertainty: the identity of Plotinus' god remained unknown; that of Isidore could never be proven; the significance of Sarapio's life was only Damascius' opinion. In the final analysis, no-one could definitely tell whether Chrysanthius was Socrates' reincarnation or just the impeccable inheritor of his wisdom.[188] The identity of the holy man, then, was often left no more precise than the nature and content of his insight; indeed, these things often receive a remarkably similar treatment. A category of spiritual significance was robustly maintained without exhaustively defining its nature. Instead, the reader is left with either a general impression or with multiple possibilities: whoever Plotinus' spiritual guardian was, however Chrysanthius was related to Socrates, it was indisputable that they were very extraordinary men.

As far as hagiographical realism is concerned, perhaps the issue most relevant to the holy man's identity, then, is not its precise theological definition, but rather the literary techniques by which it was suggested. The fact that the identities of holy men were so often shrouded in uncertainty was as much an advantage as a constraint for the hagiographer: by being impossible, exhaustivity became unnecessary; typologies could comfortably rest on a symbolic base which was *schattenhaft*. In this way, typology too contributed towards the literalizing tendency of hagiography by which many, ordinary details of the sensible world acquired profound spiritual meanings. But this was true in a second, less obvious, sense. Implicitly, one thing hagiographers achieved when they compared a holy man to Socrates or Abraham or Moses was to reduce the archetype's potential complexity and to render its message straightforward and uncontroversial. For example, what Moses stood for as a hagiographical yardstick was clearly far simpler than the treatment his story received from biblical exegetes.[189] The wider the range of figures from which typological comparisons were drawn, the simpler the message of any single one. This is shown by Cyril when he imagines the impression left on Cyriacus by the Old Testament:

> (God) glorified Abel on account of his sacrifice, honoured Enoch by translation
> for being well-pleasing, guarded Noah as the spark of the race on account of

---

[187]   Matthew 17.2–13; Mark 9.2–12.

[188]   Eunapius, *Lives* 501.

[189]   One very extensive example from late antiquity is Gregory of Nyssa's *Life of Moses* (*De Vita Moysis*), ed. Jean Daniélou, *La Vie de Moïse* (Paris, 1968), which is divided into a historical and an exegetical section. Something similar can be said about the wanderer Odysseus: Jean Pépin, 'The Platonic and Christian Ulysses', in Dominic J. O'Meara (ed.), *Neoplatonism and Christian Thought* (New York: State University of New York Press, 1982), pp. 3–18.

his righteousness, made Abraham the father of nations on account of his faith, accepted the devout priesthood of Melchizedek, raised up Joseph and Job as models, for our life, of continence and endurance, made Moses a lawgiver, let Joshua son of Nun control the sun and moon, appointed David prophet and king and ancestor of an awesome mystery, changed the fire of the Babylonian furnace into dew, taught the lions of Daniel to fast in their den, and made the sea-monster a prophet's chamber.[190]

The simpler an archetype became, the more it became synonymous with a single idea, the more easily it lent itself to typological comparison with recent holy men. This was especially true if it could be reduced to a simple action or human situation: Abraham abandoning home, Moses providing water, Socrates ignoring intimidation. The details of a holy man's life did not have to be interpreted in terms of an abstract philosophical principle (as for example in the case of his appearance) but in terms of another event already authenticated as an instantiation of some higher truth. Thus typology brought philosophical truths one step closer to the holy man's life and world; his identity, though ultimately hidden, now corresponded concretely to certain easily graspable and repeatable classes of action.

Hagiographical realism supplied another tool when it confronted the holy man's identity. It benefited not just from the great significance acquired by the few, simple things that could be said about the holy man; equally significant were the things that could not be said. As we have seen, not everything that the holy man understood, everything he was, could be communicated. In various ways, hagiographers, especially pagan ones, exploited these inevitable areas of silence and uncertainty between the modest fragments of information. Sometimes, this took the form of a more or less symbolic ethic stemming from the holy men themselves. The *Philosophical History* reports how Asclepiades was born with his mouth and finger attached as a symbol of future philosophical achievement.[191] The ancient Pythagoreans had been bound by an oath of silence,[192] an attitude echoed in more recent times by the reluctance of Plotinus and his companions to divulge the teachings of their master Ammonius Saccas.[193] The philosopher hermit Antoninus refused to discuss religious questions publicly.[194] In other cases, as we saw above, the hagiographer himself highlighted an explicit area of uncertainty, for example by admitting ignorance of a holy man's guardian

---

[190]   Cyril, *Lives* 223.14–24.
[191]   Damascius, *Philosophical History* 76.
[192]   Iamblichus, *On the Pythagorean Life* 34(246).
[193]   Porphyry, *Life of Plotinus* 3.
[194]   Eunapius, *Lives* 472.

divinity. The two tendencies could be connected: it is precisely her spiritual identity which the gods forbid Antoninus' mother, Sosipatra, to reveal.[195] As we shall discuss at length in the next chapter, Severinus is one of a number of Christian holy men who decline to declare their country of origin.[196]

The effectiveness of these techniques reflects the basically unempirical spirit in which hagiographies were read. Certainty was impossible in the sensible world: in Plato's famous formulation, one could have beliefs about it but not true knowledge.[197] A simple lack of information therefore failed to disturb preconceptions about holy men which were capable of being confirmed by very meagre information. But we can go further than this: for hagiographers the gaps were not just neutral and inevitable; they were skilfully created and could become spaces in which beliefs about holy men flourished. This is because a measure of uncertainty actually encouraged the reader's preconceptions: *omne ignotum pro magnifico.*[198] The missing information was not mysterious in the same way as that between the fragments of evidence half way through a detective novel – temporarily lacking, but capable of completion in a manner which eventually reveals familiar human motivations. Rather, with their interest already geared towards spiritual truths, hagiographical readers would assume that this was what any missing information indicated: deeper and more spectacular confirmations of their unshakable convictions. Eunapius seems to have understood this particularly well. In his critique of Iamblichus' biography of Alypius, he offers what almost amounts to a literary theory of realism: it is only by saying less than the truth that a writer stays true to his subject.[199] Like the other techniques examined in this chapter, silence became a feature of realism in the twofold way mentioned above: an inevitable consequence of a transcendental world view, it in turn became an earthly symbol of it, and one capable of hagiographical exploitation.

---

[195]   Ibid. 469 (p. 411). In the same way, the mysterious identity of the two wandering old men who first discover her is also never resolved: ibid. 467. This process of concealment mirrors Apollonius' refusal to discuss past and future lives, Philostratus, *The Life of Apollonius of Tyana* 8.7.

[196]   Eugippius, *Letter to Paschasius* 7–10.

[197]   Plato, *Republic* 6.509–11; *Timaeus* 27D–28A, ed. and tr. R.G. Bury in *Plato* vol. 9 [*Timaeus, Critias, Cleitophon, Menexenus, Epistles*], Loeb Classical Library (London/New York, 1929).

[198]   'Everything unknown in the place of the magnificent': Tacitus, *Agricola* 30.3, eds Robert Maxwell Ogilvie and Ian Archibald Richmond (Oxford, 1967).

[199]   Eunapius, *Lives* 500.

Reader, Writer, Holy Man: 'Historicity' and the Scope of 'the Hagiographical'

This chapter has characterized hagiography as a form of literary realism. The claim depends on an understanding of the basic, philosophical notions of reality which informed the genre. But this notion of reality continued to place a major emphasis on the literal; this, indeed, was part of its commitment to truthfulness even in a theoretical sense. There were many ways in which the phenomenal world's contents could be interpreted as confirmation of higher truths; many ways in which higher truths could be felt to manifest themselves in the phenomenal world.

So far, this realist stance has been treated purely as a feature of hagiography as a literary genre. It could, theoretically, remain only this: as we saw earlier, it is perfectly possible to see literary realism as an effect of language with no necessary direct relation to a world prior to the text (see p. 34). But as is clear from the third term in our title, the current book posits a significance beyond this, and it is this concept of 'historicity' which occupies more space than any other throughout the remainder of the book. But what exactly does, or should, this term mean? Perhaps the most intuitive way in which we might consider a text as historical is to see its author as part of a chain of information, linking the work's subject – in this case a holy man or holy men – to its recipient reader or hearer. (This may, of course, be a more or less direct relationship depending on how many sources the hagiographer exploits and how many versions of the text come into being.) The test of its historicity could therefore be defined as the extent to which information remained stable at each stage in this chain of transmission.

To a certain extent, this metaphor is legitimate in the case of hagiography: by earnestly promising to relate the truth, the authors of this genre invited precisely this sort of judgement. The question of how historical the hagiographical genre is according to this criterion, and indeed how historical specific hagiographies are, should and will continue to be debated. We have already discussed some of the main reasons why it should have been imperfect such as the inevitable compromises hagiographers made as they balanced literal truthfulness against other considerations. To this we may add that the simple intention to tell the truth, however sincere, does not of itself guarantee the stability of information over time. This can be shown by something as simple as a game of Chinese Whispers which often produces a surprisingly contorted message. Nonetheless, this question is somewhat peripheral to the main argument of the current book, and will only be addressed on an *ad hoc* basis. In general, we can tentatively say that the realistic stance taken by hagiographers, which included a genuine ethical pressure to write truthfully, probably made the genre a somewhat more effective vessel for the transmission of information than is sometimes assumed.

But the stability of specific information down the chain of information need not necessarily be considered the only valid criterion of historicity. For one thing, since the hagiographer is usually the only source for a given piece of information, the historian usually has no way of assessing this stability beyond the measure of his own notion of plausibility. Another problem is that the idea of the chain of information can make its component links seem too distinct. Rapp has rightly highlighted the potential for slippage between the roles of hagiographer, eyewitness, and disciple in Christian desert literature.[200] We can, perhaps, go further than this: wherever sanctity was concerned, there was the potential for an overlap, even a circular relationship between what appear at first sight to be fairly straightforward roles: namely those of holy man, disciple/eyewitness, hagiographer and indeed reader. These distinctions applied less to classes of people than to types of activity, and were therefore flexible. Interpretation was not just the possession of the hagiographer as a writer, but was necessary whenever, and by whomever, spiritual information was encountered.

To illustrate this point, let us consider the relationship between the hagiographer and the reader. Obviously, the hagiographer assumed a certain authority: he had either personally known or heavily researched his subject and often claimed some form of higher inspiration. However, his inferiority *vis-à-vis* his extraordinary subject entailed a stance of humility and an awareness of limitations. From the reader's point of view, both elements were important. It was necessary for him to trust the contents of the account immediately in question. But it was also important that the hagiographer's mode of understanding served as a paradigm of an appropriate ethic towards the truth on anyone's part, including that of the reader.

What did this ethic consist in? It certainly allowed further dissemination of hagiographical stories: Athanasius would no doubt have approved of Ponticianus' enthusiastic retelling of the Antony story for example.[201] It also held up its subjects as models worthy of imitation; an intention some hagiographers, such as Theodoret and Palladius, make explicit.[202] But the legitimacy of such dissemination touches on something deeper. As Williams has argued, one consequence of hagiography being both realist and edifying is that, in various complex ways, it encouraged the reader to apply its lessons to his or her own

---

[200] Rapp, 'Storytelling as Spiritual Communication in Early Greek Hagiography', p. 439.

[201] Augustine, *Confessions* 8.6.14.

[202] Theodoret, *History* 30.7; Palladius, *Lausiac History* Foreword 1. For discussion of this didactic function see Rapp, 'The Origins of Hagiography and the Literature of Early Monasticism', pp. 119–38.

world.[203] Indeed, one might say that the test of a hagiography's effectiveness lay not only in its accuracy but in its ability to inspire in its readers the appropriate understanding of reality and attitude towards it. In the final analysis, it didn't matter how many links there were in the chain of information between Antony and Augustine; the story was still able to have a profound effect on the latter's life.[204] As devotional literature, hagiography always contained this didactic potential. The reader – the act of reading – was not necessarily the final destination of its message.

Although this didactic message is implicit in all hagiography, it receives a more thorough philosophical treatment in pagan works. This may partly be because, as we have already seen, a number of such works were conceived as introductions to longer philosophical volumes; their ability to awaken readers to higher things was therefore inherent in their form. But these works also contain indications of what such a didactic process implied practically, and what its consequences were for the reader. This can be seen when we consider not merely the content of spiritual stories, but the extent to which their message was made explicit or left to the reader to interpret.

For example, the anecdote about the furtive portrait with which Porphyry opens his *Life of Plotinus* contains several possible levels of meaning. The doctrine of Soul's superiority to body is put into the philosopher's own mouth, but the self-conscious recognition of the limitations of Porphyry's own biographical form of portraiture remains only implicit.[205] Indeed, as we saw in the case of Plotinus' enigmatic pronouncement about religion, Porphyry actively highlights areas of incomplete understanding, and one effect of this is to stimulate the reader's own interpretation. Something similar can be said of Marinus' *Life of Proclus* and Damascius' *Life of Isidore*. The unifying structures of these works, which mirror the Neoplatonic *scala virtutum*, are extremely subtle and were detected only in modern times by H.J. Blumenthal[206] and Dominic O'Meara respectively.[207] The *Life of Proclus* in particular is reserved when it comes to explicit interpretation by the author. For example, immediately after declaring Proclus' arrival in Athens to be an omen of troubled times, Marinus states in the next chapter that 'it was the hour when visibility was failing. Even as they were talking, the sun sank low and the moon appeared for the first time in her new cycle.'[208] Although this

---

[203]   Williams, *Authorised Lives*, pp. 183–5.

[204]   Augustine, *Confessions* 8.12.29.

[205]   Edwards, 'A Portrait of Plotinus', pp. 482–3.

[206]   H.J. Blumenthal, '*Marinus*' Life of Proclus', *Byzantion* 54 (1984), p. 474.

[207]   Dominic J. O'Meara, 'Patterns of Perfection in Damascius' *Life of Isidore*', *Phronesis* 51 (2006), p. 75.

[208]   Marinus, *Life of Proclus* 11 (tr. Edwards, p. 73).

chapter concerns Proclus' lunar worship, the context makes it hard to believe that only a literal meaning is intended; rather, the reader is probably supposed to interpret it as a further sign of the decline of philosophy in a Christian age. (The significance of this image is confirmed in the work's penultimate chapter where the darkness of an eclipse portends the 'eclipse of the light of philosophy'.[209]) The didactic process thus takes the form of encouraging in the reader a certain interpretative autonomy.

If, in philosophical terms, the reader's condition was closely analogous to that of the hagiographer then it is no surprise that a similar relationship was reflected in the way holy men were reported to interact with others. The importance of ultimate spiritual autonomy was captured in Socrates' depiction of himself as a midwife of other people's ideas.[210] For a holy man to teach was less to transmit information than to awaken in others the desire and ability to seek the truth; to be, like the philosopher Athenodorus, 'a spark which set fire to whatever was next to it'.[211] In a similar vein, Iamblichus describes how Pythagoras' teaching methods involved paying a young athlete to solve mathematical problems; when his enthusiasm made bribes unnecessary, and the philosopher pretended to be poor, the athlete, by now intrigued, agreed to pay for continued tuition.[212] '"Much learning does not teach men to have understanding"' wrote Julian quoting Heracleitus.[213] In keeping with this ethic, hagiographers, both pagan and Christian, often depicted holy men themselves as the correct models of spiritual autonomy. Honoratus, for example, somehow taught himself as a boy many moral maxims which would guide him through later life.[214] Similarly, Plotinus was not, as his predecessors had been, the mere recipient of teachings collated over generations but his own man in all his meditations.[215] Readers could, and were probably intended to, apply these lessons in their own lives.

What are the implications of this for the historicity of hagiography? We have seen that the stability of data down the chain of information is too limited a

---

[209]   Ibid. 37 (p. 114).

[210]   Plato, *Theaetetus* 149–51, ed. and tr. Harold N. Fowler in *Plato* vol. 7 [*Theaetetus, Sophist*] Loeb Classical Library (London/New York, 1921; repr., 1977).

[211]   Damascius, *Philosophical History* 66G (tr. Athanassiadi, p. 179); according to a similar image by Eunapius, Iamblichus' pupils used to 'fill themselves full as though from a spring that bubbles over and does not stay within its limits', Eunapius, *Lives* 460 (tr. Wright, p. 373).

[212]   Iamblichus, *On the Pythagorean Life* 5(21–5).

[213]   Julian, *To the Uneducated Cynics* 187D, quoting Heracleitus fragment 16 (tr. Wright, vol. 2, p. 23).

[214]   Hilarius, *Life of Honoratus* 1.7.

[215]   Porphyry, *Life of Plotinus* 14.

notion of historicity for it assumes that what the genre served to disseminate was essentially only information. But we have argued here that something else, something more ethical was also passed on: a picture of the world and a stance towards it. The less distinct and rigid we assume the various stages in the chain to be, the less that hagiography appears merely as a form of writing. Rather, it appears as something broader, namely a set of attitudes exemplified in a written genre but applicable beyond it: to an *unmittelbar erscheinende natürliche Welt*,[216] and to forms of experience, not yet recorded in texts; even, perhaps, to people who were not (or not yet) holy men. In so far as 'the hagiographical' was something which included a written form, but was not restricted by it, hagiographies can legitimately be accorded a certain historicity.

This claim is not eccentric. For one thing, it is a good way to understand the late antique tendency observed by John Liebeschuetz of reading spiritual messages into chance and natural phenomena.[217] Nonetheless, the almost complete anonymity of the period's readers, or at the least the invisibility of reading as an activity, severely limits how far we may speculate about this role beyond theoretical probabilities. Instead, it is to holy men themselves that we must turn to understand the hagiographical as a broader process and set of attitudes. As the next chapter will argue, just as there is no reason to assume that the reader represented the end of the hagiographical chain of information, we should equally avoid assuming that the holy man was, at least in any straightforward sense, its ultimate source.

---

[216]   Auerbach, 'Figura', p. 470.

[217]   J.H.W.G. Liebeschuetz traces the development to the third century: *Continuity and Change in Roman Religion*, (Oxford, 1979) p. 227. It was a tendency observed by the most secular historian of the fourth century, Ammianus Marcellinus: even his greatest hero, the emperor Julian, was 'superstitiosus magis quam sacrorum legitimus observator': *Res gestae* 25.4.17, ed. Wolfgang Seyfarth (2 vols, Leipzig, 1978).

Chapter 2
From Hagiography to Charisma

Severinus: Saint and Image

Perhaps we are obliged to ask the question from which country he came since it is customary for a biographer to take this as his start. Yet I must confess I have no certain information on this point. Many priests and spiritual men, but also noble and religious laymen, natives as well as others who came to him from far away, guessed and asked each other to what nation the man belonged who worked such great miracles before their eyes, but nobody dared to ask him openly; at last a certain Primenius, a noble priest of Italy, and a man who commanded every possible authority ... after many days of intimate friendship burst out, as in the name of them all, with the question, saying: 'Holy master, what is the province from which God has deigned to send such a great light as His gift to these districts?' The man of God first replied in joke: 'If you think I am a runaway slave have money ready to offer for me when I am claimed'. But then, turning serious, he added something like this: 'What good does it do a servant of God to make known his birthplace or family? By keeping silence about it, he can more easily avoid pride, which is on his left side; without letting his left hand know,[1] he wishes to perform every good work by the grace of Christ, and thus to be made worthy of the company of those who stand on his right side[2] and to be enlisted as a citizen of the heavenly fatherland. If you realize that I, though I am unworthy, strive for this, why must you know my country on earth, for which you ask? This, however, you should know: that God, who has made you a priest, has also ordered me to come to these people in their hour of need'. By this reply, the priest was silenced, and nobody else, either before or after this, ever dared to ask the holy man a similar question. His language, however, proved him a true Latin. Earlier in his life, as is known for certain, he had gone to some desert in the east, burning with desire for a more perfect life; afterwards, compelled by divine revelation, he had left there and gone to the towns of Noricum Ripense, bordering on Upper Pannonia, towns which were afflicted by frequent raids of the barbarians. This he used to indicate in veiled language, as if he

---

[1]   Matthew 6.3.
[2]   Matthew 25.33.

were speaking of somebody else (*sicut ipse clauso sermone tamquam de alio aliquo referre solitus erat*), mentioning by name some cities of the east and hinting at the dangers of the endless journey which he had miraculously overcome. What I have told here is all that I have ever heard when our conversation turned on blessed Severin's home – even in his lifetime.[3]

Severinus of Noricum: ascetic, prophet, diplomat and military chief during the twilight decades of Roman rule on the troubled upper Danube frontier. His *life*, written in 511 by Eugippius, abbot of the Southern Italian monastery of Lucullanum originally founded by Norican refugees, has long been regarded as a extremely rich and almost unique source for the sombre history of the Roman Empire's provincial disintegration.

It is not primarily for these reasons, however, that this chapter begins with a discussion of Severinus. Rather, our interest lies in what this saint reveals about the process by which the life of a spiritual leader was committed to writing, and about the scope of the hagiographical. Like other hagiographies, the *Life of Severinus* has been subjected to many critical questions relating to its genre: what, if anything, does it tell us about the real Severinus and where does he end and the legendary saint begin? Until about 20 years ago, many scholars such as Lotter,[4] Rajko Bratož[5] and Thompson treated Eugippius' work as a mine of information about late Roman Noricum. Although this approach has not been completely abandoned, recent years have seen a gradual shift towards an analysis of the *life* as a piece of hagiography, as a vehicle for expressing a certain idea of sanctity. In a major essay collection published in 2001 Walter Pohl summarized this trend: 'Die hagiographische Stilisierung kann nicht einfach entfernt werden wie eine Schicht, die sich über den "historischen Severin" gelegt hat.'[6] In this collection, readers of the *life* had more to say about Eugippius' concerns as the abbot of an early sixth century Italian monastery than about the distant world of the now disintegrated frontier of half a century earlier. Against the background of this general trend, it is particularly instructive to consider the changing treatment of the famous *Letter to Paschasius* which prefaces the *life*

---

[3]   Eugippius, *Letter to Paschasius* 7–10, tr. Ludwig Bieler, *Eugippius: The Life of Saint Severin* (Washington D.C, 1965), pp. 49–50.

[4]   Lotter, *Severinus von Noricum* (Stuttgart, 1976).

[5]   Rajko Bratož, *Severinus von Noricum und seine Zeit: Geschichtliche Anmerkungen* (Vienna, 1983).

[6]   'The hagiographical stylization cannot simply be removed like a sheet which has come to rest over the "historical Severinus"': Walter Pohl, 'Einleitung: Commemoratium – Vergegenwärtigungen des heiligen Severin' in Walter Pohl; Maximilian Diesenberger (eds), *Eugippius und Severin* (Wien, 2001), p. 12.

and part of which is quoted above. For Lotter, the letter contained a few scraps of hard information about Severinus (his excellent Latin, his apparent legal knowledge and experiences far beyond the province) which formed the basis for a reconstruction of his mysterious identity. But few scholars have been convinced by his identification of Severinus with a consul of the same name.[7] By contrast, the contributors to *Eugippius und Severin* were much more inclined to question the reason for the mystery: did Eugippius really not know?[8] And if he did, what was his reason for omitting to identify Severinus' earthly background?[9] Is this image of 'a hero from nowhere' unique or are there other examples?[10]

Although we can never be certain, some of the answers may be more straightforward than has hitherto been realized. To begin with the first of the questions posed above, everything suggests that Eugippius wrote truthfully when stating he knew nothing of Severinus' origins because the saint himself had actively concealed them. What he records is the very opposite of a private memory; rather, it is presented as the first thing all those the saint encountered (both visitors and members of his circle) remembered about him. Nor was this manner of speaking mysteriously (*clauso sermone*) a single incident, but a habit, built up over time (*referre solitus erat*). Eugippius' claim to have reported the testimonies of community members old enough to remember Severinus should be regarded as limiting further the possibility of total retrospective invention;[11] the wider we

---

[7] Lotter, *Severinus von Noricum*, pp. 246–54. For a review of the arguments and its weaknesses see Pohl, 'Einleitung', pp. 9–11, 25–31; and Thompson, *Romans and Barbarians*, pp. 113–15; Philippe Régérat, 'Introduction', Eugippe, *Vie de Saint Séverin* (Paris, 1991), pp. 99–101; Andreas Schwarz, 'Severinus of Noricum between Fact and Fiction', in Walter Pohl and Maximilian Diesenberger (eds), *Eugippius und Severin* (Vienna, 2001), pp. 9–11, 25–31.

[8] Ian Wood, 'The Monastic Frontiers of the Vita Severini', in *Eugippius und Severin*, p. 46: 'Whether or not we believe Eugippius ... (Severinus) is presented as if coming from nowhere ... his history is positively ignored as being irrelevant.'

[9] S.J.B. Barnish suggests that Eugippius' silence responds polemically to the way that Ennodius' biographies of Epiphanius and Antony celebrate their saints' nobility, 'Ennodius' Lives of Epiphanius and Antony: two models of Christian gentlemen', in *SP* 24 (1993), p. 19. Philippe Régérat assumes the suppression is an artifice on the author's behalf, and also suggests a remarkably banal motivation which lacks a clear ideological significance: 'peut-être est-ce là un artifice qui permet à l'auteur de commencer son récit avec l'arrivée de Séverin dans le Norique, sans s'attarder sur les détails jugés secondaires', 'Introduction' to Eugippe, *Vie de Saint Séverin* (Paris, 1991), p. 21.

[10] The phrase is Walter Goffart's, who also asks 'Does such concealment occur elsewhere in hagiography? It is unique in my ... experience; editors of Eugippius offer no parallel instances'. 'Does the Vita S. Severini have an underside?' in *Eugippius und Severin*, p. 34, footnote 8.

[11] Eugippius, *Letter to Paschasius* 2.

stretch the circle of people privy to the secret, the less likely it is that the secret would have made sense as a convincing and interesting part of the portrait.

As for the second question about the apparent uniqueness of this secretive device, several informative parallels in other hagiographies appear to have gone unnoticed. As we have seen, Hilarius refuses to disclose Honoratus' identity for very similar ideological reasons (spawning very similar modern attempts to resolve the mystery).[12] In other early Western hagiographies, identity concealment is, as with Severinus, attributed to the holy man himself as a personal policy. Constantius claims that, when journeying through the Alps, Germanus 'in his humility ... was most careful to let no one know who he was'.[13] Ferrandus depicts Fulgentius at a public banquet reluctant to reveal his illustrious origins out of humility, although, unlike Severinus, his attempts at anonymity ultimately fail.[14] Something similar is true of the Jura fathers Romanus and Lupicinus who went to great efforts to keep a low profile after working miracles.[15] There are close Eastern parallels to these Western examples. Pachomius tried to hide amongst his monks when Athanasius was visiting the Upper Thebaid.[16] Palladius and Theodoret mention a number of examples of holy men concealing their skills or their identity out of humility.[17] The case of Plotinus, who refused to mention his homeland, birthday, or parents, is a famous pagan example of the same policy (see p. 49).

In the absence of any direct evidence to the contrary, it seems probable that Eugippius' *Letter to Paschascius* genuinely reflects the image the saint carefully and consistently projected; the passage therefore does nothing to undermine the previous chapter's argument that hagiographical claims to truthfulness should be taken seriously. But although the case of Severinus is interesting in its own right, and will be discussed further in more depth, it also exemplifies issues of broader relevance to late antique hagiographies and the holy men they described. Modern historians, by either seeking Severinus' true identity or examining his hagiographical image, have accepted a conceptual dichotomy which is too stark

---

[12] 'Few documents are more frustrating ... than those biographies of holy men which ... virtually ignore ... mundane details of geographical or chronological exactitude', David Woods, 'The Origin of Honoratus of Lérins' in *Mnemosyne* Ser. 4 46.1 (1993), p. 78; Adalbert de Vogüé, 'Sur la patrie d'Honorat de Lérins, évêque d'Arles', in *RB* 88 (1978).

[13] Constantius, *Life of Germanus* 31, tr. F.R. Hoare in *The Western Fathers being the lives of SS. Martin of Tours, Ambrose, Augustine of Hippo, Honoratus of Arles and Germanus of Auxerre* (London, 1954), p. 311.

[14] Ferrandus, *Life of Fulgentius* 24.

[15] *Lives of the Jura Fathers* 43, p. 114.

[16] *Life of Pachomius* 30.

[17] Palladius, *Lausiac History* 18.16, 34.6; Theodoret, *History* 3.9, 12.4, (25.2).

and which effectively treats the subject and the writer as occupying entirely distinct roles in a notional chain of information. According to this model, the responsibility for the idealized image of Severinus is bound to have lain with his hagiographer. But as we have seen, the 'real' Severinus, far from being concealed behind this stylized image, may in fact have embraced it, employed it, and found it to be a highly effective aspect of his charismatic style. The significance of his identity to the present study thus lies not only in its hagiographical content, but in the possibility that this content was his own creation.

The case of Severinus reveals the possibility of an alternative model for interpreting late antique hagiographies. It is a model which will be explored throughout this chapter and contends that the notion of the hagiographical can very profitably be applied to many contexts beyond the formal act of literary composition on which we admittedly depend for so much of our information about spiritual leadership in late antiquity. Indeed, to examine the problem from the opposite viewpoint, the literary characteristics of hagiography make more sense once they are recognized as continuous with, and ultimately dependent on, much more general attitudes towards sanctity in the period. Careful analysis of hagiographies suggests these attitudes to be characteristic of, amongst others, holy men themselves, disciples of holy men, enthusiasts who recounted their lives orally and, implicitly, readers of hagiographical texts, a cluster of possible relationships sometimes disguised by the rather static image of a chain of information. Whilst this approach involves shifting attention, as it were, 'upstream' from the writer, it does not involve a simple restatement of the question 'how historically accurate are hagiographies?' Rather, the question it poses could be thought of as 'how hagiographical were the lives/lifestyles of holy men and the processes by which they became known?' This question aims to derive a certain historicity from what can be understood as a truthful and realistic genre, not because the historical truth somehow resides beneath the hagiographical surface, but because the genre's very hagiographical nature is representative of the broader attitudes in question.

As explained in the Introduction (see pp. 17–18), the move from realism to historicity involves the extension of the notion of textuality beyond the boundaries of a written genre to a lived world of behaviour and experience. But this move cannot be justified on methodological grounds alone. The transition from one notion of textuality to another is highly complex and must be explained in a way which is specific to the historical context. Although there are a number of reasons to believe that such a method can be highly fruitful when applied to the spiritual life of late antiquity, certain powerful objections can also be raised against it, and these too must be carefully considered.

The method proposed in this chapter rests on a series of basic premises. Firstly, that holy men could and did influence their own image; secondly, that as they did so they employed tools and techniques consistent with and recognizable from written hagiography; thirdly, that the reaction of people receptive to hagiographical information is likely to have been similar in whatever form, and at whatever stage they encountered it: be that as readers of literary texts, as learners through hearsay (the route by which Augustine learnt about Antony for example), or as followers witnessing spiritual achievements at first hand.

In all these respects, Severinus constitutes a fascinating example. A major part of his particular style of self-presentation was the cloak of mystery in which he wrapped himself. It is not just the permanent buzz of speculation amongst his followers and visitors that attests to the effectiveness of this device, but rather the amount of scholarly ink the question of his identity has caused to flow in more recent times. As the previous chapter showed, mystery had a number of important functions in hagiographical character descriptions (see pp. 68–9), and there is every reason to believe that it served Severinus himself in precisely the same way. It relieved him of the need to provide a substantial supply of spiritually significant information about himself which might then be vulnerable to dispute; instead his image could safely and steadily gestate in his followers' imaginations. But to understand fully how it did this, we must appreciate the complexity of what his silence implied. Although he made no direct claim to sanctity, the suppression of conventional biographical information pitted the concepts of earthly and spiritual identity against each other in a way which unambiguously associated him with the latter. Furthermore, his silence, though thorough, was not total: his 'obscure words' contained enough information to evoke powerful religious connotations which were magnified by their very lack of specificity. His immense and dangerous physical pilgrimage clearly evoked ideas of impressive spiritual progress, especially since he had apparently abandoned his homeland in a way often associated with the Patriarch Abraham. His references to cities in the East, and miracles on the way, reminded listeners of the famous monks of Egypt. That he had come from happier lands to a frontier region which, even in less troubled times, was regarded as challengingly backward, underlined both his mercy and spiritual constancy. If 'no prophet is accepted in his home town,'[18] if a holy man was 'the "stranger" *par excellence*,'[19] then Severinus did everything he could to emphasize his foreignness. Ultimately, his allusions to lands beyond Noricum evoked the idea of a world beyond this whose direct instructions he was obeying in (otherwise inexplicably) coming to the province.

---

[18]   Luke 4.24; Matthew 13:57; John 4.44.
[19]   Brown, 'Rise and Function of the Holy Man', p. 91.

But these spiritual connotations are only part of the story. Paradoxically, Severinus' habits of self-presentation also allowed him to make a powerful statement about his secular background. The entire style can be interpreted as an extended and sophisticated application of *praeteritio*: the rhetorical device by which an author refers to a subject precisely by announcing his intention not to do so. The possibility of slavery is jovially negated; the serious-minded motivation for concealing his background – to avoid vainglory – effectively asserts that his background is of a type susceptible to this vice. His educated speech and apparent good breeding, things which can be disguised if genuinely necessary, contribute to the effect. In this sense it is misleading to describe Severinus as a 'hero from nowhere', or to maintain that his background was 'positively irrelevant'. The elimination of specifics does not result in nothing, but rather in an idea which is more abstract and wider-ranging in its connotations. A very similar effect is achieved in the *Life of Honoratus* where the suppression of detail is accompanied by a vivid portrait of a privileged Roman upbringing which included games, school, hunting and an easy-going pagan father. The author both evokes a picture and divorces it from any specific location.[20] The effect is rather like the idealized landscape portraits popular in nineteenth-century Germany, in which features felt to be generic to the nation's villages and countryside were blended together to create the impression of a notional, quintessential *Heimat* which transcended the specificities of any particular region.[21] In Severinus' case, visitors and disciples, though unable to pin him down, remained convinced of his aristocracy and were left with a general impression of *romanitas* which, no less than his spiritual achievements, was magnified by a lack of detail. Even as a Christian ascetic on the barbarous Danube frontier, Severinus, like his distant predecessor Ovid, was still close to the idea of Rome.

In summary, what constituted Severinus' image were connotations as capable of functioning in immediate social contexts as they were on a literary level: hagiography thus had its close counterpart in charisma. But his charisma consisted of more than the mere sum of these connotations. To read a text is not just to comprehend a series of statements, but to understand their mutual interaction, to accord to them as a whole the appropriate significance, to recognize the 'codes' which govern the discourse to which they belong and in

---

[20] This use of *praeteritio* is observed on a literary level by Jean-Pierre Weiss, 'Honorat héros antique et saint chrétien: étude du mot *gratia* dans la *Vie de Saint Honorat* d'Hilaire d'Arles', in *Augustinianum* 24 (1984), p. 266.

[21] See Alon Confino, *The Nation as Local Metaphor: Württemberg, Imperial Germany, and National Memory 1871–1918* (Chapel Hill, 1997), esp. 191–209.

which they participate.[22] As Gérard Genette showed throughout his magisterial *Palimpsestes*, in the case of a literary work these codes are extremely rich, and present in everything from a work's linguistic style to the colour and typeface used on its front cover.[23] But for all its complexity, the literary text, as well as the constraints of the physical acts necessary to appreciate and create it (reading, writing etc.), at least create a focal point for these codes. To attribute to real life any kind of textuality entails not just an analysis of contents but an explanation of how an equivalent set of codes established the parameters of the discourse which first allowed the events in question to be identified, grouped, and appropriately evaluated. How was Severinus able to transform a set of statements, attributes and behaviours into a narrative which could be noticed, followed, and understood by an audience? How did the events which constituted his life come to stand out from the immeasurable number of other events happening in the background around him?

With only one detailed written description of Severinus' life available,[24] any answer to these questions will necessarily be extremely limited. Even Max Weber, who made charisma an object of scholarly discussion, also accepted the limitations inherent in any analysis intended to capture the precise quality of a first hand encounter with a successful leader.[25] Nonetheless, in the few surviving details in the *Letter to Paschasius* we can recognize not only connotations of leadership likely to have been powerful to those willing to hear them, but also certain mechanisms which established out of them a narrative structure. It would be misleading to regard these mechanisms as completely separate from the spiritual connotations mentioned above – many pieces of information played both roles – but nonetheless a certain distinction can be drawn. For example, Severinus' mysterious and exotic past was attractive for many reasons, but his travels, and the foreignness which resulted from them, delineated a particular sphere of significance, and created a particular phase in his life, over which he

---

[22]   'However familiar, however casual the act of opening a novel or a newspaper or turning on a television program today, nothing can keep this modest action from setting up in us, at one blow and in its entirety, the narrative code we are going to need', Roland Barthes, 'Introduction to the Structural Analysis of Narratives', in *The Semiotic Challenge*, tr. Richard Howard (Oxford, 1988), p. 128.

[23]   Gérard Genette, *Palimpsestes: La littérature au second degré* (Paris, 1982).

[24]   The only other source is a fleeting reference to *inlustrissimum virum Severinum* by Ennodius, *Vita Beati Antonii monachi Lerinensis* 9, ed. Friedrich Vogel, MGH Auct. Ant. 7 (Berlin 1885).

[25]   This is implicit in his attempt to analyse it objectively: 'How the quality in question would be ultimately judged from any ethical, aesthetic, or other such point of view is naturally entirely indifferent for purposes of definition', Max Weber, *On Charisma and Institution Building: Selected Papers*, ed. S.N. Eisenstadt (Chicago, 1968), p. 48.

exercised great control and freedom of expression. Severinus' past life, which, like all lives, probably contained much information unworthy of hagiography, was safely cordoned off with the exception of a few carefully chosen allusions. We can well imagine that the mere presence of powerful foreigners in Noricum's small frontier towns always had the potential to generate great public interest and thus provided Severinus with a potentially curious audience. His exotic past life gave him both something to talk about and the means not to talk about it.

Another type of narrative mechanism was present in the two strands that constituted his image – the ascetic and the aristocrat – and related specifically to the way these two figures interacted. It has been observed that Severinus brought much needed leadership in a religious guise to the insecure and impressionable inhabitants of a province where familiar secular institutions had largely collapsed.[26] A reading of the *life* sympathetic to Eugippius' literal meaning suggests this may have been true in a quite specific and practical sense: in the dire conditions of the day, the providential, biblical significance Severinus gave to events may have served as a crucial organizational tool. The final evacuation of part of the province by the Roman population which Severinus, like a Moses figure, purportedly recast in the terms of the Hebrew Exodus,[27] could be seen as a hagiographer's attempt to explain away a mission which had ultimately failed to save Roman Noricum. More generally, whilst scholars have observed the biblical underpinnings of many of the events reported in the *life*, the working assumption has generally been that such comparisons were essentially a literary phenomenon.[28] But it could equally be argued that Severinus, shrewdly cognizant of political reality, urgently preached this significance to garner support for such necessary, radical action. In a similar way, many seventeenth-century English Puritans travelling to the Promised Land of the New World were encouraged to see in their journey a literal fulfilment of Scripture.[29] Severinus' personal example of having long ago like Abraham abandoned his own homeland may have helped the reluctant to detect meaning in the physically dangerous and emotionally difficult step that now confronted them.

Although Severinus' image was rooted in a stark conceptual contrast between a spiritual and an earthly notion of identity, these things in tandem

---

[26] Ron F. Newbold, 'Power Motivation in Sidonius Apollinaris, Eugippius, and Nonnus', in *Florilegium* 7 (1985), pp. 1–16.

[27] Eugippius, *Life of Severinus* 40.4–6.

[28] Marc van Uytfanghe, 'La Bible dans la "*Vie de Saint Séverin*" d'Eugippe', in *Latomus* 33.2 (1974), pp. 324–52; Régérat, '*Vir Dei* als Leitbild in der Spätantike: Das Beispiel der *Vita Severini* des Eugippius' in J. Dumner and M. Vielberg (eds), *Zwischen Historiographie und Hagiographie* (Stuttgart, 2005), p. 77.

[29] As observed by Williams, *Authorised Lives*, pp. 1–4.

involved a relativization, not a total effacement of the latter. Just as the outline of
how much he had renounced made his spiritual achievement more impressive,
it was precisely having renounced it so visibly that he could hint constantly at
its reassuring benefits whilst remaining immune from suspicions of vainglory.
It is probably true that the dire conditions in Noricum made its inhabitants
particularly receptive to charismatic, religious leadership. However, it may be
equally true that they were more able to accept the exotic and ascetic Christian
form this leadership took because Severinus delivered it in an accent whose
ancient connotations of authority they could easily understand.[30] Therefore these
two aspects – saint and aristocrat – provided more than merely a double list
of qualities; in combination, they fulfilled the basic criterion of hagiographical
realism explored in the previous chapter: the location of spiritual significance in
familiar and plausible information.

Self-Conscious Saints

The case of Severinus neatly illustrates the model with which this chapter is
concerned. But as with any model the question remains how far, and in what
way, we are justified in applying it to other cases. One can certainly imagine how
the example of Severinus' mysterious style might encourage a literal reading of
similar policies by saints such as Germanus of Auxerre and Fulgentius of Ruspae.
There is perhaps some evidence that Hilarius echoed the policy of silence already
practised by his master Honoratus; the author's concealment of Honoratus'
origins has the secondary function of disguising his own, and in the *Life of
Hilarius* written by the younger Honoratus, the pattern of concealment (still
presented as a rejection of biographical convention, but fast becoming one in
its own right), is repeated.[31] On a broader level, what about other holy men and
other hagiographical techniques? Should we see in Sulpicius Severus' claim that
he relied heavily on information from Martin's own mouth evidence for similar

---

[30]   In a similar way Constantius identifies Germanus' earlier secular career (inc. law,
military experience, eloquence) as part of God's plan for his eventual episcopacy, *Life of
Germanus* 1. Raymond van Dam suggests that Martin's military experience was a reassurance
against barbarians, *Leadership and Community in Late Antique Gaul* (Berkeley, 1985), p. 126.

[31]   'dignum duco nequaquam more rhetorico patriam parentesque memorare': Honoratus,
Life of Hilarius 2, ed. Samuel Cavallin, *Vitae Sanctorum Honorati et Hilarii, Episcoporum
Arelatensium* (Lund, 1952). Like his mentor, Hilarius was unknown in the city before the
election. The parallel is observed in passing by Ralph W. Mathisen, *Ecclesiastical Factionalism
and Religious Controversy in Fifth-Century Gaul* (Washington D.C., 1989), p. 89.

tendencies of self-expression?[32] Having recognized such texts as committed to truthfulness, should we habitually try to explain the image of sanctity they contain as first and foremost a product of the holy man, and only secondarily of his hagiographer?

Far from being fanciful or unusual, this is, I suspect, a very real possibility which should at least be considered as a matter of course. As Severinus and his followers show, the model finds support partly in the social contexts hagiographies describe and from which they often emerged. The Neoplatonic schools of philosophy in cities such as Athens and Alexandria were the milieux in which pagan holy men moved. Here, one's status depended partly on that of one's master, and educational reputations spread far beyond the teacher's city; generations of students and teachers could thus be linked back over decades and through different educational centres and long lines of succession. Eunapius, for example (as he was probably well aware) had a place in an academic 'family tree' going back as far as Plotinus, the first subject of his collective biography.[33] As Edward J. Watts has argued, much of this author's information probably derives from a sophisticated oral tradition characteristic of this academic environment,[34] a claim supported by the fact that he only highlights written sources.[35]

A similar point can be made about the deserts of Egypt and the Levant which were the cradle of Christian monasticism. The principal focus of the literature that emerged from this context are the spiritual achievements of monks as reflected in their ascetic feats. But no less than the philosophical schools, this was also a world in which human relationships – between a master and pupil, between a monk and his neighbour – were crucial to an individual's identity. Individual ascetic achievements were therefore a matter of considerable collective interest and speculation. It is with this social context in mind that Graham Gould convincingly argues that the *Sayings of the Fathers* (*Apophthegmata Patrum*), far from being a literary idealization of monastic life, is in fact deeply rooted

---

[32] Sulpicius originally claims to record only tested information, since things to which Martin alone was witness are unknowable: *Life of Martin* 1.7–9. Nonetheless, Martin's own testimony is later used as proof: ibid. 24.8. Similarly, Ferrandus felt able to avoid the charge of falsification by recording either what Fulgentius had told him, or what he and his correspondent Felicianus had witnessed: *Life of Fulgentius* 3.

[33] Eunapius was the pupil of Chrysanthius, who had studied with Aedesius (*Lives* 500) Aedesius was Iamblichus' leading student (ibid. 458), himself a close associate of Porphyry (ibid. 457), Plotinus' student (ibid. 455). The link is almost made explicit at ibid. 458. For Eunapius' communitarian aspect see Goulet, *Etudes sur les vies des philosophes*, p. 20; Watts, 'Orality and Communal Identity in Eunapius' *Lives of the Sophists and Philosophers*', pp. 334–61.

[34] Ibid.

[35] E.g. a *Life* of Alypius by Iamblichus: Eunapius, *Lives* 460–61.

in a rich tradition of oral communication fostered by the desert.[36] In a similar vein, Rapp finds evidence for an active oral tradition in Theodoret's *Lives* and Palladius' *Lausiac History*.[37] We might add that spiritual tourism by such figures as Palladius and Egeria can only have bolstered these traditions by disseminating stories about monks not only beyond but also further within and around the desert world.

On one level, these arguments concern the texts and our perception of them. For Gould, an awareness of an underlying oral culture increases the texts' historicity by placing their contents closer to the events they describe.[38] Rapp's emphasis is more stylistic: by being simple, plain, and unadorned, such accounts leant themselves to a certain literary realism, although we cannot assume that this verisimilitude guaranteed historicity.[39] But either way, there is a sociological as well as a literary point to be made. As Gould shows, the desert offered monks both an obligation to be open, and an opportunity for self-expression;[40] the oral tradition both reflects this and facilitated it. Therefore, just as desert literature contains lots of evidence of monks talking about other monks, it also reports many instances of monks talking about themselves. These may be substantial anecdotes of spiritual experience such as the hermit Paul's account to Cyril of his struggle with sexual desire and other sins.[41] They may also be straightforward formulae which encapsulate their personal spiritual achievements over time: Cyril also reports how '(Cyriacus) stated categorically to me, "In this long period of thirty-one years in which I was canonarch and treasurer the sun never saw me either eating or in a temper."'[42] Similarly, Macarius told Palladius that he hadn't spat on the ground in the 60 years since his baptism.[43]

The opportunity to relate one's own spiritual life could easily become a temptation. Desert literature is deeply aware of the problem of vanity. A whole section of the *Sayings of the Fathers* concerns the risk of doing things for show: for

---

[36]   Gould, *The Desert Fathers*, pp. 18–25. An negative by-product of this culture is explored by Maud W. Gleason: 'Visiting and News: Gossip and Reputation Management in the Desert', *Journal of Early Christian Studies* 6.3 (1998), pp. 501–21.

[37]   Rapp, 'Storytelling as Spiritual Communication in Early Greek Hagiography', pp. 439–41.

[38]   Gould, *The Desert Fathers*, p. 25.

[39]   Rapp, 'Storytelling as Spiritual Communication in Early Greek Hagiography', pp. 442–4.

[40]   Gould, *The Desert Fathers*, pp. 31–2.

[41]   Cyril, *Lives* 7.20–74.26.

[42]   Ibid. 227.1–5.

[43]   Palladius, *Lausiac History* 18.28.

example, becoming famous for one's diet.[44] Surrounded by disciples, a reputation for sanctity could become a pressure for Christians and pagans alike: we only have to think of the students of Iamblichus,[45] and the disciples of Pachomius[46] pestering their masters for miracles; or of Honoratus' followers gathering on the shore as he crossed to Lérins.[47] Because we encounter it in a written form, it is easy to treat a phrase such as 'Abba, give me a word' as, first and foremost, a literary formula, but it may also have functioned as a conventional mode of address which placed both the disciple and the holy man in a self-conscious position and brought certain expectations to their subsequent conversation.[48] These two possibilities are in no way contradictory: the more recognizable 'Abba, give me a word' was as a literary formula, the greater the expectation it placed on those who uttered it and on its immediate addressees.

For all these reasons it should be clear that the possibility of holy men moulding their own reputations is a very real one. Nonetheless, the applicability of textual formulae to contents other than the written text means that the default attribution of all idealized details to the saint would be no more satisfactory than the existing tendency which sees them habitually attributed to the hagiographer. Indeed, the *Letter to Paschasius* cited above is highly unusual because it occurs in the explicit context of a hagiographer explaining in detail what he doesn't know and why. In the overwhelming majority of cases, hagiographers reveal nothing about the origins of specific information (most of the rest of Eugippius' *Life of Severinus* is no exception); they simply present it as trustworthy and uncontroversial.

To demonstrate that the hagiographical had an existence beyond the literary text, we cannot therefore rely only on the opinions of the authors of this genre, but must look in other places. Spiritually-minded autobiographical writings are useful because they describe a reader's own experiences and/or appear to lay claim to a certain conception of sanctity in terms familiar from hagiography: such works are the subject of Part II. Also useful are references which reveal the possibility of an alternative, more sceptical perspective on holy men (or on those who aspired to that status) than is provided by partisan hagiographers about their subjects.

What constituted sanctity was subjective: one person's holy man was another person's fraud or dupe or villain. This is immediately clear if one compares, for

---

[44] *Apophthegmata Patrum* 8.22, 27, ed. Jean-Claude Guy, *Les Apophthegmes des Pères: Collection Systématique*, Sources Chrétiennes 387 (Paris, 1993).

[45] Eunapius, *Lives* 459.

[46] *Life of Pachomius* 112.

[47] Hilarius, *Life of Honoratus* 3.15.

[48] For the role of the Abba's word in the desert see Gould, *The Desert Fathers*, pp. 37–52.

example, Athanasius' description of pagan philosophers[49] with, say, Eunapius' description of Christian monks.[50] A subtler strand in some hagiographies is where the possibility of scepticism towards holy men is recognized precisely in being explicitly refuted. For example, in the *Life of Hilarion* Jerome assures his readers that his subject's peregrinations were 'not the result of any restlessness or childish caprice'.[51] Similarly, Hilarius records how, on leaving their homeland, Honoratus and his brother feared that their decision would be attributed to 'mere youthful foolhardiness' (in fact, as it turns out, they were 'true sons of Abraham').[52] Theodoret of Cyrus makes great efforts to show that Symeon Stylites' distinctive form of pillar-based asceticism was not his own hair-brain idea as some people suspected, but (at a stretch) had biblical precedents (see p. 66).[53] Although anonymous and immediately refuted, the opposition such statements anticipate reveal late antique society to be more capable of and sophisticated in its scepticism than the monotonous adulation of hagiographers might otherwise suggest.[54]

In other texts, the author himself voices a sceptical viewpoint towards holy men. One particular form of scepticism – namely the charge of affectation – paradoxically serves as good evidence that holy men could sometimes engineer their own image, precisely by showing that such attempts were not universally effective, even amongst their notional co-religionists. An extensive section of the fifth century *Regula Magistri* launches a withering attack on a type of monk known as a gyrovague. Of dubious motivation, these men were accused of roaming the Empire unsupervised, unreasonably demanding hospitality from strangers. Most revealing from our viewpoint are their apparently common attempts to pass themselves off as sages by bowing their heads in a show of humility, whilst at the same time showing off with exaggerated tales of their journeys.[55] Similarly, Eunapius, in one of his most polemical portraits, attacks the career philosopher Priscus for building his reputation on a haughty reserve and strategic silences – a fakery which contrasts markedly with the easy affability of his hero Chrysanthius.[56] Their central value judgement aside,

---

[49] Athanasius, *Life of Antony* 72–3, 80.5.

[50] Eunapius, *Lives* 476.

[51] Jerome, *Life of St. Hilarion* 43.

[52] Hilarius, *Life of Honoratus* 2.12 (tr. Hoare, p. 257).

[53] Theodoret, *History* 26.12.

[54] See footnote 75, p. 41.

[55] *Regula Magistri* 1.13–74, ed. and tr. Adalbert de Vogüé, Sources Chrétiennes 105–7 (3 vols, Paris, 1964–65), vol.1, p. 333).

[56] Eunapius, *Lives* 482. A portrait of philosophical affectation in a similar spirit is given by Julian, *To the Uneducated Cynics* 201A (tr. Wright, vol. 2, p. 57).

what is remarkable about these descriptions is that they criticize techniques one might easily consider hagiographical: a friendlier interpreter might be moved by a philosopher's silence and reserve instead of finding it phoney; he might be impressed by the scale of a monk's journeys. Conversely, as one commentator astutely observes, a less generous judge than Eugippius might well have considered Severinus a gyrovague *par excellence.*[57]

Of course, all these cases provide direct evidence only for the specific holy men or groups of holy men to which they refer; but taken collectively, they nonetheless enhance the claim advanced earlier in this chapter that holy men could influence their own reputations using hagiographical techniques. To put it another way, they suggest that there was a fundamental structural similarity between the type of charisma exercised by holy men and the hagiographical texts devoted to them, particularly in the sense that both displayed the strong influence of previous models.[58] This is especially obvious in cases where writers judge (would-be) holy men negatively by highlighting the abuse of models of spirituality borrowed from elsewhere. But it is corroborated, perhaps in a more surprising way, by the willingness of many hagiographers to concede the consciously imitative nature of their subjects' quest for sanctity. For instance, Athanasius is explicit about Antony's desire to follow in the footsteps of a local holy man and Elijah.[59] The philosopher Antoninus spends his life trying to fulfil the sacred prophecy his god-like mother Sosipatra has made about him.[60] Severinus speaks of himself 'as if of another'; in ways, in other words, that would have sounded more natural in the third person. According to Ennodius of Ticinum, Epiphanius simply became whatever biblical character he was reading about at the time.[61] Such self-conscious comparisons reinforce

---

[57]   Ian Wood, 'The Monastic Frontiers', p. 49.

[58]   The relationship between sacred biography and charisma is usefully considered in Michael A. Williams (ed.), *Charisma and Sacred Biography (Journal of the American Academy of Religion Studies* 48 (1982), and especially by Charles F. Keyes, 'Introduction: Charisma from Social Life to Sacred Biography', pp. 1–22. As his title implies, Keyes tends to consider the causality the other way round; he also emphasizes the constraint placed on the text by the life (pp. 15–16), rather than the extent to which they may reflect the same patterns.

[59]   Athanasius, *Life of Antony* 3.3–5, 7.13.

[60]   Eunapius, *Lives* 470.

[61]   Ennodius, *Life of Epiphanius* 30–31. Similarly, John Chrysostom argues that 'when a person is continually with others, he becomes like them in character'; thus monks become like prophets and apostles: John Chrysostom, *Comparatio Regis et Monachi* and *Adversus Oppugnatores Vitae Monasticae* 2, ed. J-P. Migne, PG 47 (Paris, 1958), tr. David G. Hunter, *John Chrysostom: A Comparison Between a King and a Monk/Against the Opponents of Monastic Life* (Lampeter, 1988), p. 71.

the concluding point of the previous chapter: namely that, just as the reader was not necessarily the final destination of hagiographical information, nor was the holy man necessarily its straightforward source. At the limit, this is because these roles were potentially interchangeable i.e. a holy man may also be a reader of holy *lives* as some saints apparently were (see p. 30). In a more general sense, it is because holy men, even in being holy men, were also the receivers and interpreters of spiritually significant information, as much as they were its projectors. In such a situation, complex relationships were generated. As Williams argues, because Antony was both a new Elijah and new John the Baptist, his imitators were also their imitators.[62] There is no contradiction between these various possibilities. As the third century philosopher Favorinus argued (coincidentally, like Honoratus, a citizen of Arles), it was in obeying previous paradigms that one became a paradigm for others.[63]

Indeed, it is the *Life of Honoratus*, perhaps more clearly than other late antique hagiographies, which illustrates how holy men might use models in their own spiritual lives. The previous chapter examined what paradigms were in play within the written *life* (see pp. 63–4). What makes the paradigmatic frame still more interesting, however, is the conscious awareness of it demonstrated by Honoratus at key moments in the narrative and which Hilarius has no hesitation in conceding. It is in imitation of Abraham that Honoratus and his brother leave home;[64] Honoratus chooses Lérins precisely because its reptilian denizens allow him to fulfil Christ's promise that his followers will have the 'authority to trample on snakes and scorpions'.[65] The spiritual significance of Honoratus' actions is apparently not, therefore, an extraneous judgement retrospectively applied by others, but rather 'always already' present in his most important decisions.

These moments serve as hagiographical codes by which Honoratus' grade and type of sanctity is measured and defined. But of course, one thing altered by the shift from the literary realm to a parallel realm of charisma is the nature of the audience: no longer a readership addressed by a hagiographer, but a group of followers attentive to the holy man and his actions. In this respect too, the *Life of Honoratus* is an unusually rich source, for it hints at the presence of such an audience around Honoratus as he enacted these sacred paradigms. For example,

---

[62]   Williams, *Authorised Lives*, p. 142.

[63]   Favorinus, *De Exilio*, ed. Adelmo Barigazzi, *Favorino di Arelate: Opere* (Florence, 1966). See Timothy Whitmarsh, *Greek Literature and Roman Empire* (Oxford, 2001), pp. 170–71.

[64]   Hilarius, *Life of Honoratus* 2.12.

[65]   Ibid. 3.15 citing Luke 10.19.

the nearby coastal population are aware of his desire to seek out the desert, and attempt to warn him against the 'terrible wilderness' (*terribilem ... vastitatem*) of Lérins; and despite going there in search of solitude, he repeated the famous words from Luke about trampling on snakes and scorpions 'now to himself, now to his followers'.[66] One reason for choosing Lérins was that it was close to 'the neighbourhood of Bishop Leontius' (in nearby Fréjus). In an influential article, Goehring argued that the monastic desert was often closer to Egyptian cities than hagiographies suggested;[67] Honoratus' hagiographer goes further by suggesting that the saint chose his desert partly on the basis of its proximity to an urban centre. Indeed, the journey to Lérins is presented as just one stage in a spiritual journey which had always been highly public and prominent. Hilarius hints that Honoratus' original departure from home had been sufficiently visible to attract scepticism in some quarters;[68] before this date, he and his brother had drawn visitors from far and wide by very visibly distributing all their wealth[69] – or perhaps not quite all, for we later discover that throughout their wanderings they continue to donate vast funds.[70] All these things may help explain the apparent paradox that throughout Honoratus' continual search for solitude the lingering sense of an audience still felt natural to Hilarius. We only have to think of the Roman crowd's reaction to the conversion of Marius Victorinus related in Augustine's *Confessions* to realize that the spiritual lives of prominent men, though personal, were not always wholly private.[71] What Hilarius' portrayal of Honoratus' spiritual career suggests, in fact, is highly compatible with Favorinus' view that someone became a worthy paradigm by successfully fulfilling earlier ones. Given that Honoratus was legitimately using the Bible as a guide to life, his self-conscious behaviour could be accepted merely as the continuous striving of one whose moral excellence had been visible from earliest childhood. This is not to say that those who observed Honoratus were always and immediately united in their judgement; but it is perhaps why, in a world highly conscious of phoney holy men, the support, or presence in the

---

[66]   Ibid. 2.15 (tr. Hoare, p. 260).

[67]   Goehring, 'The Encroaching Desert', pp. 73–88.

[68]   They were concerned it would be interpreted as 'mere youthful foolhardiness', ibid. 2.12.

[69]   Ibid. 2.10.

[70]   'Their possessions ... were still large and now they were completely dispersed', Hilarius, *Life of Honoratus* 2.11 (Hoare, p. 257). Similarly, Fulgentius' building of a monastery 'at his own expense' (Ferrandus, *Life of Fulgentius* 51, tr. Robert B. Eno in *Fulgentius: Selected Works* (Washington D.C., 1997), p. 45), indicates continuing wealth despite allegedly having given all his property away upon renouncing the world: ibid. 14 (tr. Eno, p. 14).

[71]   Augustine, *Confessions* 8.2.5.

crowd of senior figures like Caprasius or the bishop of Fréjus was so important. At least in the eyes of Hilarius, what made a comparison between Abraham and Honoratus legitimate, was ultimately that he had succeeded in the extremely difficult aim of living up to his timeless example.

Eucherius' Lérins: A Hagiographical Stage Set?

The *Life of Honoratus* goes further than many other hagiographies in acknowledging the existence and role of a holy man's audience. Even this testimony, however, has limitations. By nature, it reflects an official version of Honoratus' story related after the saint's death; within the text, the audience play their role, but their voice is subsumed into the work's real subject, namely the saint's life story. What it leaves unclear, in other words, is the immediate atmosphere that prevailed around the saint during his lifetime, the collective mentality necessary for the establishment of his reputation. This limitation applies particularly where the text's pivotal moment is concerned i.e. the events surrounding the crossing to Lérins. Although Hilarius had been among the saint's followers, he was presumably not an eyewitness to these events since he claims to have been recruited to the community some time after its foundation.[72]

The purpose of the present section is to show that Eucherius of Lyons' *In Praise of the Desert (De Laude Eremi)* can be read in such as way as to cast some light onto the atmosphere around Honoratus, and thus partially redress the limitations of the hagiography in isolation. For although some extremely revealing points of contact exist between the two texts, *In Praise of the Desert* offers evidence of a different and exceptionally valuable kind. There are several basic reasons for this: as a prominent member of the Lérins community, Eucherius was an associate of Honoratus, as well as of his hagiographer Hilarius to whom he dedicated the work. We can say with confidence, therefore, that the work emerged from Honoratus' close milieu; indeed, it was almost certainly composed by Eucherius at Lérins when Honoratus was still alive, and very probably while he was still abbot. However, the focus of the *life* is different: the island, its community and their place in Christian reality rather than the holy man.[73] This section will attempt to show that the information Eucherius offers

---

[72]   Hilarius, *Life of Honoratus* 5.23–4.

[73]   The difference between the two texts is seen as fundamental in a brilliantly argued article by Conrad Leyser: '"This Sainted Isle": Panegyric, Nostalgia, and the Invention of Lerinian Monasticism' in W.E. Klingshirn and Mark Vessey (eds), *The Limits of Ancient Christianity* (Michigan, 1999), pp. 188–206. He regards them as *oeuvres de circonstance* which represent different visions of the community's history at different stages in its development,

is not irrelevant or contrary to that provided in the *life*, but rather helps explain some of its silences.

The value of *In Praise of the Desert* as a source for the early Lérins community, one of the earliest and most important monasteries in fourth century Gaul,[74] has often been recognized, and the present work will aim to contribute something to an understanding of the institution in the course of our own discussion of the holy man and his audience. Scholarly debate has revolved around several questions: the role of Eastern prototypes in the Lerinians' self-conception;[75] the style of the regime that prevailed there (usually seen as moderate, more akin to traditional Roman *otium* than to Egyptian monasticism);[76] and the contribution made by Lérins to the history of the idea of the desert. It has been observed that *In Praise of the Desert* is unprecedented in two senses: the only late antique work which attempts to gather all the various Christian connotations of the concept under a single title, it is also the first Latin work to apply the term *eremus* directly to a location which was not a desert in the traditional sense (e.g. Levantine or African).[77] The earlier Gallic saint Martin may have 'desired the desert' (*eremum*

---

and tell us little about the ascetic life practised there. The essential disagreement between our views will become clear in the course of the argument.

[74]   'ingenti fratrum coenobio': Cassian, *Conlationes* 11, ed. M. Petschenig, CSEL 13 (Vienna, 1886, repr. Verlag der Österreichischen Akademie der Wissenschaften, 2004). Praefatio (ed. M. Petschenig, p. 311).

[75]   It has generally been accepted that the relationship was one of close imitation: e.g. Pierre Courcelle, *Les lettres grecques en Occident* (Paris, 1948), p. 216; Maria-Elisabeth Brunert, *Das Ideal der Wüstenaskese* (Münster, 1994), p. 183; Maria-Elisabeth Brunert 'Die Bedeutung der Wüste im Eremitentum', in Uwe Lindemann and Monika Schmitz-Emans (eds), *Was ist eine Wüste?* (Würzburg, 2000), p. 69. Robert Markus argues that the emphasis on isolation contrasted with the Augustinian model: *The End of Ancient Christianity*, p. 161.

[76]   Which has generally been seen as mild: Pricoco, *Monaci, Filosofi, e Saggi*, pp. 81, 164–7; Rosemarie Nürnberg, *Askese als sozialer Impuls* (Bonn, 1988), p. 111; Brunert, *Das Ideal der Wüstenaskese* (Münster, 1994), p. 68; Nouailhat, *Saints et Patrons*, p. 225; Carsten Scherliess, *Literatur und Conversio: literarische Former im monastischen Umkreis des Klosters von Lérins* (Frankfurt, 2000), pp. 84–5; Markus, *The End of Ancient Christianity*, p. 162; Fisher, 'Liminality: the Vocation of the Church (I); the Desert Image in Early Christian Tradition', p. 181. This assumption is questioned by Leyser, *Authority and Asceticism from Augustine to Gregory the Great* (Oxford, 2000), p. 41, f. 30. There has been disagreement on the question of whether or not the community used a written rule. Pricoco argued that Honoratus governed personally and charismatically: *L'isola dei Santi*, pp. 77–93; Adalbert de Vogüé associated the pseudonymous *Regula Sanctorum Patrum* with Honoratus and his community: *Les règles des saints pères* (Paris, 1982), p. 80ff.

[77]   Opelt, 'Zur literarischen Eigenart von Eucherius' Schrift *de laude eremi*', pp. 205–8; Jean Leclercq, '"Eremus" et "Eremita": Pour l'histoire du vocabulaire de la vie solitaire', in *COCR* 25.1 (1963), p. 18.

concupivit)[78] from an early age and, according to his hagiographer Sulpicius, founded a monastery outside Tours which offered the 'solitude of a desert' (*eremi solitudinem*),[79] thus achieving equivalence with its Egyptian prototypes. But the Lerinians went a step further by appropriating the term directly; a sign of their self-confidence, according to Pricoco,[80] but also a milestone on the linguistic journey which saw the vocabulary of the desert loosen and become more metaphorical until, by the early middle ages, it could signify any lonely spot (e.g. forest, cave, remote island) suitable for the contemplative life.[81]

In Praise of the Desert is deceptively easy to summarize. It essentially consists of a series of very strong value judgements about the spiritual power and value of the desert; indeed, it initially seems to be little more than a placid synthesis of its various Christian connotations. It is the place where God dwells and can most easily be found.[82] Indeed, God created deserts for this very purpose.[83] At one point, love of the desert is directly equated with love of God.[84] The evidence for these assertions is overwhelmingly biblical, and much of the work consists in a list of stories that took place in the desert, excerpted from both Testaments. But these stories did not mark the end of God's work through the desert: crucially, he still reveals himself there through miracles today, sometimes even in ways that echo Scripture, such as by providing 'manna' for hungry monks.[85] The benefits enjoyed by desert dwellers are therefore innumerable: they become 'a temple of God'[86] and 'go beyond this world'.[87] All these claims are delivered in an emotive, affectionate tone: Eucherius personifies the desert, describes its miracles as personal triumphs,[88] and addresses it in the second person, and even vocatively.[89] The relevance of this tone becomes clearer when we recognize that Eucherius'

---

[78]   Sulpicius, *Life of Martin* 2.4.

[79]   Ibid. 10.4.

[80]   Pricoco, *L'isola dei Santi*, pp. 185–7. A view rejected by Leyser, '"This Sainted Isle"', pp. 195–7.

[81]   E.g. Brunert, 'Die Bedeutung der Wüste im Eremitentum', p. 69.

[82]   Eucherius, *De Laude Eremi* 3, ed. Salvatore Pricoco (Catania, 1965).

[83]   Ibid. 5.

[84]   Ibid. 1.

[85]   Ibid. 29.

[86]   Ibid. 41, tr. Tim Vivian, Kim Vivian, Jeffrey Burton Russell in *Lives of the Jura Fathers* (Kalamazoo, 1999), p. 213.

[87]   Ibid. 31 (tr. Vivian et al., p. 208).

[88]   E.g. Eucherius, *In Praise of the Desert* 21.4.

[89]   Despite its reputation for literary eccentricity (esp. Opelt, 'Zur literarischen Eigenart'), these tendencies perhaps have something of a contemporary echo in Rutilius' praise for Rome: Rutilius Namatianus, *De Reditu Suo* 1.43ff, ed and tr. Jules Vessereau and François Préchac, *Rutilius Namatianus: Sur son retour* (Paris, 1961).

praise applies not just to a category of landscape but also to a very specific object: it is Lérins – *his* Lérins – that he honours above all.[90]

In view of this double content – a thematization of the desert on the one hand, the inclusion of Lérins within this tradition on the other – it is understandable why *In Praise of the Desert* has been seen as a milestone in the process which turned the desert from being a literal concept into a more metaphorical one. A close reading, however, reveals a more complex logic at work within the text:

> There ... also is to be found that 'living bread that comes down from heaven' (Jn 6:51); from those stones gush forth refreshing fountains and streams of living water capable not only of satisfying thirst but of saving souls ... the material desert becomes a paradise of the spirit.[91]

In this passage, as in many others, Eucherius shows himself unwilling to abandon the desert's literal meaning even whilst explaining its spiritual, metaphorical function: the water found in the desert is still a physical blessing; the desert remains a material entity. But we can go further than this. One of the text's most striking features is the superficiality with which he treats what we might call the desert's deeper connotations which, though acknowledged, go almost entirely unexplored.

This is especially clear in the case of the Eastern monastic tradition which is restricted to a small section on John and Macarius and, at the very end, a brief and entirely general acknowledgement of Gaul's debt to Egypt.[92] But this tradition causes no prolonged wonderment: he acknowledges that John and Macarius were guided through the desert 'by grace in the form of silent revelations or of eloquent signs',[93] but attempts no further comment nor description. The desert's famous perils, its daemons and physical dangers, go unexplored and are instead restricted to more modest hardships: the greater initial appeal of other landscapes,[94] or the description of monks as indifferent to their appearance.[95] The only common quality frequently emphasized is solitude. However, solitude does not require the radical expression found in the *Life of Antony*, for example; rather, it appears not to stretch beyond simple separation from family and homeland. It is, so to speak, separation conceived of separately, as a state shorn of the complex connotations it had acquired on its route through the Egyptian desert.

---

[90] Eucherius, *In Praise of the Desert* 42.

[91] Eucherius, *In Praise of the Desert* 39 (tr. Vivian et al., p. 212).

[92] Eucherius, *In Praise of the Desert* 42.

[93] Ibid. 27 (tr. Vivian et al., p. 207).

[94] Ibid. 6, 40.

[95] Ibid. 43.

A similar pattern can be observed where the biblical desert is concerned. Given the extensiveness of its treatment, one might imagine that the desert's holiness derived chiefly from the events of sacred history that had unfolded there, as they did, for example, for the early Holy Land pilgrim Egeria who made great efforts to locate and record the precise location of major biblical episodes.[96] In fact, Eucherius provides little more than a list whose conceptual unity rests heavily on the oft-repeated buzzwords *eremus* and *desertum* i.e. on the simple physical setting.[97] Indeed, Eucherius' chief concern seems sometimes to be that the desert's literal meaning will be overlooked. This is especially true when confronting allegorical information. Acknowledging the theologically crucial role of the Exodus in foreshadowing the New Covenant, Eucherius again stresses the events' literal meaning: 'these symbolic events remain true realities in themselves. So the desert still deserves to be praised *even if* (*etiam si*) the things done there must be understood as referring to deep mysteries'.[98] Similarly, the concept is never reduced, by metonymy, merely to the monastic lifestyle: that the desert's destiny in that role remained, for a long time, unrealized[99] shows, rather than disproves, that he imagines it first and foremost as a physical place.

If Eucherius' desert remains fundamentally and literally a landscape, it is also very abstract; that is to say, its existence as a category is far more important than any details of its history; everywhere the whole triumphs over its parts. Thus, for example, God's instruction to Moses to take off his sandals at Exodus 3:5 seems to be ingeniously interpreted as a reference to the sacredness of the desert *qua* category rather than to the individual spot in question.[100] But why should Eucherius' treatment of the desert tradition take this form? The answer, surely, is that only by fashioning the category in this way can it incorporate Lérins satisfactorily. Indeed, it seems to be in order to embrace Lérins in a sacred tradition that the category exists at all: this would appear to be the text's central objective. Too much information about the desert would have been both unnecessary for this aim and indeed deleterious to it. On the one hand, it could have led to a too literal characterization which

---

[96]   J. Wilkinson refers to her 'assured literalism': 'Introduction', *Egeria's Travels to the Holy Land* (Warminster, 1981), p. 39.

[97]   Eucherius, *In Praise of the Desert* 34 (tr. Vivian et al., p. 210).

[98]   Eucherius, *In Praise of the Desert* 15 (tr. Vivian et al., p. 203).

[99]   Ibid. 5.

[100]   Eucherius, *In Praise of the Desert* 7. The particularity of this stance is underlined by a comparison with the pilgrim Egeria's discovery of the exact spot : *De Itinerario* 4.8, ed. and tr. Pierre Maraval and Manuel C. Díaz y Díaz, *Egérie: Journal de Voyage* (*Itinéraire*) *et Lettre sur la bienheureuse Egérie*, Sources Chrétiennes 296 (Paris, 1982).

would have risked excluding Lérins which was not a desert in any conventional sense; on the other, it could have slid too far towards metaphor, in which case Lérins would have seemed just like any other monastery. By categorizing it as he does, Eucherius balances the difficult task of retaining the concept's fundamental literalness whilst widening it beyond its traditional boundaries. Except in a few places, such as his bet-hedging claim that 'desert lands are often covered with fine sand (*saepe in eremo tenuis soli pulvis occurrat*)'[101] this aim is achieved by repeatedly mentioning the desert as if it were an uncontroversial geographical category. In this way, Lérins could become an integral chapter to this sacred history rather a dubious addendum.

Seen from this perspective, one suspects that what *In Praise of the Desert* expresses is only secondarily and superficially a theological theory, but rather a statement of the Lérins community's self-conception and identity, and therefore very possibly part of the explanation for its success as an institution. But if this is true, we must not imagine that it could be achieved and sustained by mere wishful thinking or that the Lerinians chose to assert their desert identity in the face of all contrary evidence. To judge by Eucherius, as important as their stance towards the desert tradition was the meticulous attention paid to those few aspects of the local environment which could justify its equation with more traditional notions of the desert. Two passages make this particularly clear:

> You (Hilarius) are now the true Israel who gazes upon God in his heart, who has just been freed from the dark Egypt of this world, who has crossed the saving waters in which the enemy drowned, who follows the burning light of faith in the desert, who experiences things formerly bitter now made sweet by the wood of the cross, who draws from Christ waters welling up into eternal life, who feeds his spirit from the bread from on high and who from the Gospel receives the divine word in thunder. Because you keep company with Israel in the desert, you will certainly enter the promised land with Jesus.[102]

> When an unexpected (*insperata*) amount of food is generously given to a monk in the desert, what is this but a gift fallen from heaven? ... When these monks dig down through the rocky ground, and water finally begins to flow ... what is this but water flowing from the rocks as if it had been struck by a blow of Moses' staff?[103]

---

[101]   Eucherius, *In Praise of the Desert* 34 (tr. Vivian et al., p. 210). The ubiquity of this sort of geographical conception is further suggested by Palladius, *Lausiac History* 15.1: 'Now the land is rainless, as everyone knows either by hearsay of by direct experience.'

[102]   Ibid. 44 (tr. Vivian et al., p. 44).

[103]   Ibid. 29 (tr. Vivian et al., p. 29).

With great ingenuity Eucherius allegorizes Hilarius' journey to the island as a re-enactment of the Hebrew Exodus by emphasizing the physical crossing of water – the short trip from the Provençale coast on the one hand, the Red Sea on the other – that both entailed. In the absence of conventional characteristics, this small physical detail of the sensible world could serve as a vital element of Lérins' desert identity. It is also significant that as in the passage mentioned earlier (see p. 95), Eucherius holds up as typical of the desert its beneficent provision of food and water. Even if Lérins contained no daemons, this was a concern of community living it indisputably shared with its Egyptian counterparts. Indeed, in the second passage cited immediately above, Eucherius declares them to be miracles: unexpected food is, like manna, a gift from heaven; successful well-digging repeats the miracle of fresh water worked through Moses in the desert.

One very significant aspect of the place Eucherius makes for Lérins within the desert tradition, is how far it reflects techniques familiar from hagiography. Like the connection between a holy man and his sacred predecessors, Lérins' entry into the desert's sacred history is facilitated hugely by the simplification of its archetypes; associated with this is a general emphasis on the literal, and great attention paid to a few physical details felt to hold great symbolic potential. In other words, *In Praise of the Desert* would appear to provide further evidence that the sort of intellectual outlook displayed in hagiography was not restricted to that written genre.

But *In Praise of the Desert* is hagiographical in a more specific sense. It does not merely mention the provision of water as a literary trope; rather, as the citation above shows, it very explicitly asks the reader to equate well-digging by pious monks with the miraculous provision of water granted to Moses in the Egyptian desert. This recalls very closely a crucial moment in the *Life of Honoratus*, which reveals the saint as a latter-day Moses:

> Water, unknown there for ages began to flow copiously (*negetae a saeculis aquae largiter fluunt*), repeating, in its origin, two miralces of the Old Testament; for when it burst out of the rock (*erumperent*), it flowed sweet though surrounded by the saltiness of the sea.[104]

The *Life of Honoratus* gives few details about this incident, presenting the water as the active, spontaneous agent, and dwelling instead on its spiritual meaning. In keeping with this, some scholars have treated it, and other elements of the *life*, as a typically hagiographical element attributable purely to literary typology.[105] But

---

[104] Hilarius, *Life of Honoratus* 3.17.

[105] 'S'il y a bien, dans le sermon d'Hilaire, trace de miraculeux, ce n'est qu'effet de rhétorique. Lorsqu'il évoque l'aridité de Lérins avant la venue d'Honorat, les "bêtes

read in combination with *In Praise of the Desert*, a very different interpretation seems likely: both texts refer to the same incident, that this incident was real, and that it was nothing other than the deliberate and successful construction of a well by monks.

This has major implications for our view of the *Life of Honoratus*. Even though Eucherius does not mention them, it justifies a reconsideration of the island's other so-called typological elements – its aridity and the snakes – in a similar spirit: not as mere inventions but as reflections of a textually influenced but sincere epistemic stance. We cannot, of course, know precisely what climatic conditions had to prevail and for how long 'in those arid wastes' (*in illis ariditatibus*)[106] for Hilarius to apply this description to the island. Similarly, we cannot know how great or frequent the threat from snakes was, but the idea that Hilarius invented them entirely seems unlikely, because he claims to have witnessed them himself,[107] and was delivering the eulogy to an audience many of whose members were almost certainly familiar with Lérins. We can say, however, that the ongoing need to define the island as a desert may well have encouraged in Hilarius a great sensitivity towards any physical characteristics which could justify the designation. In Hilarius' own description, the 'barrier of the straits'[108] seems to play the same symbolic role in defining the environment as it does in the work which Eucherius addressed to him.

Another thing suggested by the comparison is that these structures, though not simply the inventions of a literary author, nonetheless reflected the presence of a charismatic figure in the shape of Honoratus. This is partly because it follows the pattern described by Max Weber in which charismatic leadership creates institutions and subsequently becomes enshrined in them.[109] But given how much of this transition was crystallized into a small cluster of definitive events, especially the well-digging incident, we may also consider it an 'inaugural act' of the type which Pierre Bordieu regarded as fundamental to the establishment of symbolic power.[110] In the case of Honoratus and Lérins, this transition between the apex of personal charisma and the institution's birth was extremely short

---

venimeuses" et les "serpents innombrables" qui peuplent le "désert redoutable" sortent de la Bible plus que de la rocaille de *Lerina*', P.Nouailhat, *Saints et Patrons* (Paris, 1988), p. 115. For M-E. Brunert too, the snakes are 'eine Erfindung des Hilarius': *Das Ideal der Wüstenaskese* (Münster, 1994), p. 199.

[106]   Hilarius, *Life of Honoratus* 2.15.

[107]   '*ut vidimus*': ibid.

[108]   Ibid. 3.15.

[109]   Weber, *On Charisma and Institution Building*, esp. pp. 54–61.

[110]   Pierre Bordieu, 'Marginalia – Some Additional Notes on the Gift', in Alan D. Schrift (ed.), *The Logic of the Gift: Towards an Ethic of Generosity* (London/New York, 1997), p. 238.

in temporal terms, but it was a large and sophisticated conceptual leap. It suggests, in any case, that Honoratus' charismatic leadership rested heavily on hagiographical narratives: narratives of which he was at once subject, controller and interpreter.

This analysis of the events which surrounded Lérins' foundation also supports the argument of the previous chapter about miracles: namely that, as part of their realist agenda, hagiographers often encouraged in their readers a certain epistemic stance towards phenomena which did not entirely depart from the regular course of events. But if, as has been argued here, the events at Lérins were real and widely recognized, then we can see how this pattern applied beyond the literary realm: the residents at Lérins had already been encouraged to treat the events as miracles long before they were recorded by Hilarius. The necessary stance, and the alertness to typology which informed it, were potentially as applicable to immediate phenomenal reality as they were to the religious text. But this stance did not spring from nowhere: rather, it was a function of the holy man's authority and a sign that his reputation was established. In this sense, the characteristic presence of miracles in hagiography reflects not just literary convention but the expectations of his followers while he lived, and his own role in encouraging and meeting them. I would suggest that, where miracles are concerned, this pattern could usefully become a normal tool of historical explanation alongside the existing tendency of seeing their constituent typologies as a characteristically textual feature which signifies a departure from historical reality. This would seem to be the most plausible way of explaining both the significant proportion of miracles which seem relatively mundane as well as the fact, highlighted by Benedicta Ward, that many people in the middle ages not only believed in miracles in principle, but believed that they had experienced them.[111] The case of Honoratus seems to have a close parallel in the *Lives of Jura Fathers*. When Romanus discovers a suitable spot for his monastery beneath a dense fir tree near a cold spring, his hagiographer compares it to the palm tree which famously sheltered the hermit Paul.[112] As Tim Vivian et al. observe, it is tempting to dismiss this as a literary topos, but to

---

[111] Benedicta Ward, *Miracles and the Medieval Mind: Theory, Record and Event 1000–1215* (Philadelphia, 1987), pp. 215–17. Although Ward's emphasis is on the late middle ages, the basic point seems equally applicable to late antiquity.

[112] *Lives of the Jura Fathers* 7. This is by no means the only occasion recorded in hagiography where ascetics are divinely guided to a particular spot in order to found a monastery. Cyril records how Euthymius and Theoctistus 'came to a terrifying gorge, extremely steep and impassable. On seeing the place and going round the cliffs above it they found, as if guided by God, a huge and marvellous cave in the northern cliff of the gorge': *Lives* 15.14–17 (tr. Price, p. 11).

do so would overlook the strong possibility that Romanus was just as aware of these precedents in his behaviour as his hagiographer was in writing.[113]

What do these interpretations suggest about Lérins as an institution and the life of its community? Firstly, that the events of its foundation were more than just accolades; rather, they may well have been the basis of its institutional identity. Against so much contrary evidence, this distinctively desert miracle served to reveal the island's desert status as surely as it revealed Honoratus as a latter-day Moses. Furthermore, since the miracles of opening the spring and chasing away the snakes removed Lérins' few fragile proofs of desert identity, it also removed the possibility of, and need for, further proofs. But it preserved them permanently in the collective memory: after this point, the few ways in which Lérins was a desert would forever outweigh the many ways in which it wasn't. That Lérins was a desert, in some fully-fledged, categorical sense was, perhaps, the greatest miracle of all.

Like that of Pricoco,[114] this interpretation sees Lérins' desert identity as a sign of its self-confidence and a factor in its success. The benefits may have been partly practical: persuaded that they were genuine desert dwellers, the Lerinians could engage in moderate forms of asceticism and avoid extreme behaviour. Their need to imitate their Eastern predecessors was limited by the abstract but meticulous respect they had paid to them. Conversely, their lifestyle could continue the tradition of Roman *otium* because of the overt but largely notional rejection of it.[115] The mere idea of the desert, once authenticated, allowed a mild regime to flourish without the uncomfortable feeling that the essence of this heritage had been abandoned.

But if, as has been argued here, Eucherius' views reflect a community identity, then the benefits went far beyond the practical. One suspects that, just as miracles had proved Lérins' desert identity, so this identity helped to create amongst its inhabitants a special religious tone. It has been argued that asceticism in our period was not only an attempt to follow the Bible's commandments and to imitate its heroes, but, in a sense, to live 'in' the Bible.[116] The collective experience of the miraculous, the willingness of their leader to authenticate it, the special religious status of their island: following the example of the well digging, all these things may well have helped other familiar events acquire a spiritual significance and, in doing so, constantly reconfirmed Lérins' desert identity.

One could certainly argue that this atmosphere depended on a very circular logic. After all, as we see in the second extract quoted above (see p. 97), there

---

113   Vivian et al., *Lives of the Jura Fathers*, p. 63.
114   Pricoco, *L'isola dei Santi*, pp. 185–7.
115   Eucherius, *In Praise of the Desert* 32.
116   Blowers, 'The Bible and Spiritual Doctrine', p. 231.

is a certain tension in the idea that a monk might both receive more food than expected, and simultaneously recognize the tendency of the desert to surprise him in this way – would he not simply end up expecting what was supposed to be unexpected? Was this a sustainable and stable way of life or did it create expectations doomed for disappointment? But surely what this paradox describes is nothing other than a hermeneutic circle equivalent in lived experience to that which defines the reader's relationship to the hagiographical text which was also read in the expectation of events which were both historically true and spiritually significant. In the same way, the willingness of the Lerinians to see sacred meanings in the world around them was no obstacle to the daily life of the monastery. It simply meant that however carefully they had planned the digging of a well, they could nonetheless treat its success as a miracle; they could remain permanently aware, for all practical purposes, of when to expect the next delivery of food from the nearby shore, but could still be habitually exhorted to treat each shipment with the sincere surprise of ones suddenly saved. An acute sensitivity to sacred paradigms did not undermine the sincerity of their reactions, but was what made them possible, in the same way that the Stanislavkian method actor must make his script second nature before he can become, night after night, the character he is required to play. At Lérins, a knowledge of the sacred and biblical past surpassed mere re-enactment of the ritual type. Rather, with an actor's and not just an audience's suspension of disbelief, it was lived with all the directness and spontaneity that the narrative imagination envied in its original, unwitting participants.

The Limits of the Hagiographical: The *Fama Effect*

The hagiographical narratives of late antiquity have long troubled historians. This chapter has suggested that they represent the logical and inevitable pinnacle of wider interpretative habits. Although the necessary interpretative habits are directly observable only through texts and, indeed, although they bear the heavy imprint of textual influence, we should not assume that they were exclusive to the literary realm. Just as they reflected a certain approach to the world, they in turn encouraged one. They had at least as much to do with holy men and their disciples as they did with hagiographers and their readers. In this sense, the realism explored in the previous chapter had a close counterpart in historicity.

The argument so far thus in no sense denies the existence of the hagiographical; rather it gives it a new and much broader definition. Nonetheless, in doing so, it has left a number of questions unanswered and the remainder of this chapter is devoted to a consideration of these problems. For one thing, the argument may seem to contain the seeds of a contradiction. In essence, the method used to support it has involved the systematic identification of those aspects of texts ideologically characteristic of hagiography, and the transposition of them onto a social realm containing the holy men themselves. But in doing so, has this chapter genuinely revealed the wider applicability of the hagiographical? Could it not be argued that it has simply taken one object of historical interest – whether it is the historical truth understood in the factual sense, or the text's intellectual content – and replaced it with another no less rigid and narrow: namely the image of the holy man as he himself projected it?

In isolation, this would indeed be unsatisfactory. The principal texts on which we have focused in this chapter have all been unusual: Eugippius gave a detailed account of his reasons for a particular sphere of ignorance; Eucherius provided a second perspective on events recorded in a hagiography. But these opportunities are very rare: in the overwhelming majority of cases, reverent hagiographers simply record information they claim to be true and which there is no possibility of comparing with another source. A relentless programme of attempting to place holy men at the fount of what was written about them is therefore impossible. But more fundamentally, it would contradict this chapter's central argument by presenting the hagiographical not as widely applicable, but as the possession first and foremost of one particular link in the chain of information, albeit a different one in the shape of the holy man. Amongst other things, this would overlook the obvious truth, proved by countless empirical studies not to mention by a simple game of Chinese Whispers, that information can be misreported, misremembered, and evolve over time. Indeed, occasionally, as in the *Life of Pachomius*,[117] or Eunapius' portrayal of Iamblichus,[118] a hagiographer himself concedes the tendency for traditions about holy men to become exaggerated even during their lifetime. Nor is this fundamentally a question of mere ability or honesty: there is no reason to doubt that late antique hagiographers such as Iamblichus, Theodoret and Cyril respected the trustees of oral tradition, but they also recognized in its inherent fluidity the need for a written record.[119] Therefore, as argued earlier (see pp. 70–71), the model presented should not, and cannot, have as its measure of historicity the precise continuity of individual details over time. Whilst this may be possible occasionally, its basis must be more general: the equal applicability of the principles and techniques of hagiographical realism at every stage of spiritual life. The model outlined would be more satisfactory if it could demonstrate not merely the applicability of the hagiographical to a world

---

[117]　*Life of Pachomius* 112.

[118]　Iamblichus himself jovially denies his rumoured ability to levitate: Eunapius, *Lives* 458.

[119]　Iamblichus, *On the Pythagorean Life* 1(2); Cyril, *Lives* 6.5–12; Theodoret, *History*, Prologue 2.

of holy men prior to the text, but also an influence beyond the sorts of subjects and situations hagiographies depict.

Nonetheless, there is one genuine and fundamental difference between the literary use of the hagiographical and its use in other contexts which poses a deeper problem. Whilst it is important to recognize the potential for an overlap between the different roles in the chain of information, an exaggerated emphasis on this overlap risks overlooking the profoundly hierarchical nature of late antique ideas of human spiritual achievement and identity. A few people were holy men; the vast majority were not, and the belief that the former constituted a very special class was fundamental not least to the existence of hagiography as a written genre.

This consideration is particularly important because of the reputation for sanctity some people acquired within their own lifetimes. There is a fundamental phenomenological difference between beliefs about other people's identity and beliefs about oneself. This was particularly true in the context of late antique holy men for whom humility was such a crucial virtue, and whose spiritual achievements were constantly threatened by pride. However much the hagiographical reflected religious life beyond holy men, and however much the spiritual lives of this elite were themselves influenced by previous models, the question remains what precisely holy men believed about themselves, how these beliefs formed and how they were sustained.

This may seem to be an exceedingly difficult question and perhaps even beyond the boundaries of what we can expect a historical enquiry to tell us. In the theological terms reflected in hagiography, sanctity was ultimately a private condition, a special insight into reality which was not fully communicable. Furthermore, one may suspect that any progress towards answering such questions of personal identity is likely to be found not in third person hagiography but in first person spiritual narrative. To some extent, this is true, and it is partly for this reason that the next chapter is devoted to works of this latter category. But nonetheless, our argument for the broader applicability of the hagiographical requires the genre if not to serve as a direct source for the holy man's personal convictions, then at least to provide a general correspondence to them. The idea that written hagiographies may sometimes contain exaggerated versions of what holy men said about themselves is only a very partial solution, as is shown by considering the case of miracles. Miracles were moments through which the divine definitively spoke. As we have seen, the challenge to the current argument is not necessarily to explain the phenomena themselves, nor even the willingness of followers to accept the interpretation given to them by a spiritual authority; rather it is the mindset of the authority who offered the interpretation, and who sometimes, perhaps, supervised the phenomenon itself. The more we place responsibility for this aspect of the hagiographical in the hands of holy men, the greater the pressure to ask questions about their own convictions, motivations and even consciences.

No hagiographical motif instantiates this problem more acutely than what German scholars sometimes refer to as the '*Fama* Effekt', a term which will be anglicized for the present discussion. Maria-Elisabeth Brunert offers a succinct definition:

> The *fama* effect is based on a paradox: the more an anchorite cuts himself off from his environment, the more he seeks to avoid contact with his fellow men, the better known he becomes.[120]

The idea behind the *fama* effect is not completely exclusive to Christianity. Plato's Myth of the Cave established, amongst other things, the absolute necessity for the philosopher's active life to be subordinate to his grasp of reality,[121] an idea which in some ways echoes the basic ethic behind the *fama* effect. It also contained the paradoxical message that those best suited to authority (i.e. those who had left the cave and seen the sun) would be disinclined to accept it.[122] Some pagan hagiographies reflect this paradox. For example, the philosopher Aedesius responds correctly to an oracle offering him a choice between the active and contemplatives lives and rightly flees to the countryside; nonetheless his celebrity makes this lifestyle impossible and he is forced to return to public affairs.[123] Similarly, it is because of Sarapio's intensely private and austere ascetic life in Alexandria that he is able to become a living lesson to others.[124]

Nonetheless, the *fama* effect is a pattern far more starkly and more consistently attested in Christian hagiographies. Usually, the motif occurs at pivotal points in the narrative, such as when a saint makes a doomed attempt to refuse his popular candidacy as an abbot or bishop – a refusal which, by indicating humility, confirms his suitability for the post.[125] In other texts, such

---

[120]   'Der FAMA-EFFEKT beruht sich auf einem Paradoxon: Je mehr sich ein Anachoret von seiner Umwelt abschliesst, je mehr er den Kontakt zu den Mitmenschen zu meiden sucht, desto bekannter wird er,' *Das Ideal der Wüstenaskese* (Münster, 1994), p. 411.

[121]   Plato, *Republic* 7. 514A–517C.

[122]   Ibid. 516 C–E. For a discussion of this paradox, see Damian Caluori, 'Reason and Necessity: The Descent of the Philosopher-Kings', *Oxford Studies in Ancient Philosophy* 40 (Oxford, 2011).

[123]   Eunapius, *Lives* 464–5.

[124]   Damascius, *Philosophical History* 111.

[125]   Athanasius, *Life of Antony* 14.2; Sulpicius, *Life of Martin* 9; Paulinus, *Life of Ambrose* 8; Jerome, *Life of St. Hilarion passim*, e.g. 33, 38; Honoratus, *Life of Hilarius* 9; Ferrandus,

as the *Life of Honoratus*, the motif constitutes a continuous process and thus
contributes to the narrative's coherence. Even before leaving home Honoratus'
charity is known in 'the whole country'.[126] No sooner does he flee this attention
in the company of his brother than the 'refugees from their good name' find
their departure produces precisely the undesired effect. Larger and larger groups
are attracted to them: 'wherever they went, there, whether they liked it or not, a
new renown was born'.[127] During the journey to Greece, the description becomes
more precise: although they have apparently travelled there to avoid admiration,
not only Latins, but also Greeks, and even unbelieving Jews admire Honoratus;
his return is apparently fêted by whole Italian regions.[128] The earthly climax is
achieved with the foundation of the monastic community, whose ethnic variety,
it is suggested, even surpasses the boundaries of empire.[129] Humanity, therefore,
is presented by Hilarius almost as a series of concentric circles, beginning with
kin and locality, and spreading out through provinces, peoples and, eventually
beyond the frontiers itself into a single family. Each time Honoratus resists the
affections of one circle, he finds himself recognized by a greater one. And only
once he has achieved a degree of separation which can be regarded as definitive,
i.e. he has been miraculously exposed as a Moses-like figure in a genuine desert,
can this escalating process reach its climax.

As a purely narrative technique, the *fama* effect contains an elegant, paradoxical
logic. However, the reader's reception of it also lends itself to paradox: on the one
hand, for it to function meaningfully, he or she must respond with wonderment
that the holy man's stubbornly pious reserve is at once the obstacle God's will must
overcome, the reason why it should be overcome, and the mechanism by which it
eventually is overcome. On the other hand, the very fact it is a motif, a recognizable
effect, with all the predictability and regularity implied by that term, will soon
complicate the sense of wonderment and make it also an object of anticipation,
a tool for explanation. Thus when Hilarius asks his audience, 'I would ask how it
came about that the demand arose here for one so far off and so unknown'[130] they
are simultaneously capable both of sharing his wonder, and also of recognizing that
his question contains the answer. Something similar is achieved when Ambrose
reminds the congregation at Vercelli of how Eusebius, after a long exile, was chosen

---

Life of Fulgentius 15–16, 33–4; Constantius, *Life of Germanus* 34–5.

[126]   Ibid. 2.10 (p. 255).

[127]   Hilarius, *Life of Honoratus* 2.12 (tr. Hoare, p. 257).

[128]   Ibid. 3.15.

[129]   'What barbarian ways did he not tame?' Hilarius, *Life of Honoratus* 3.17 (tr. Hoare,
p. 261).

[130]   Hilarius, *Life of Honoratus* 6.25 (tr. Hoare, p. 269).

as their bishop.[131] He may be marvelling at an event that went against conventional social practice, but for precisely this reason, it fulfils an alternative, and sacred, set of expectations. Amazing in human terms, it becomes entirely recognizable as a narrative pattern reflecting, and pointing to, God.

The *fama* effect is relevant here because of the threat it appears to pose to any argument which involves the wider, extra-textual applicability of the hagiographical. It is not merely a question of plausibility on a general level: this would be true of any miraculous occurrence. More important is that the motif posits and indeed requires a radical difference between the saint's perception of himself and the view of him held by everybody else: readers of his written *life*, contemporary followers and, ultimately, even God. In this sense, it is not just implausible, but necessarily and logically impossible to equate the holy man's own stance with the hagiographical without in some way fundamentally altering the character of one or the other. On the one hand, we may regard it as simply inconceivable that humility as genuine and single-minded as that attributed to a saint like Honoratus could attract such widespread attention with such consistency: should we therefore see the miracle as a symbolic representation of more mundane processes? But of course, the mysterious rule itself demands our amazement, and the more we disbelieve its surface form, the more we compromise hagiography's status as a truth-telling genre. If, on the other hand, we suspect that holy men were aware of the ramifications of their actions, we detract from their status as true spiritual leaders, at least in the full-blooded theological sense promoted by the original texts; we may even be inclined to transform them into somewhat manipulative, insincere figures, differing from gyrovagues only in the extent of their artifice. As Weber recognized, this is a charge to which the ascetic leader is particularly vulnerable for he is 'certain to become god's instrument. For this reason, the ascetic's humility ... is always of dubious genuineness.'[132] When, for example, we read of Ambrose attempting to escape a Milanese church desperate to embrace him as its leader,[133] and then recall his childhood ambition to become a bishop,[134] we may be tempted to compare him to a figure like Shakespeare's Richard III, who stages a public

---

[131] 'As soon as they saw the holy Eusebius, who had previously been unknown to them, (they) preferred him to their own countrymen ... and required no more than to see him in order to elect him', Ambrose, *Epistula* 63.2, ed. Michaela Zelzer, CSEL 82.3 (Vienna, 1982), tr. J.H.W.G. Liebeschutz, *Ambrose: Political Letters and Speeches* (Liverpool: Liverpool University Press, 2005), p. 296.

[132] Weber, *On Charisma and Institution Building*, p. 280.

[133] Paulinus, *Life of Ambrose* 6–7.

[134] Ibid. 4.

refusal of the crown after years scheming to acquire it.[135] Avoiding a charge of this sort, historians of late antiquity have tended to treat the *fama* effect as a polite and harmless ritual, engaged in without total sincerity.[136]

It was stated earlier that we should think of hagiographical realism not just in terms of the literary effects of such texts, but also in terms of their applicability to more general spiritual circumstances. A parallel point can be made about the historicity of the genre when viewed by the modern scholar: it is not enough merely to defend the plausibility of hagiographical claims, we must also consider the effects of expectation amongst those people who came to be regarded as its proper subjects. And this is why the concept of 'enacted biography' becomes, at least in the case of holy men, so complex (see p. 21). For the more we argue that the bounds of the hagiographical extended beyond the literary text, the more we must identify and explain the inevitable moment that a person recognized its characteristic patterns in his own life. That this was indeed possible is a necessary part of our argument that hagiography was, in the full sense of the term, a truth-telling genre but, as the *fama* effect illustrates, it is a claim replete with historical and philosophical problems. The central question that remains to be answered, therefore, is did holy men know they were holy men and, if so, how? This will be discussed in Part II as we move from the social to the personal realm.

---

[135]   William Shakespeare, *Richard III* Act 3, Scene 7 (ed. J. Lull, pp. 146–52).

[136]   Thomas Hodgkin, *Italy and her Invaders* (1880–89), vol. 2., p. 248: 'the harmless comedy of the *nolo episcopari*, which was so commonly played in those days'. Similarly, Mathisen calls Hilarius' flight after Honoratus' death '*de rigueur*' suggesting he was 'hoping, perhaps, to be able to fulfil the *topos* of being *raptus ad episcopatum*': *Ecclesiastical Factionalism and Religious Controversy in Fifth-Century Gaul*, p. 88.

PART II

Chapter 3
In Search of the First Person

Hagiography and Autobiography

The previous chapter argued that the hagiographical needed to be understood not just in literary but also in social terms; the current chapter extends that wider perspective to examine sanctity, as it were, from the other side, from the more intimate and experiential perspective of the first person. As Brown recognized, this perspective is an equally important element of the phenomenon, albeit one which has received much less scholarly attention.[1]

It is for this reason that the present chapter is concerned with first person spiritual writing. But important questions need to be asked about this material and its possible uses. It is often said that the ancient and mediaeval worlds produced nothing as singular and coherent as a recognizable genre of 'autobiography';[2] in keeping with this, we shall use it only as a convenience term to denote any first-person writing. The quantity of such writing in our period is far outweighed by third person writing; what does exist is highly diverse in form and character and ranges from short personal interventions in hagiographies to a few full length autobiographies of which by far the best known and most important is Augustine's *Confessions*. Although inevitable, a heavy reliance on one very extraordinary text, and a diverse scattering of many more minor ones, is an uncomfortable basis from which to generalize.

Nonetheless, it is possible to detect many points of contact between the concerns of late antique hagiography on the one hand and those of autobiography on the other. The focus of much of the period's first-person writing is, broadly speaking, spiritual, religious and philosophical. (The military recollections of Ammianus Marcellinus, like other autobiographical writings with a very different focus, will not form part of our discussion although, as we saw in the introduction, these too have been subjected to questions about their historicity – see p. 21.) The same focus applies not only to personal interventions by

---

[1]   Brown, 'The Rise and Function of the Holy Man. 1971–1997', p. 368.

[2]   Lejeune, *Le Pacte autobiographique*, pp. 13–14, 314–17; F. Prinz, 'Hagiographie und Welthaftigkeit: Überlegungen zur Vielfalt des hagiographischen Genus im Frühmittelalter', in Dorothea Walz (ed.), *Lateinische Biographie von der Antike bis in die Gegenwart* (Heidelberg, 2002), pp. 49–58.

hagiographers but also to self-standing works. One example of an author who describes the spiritual life from both a third and first-person perspective is Porphyry, the author of the *Life of Plotinus* and the *Life of Pythagoras*, but also of the self-referential *Letter to Marcella*. This latter work, traditionally dated to the very early fourth century, has been described as 'an easy abstract of Porphyry's ethical teachings'[3] and depicts the philosopher addressing to his wife a series of consolations before embarking on a long journey. The possible anti-Christian application of many of his arguments, as well as an oblique reference to the 'affairs of the Hellenes' (τῆς τῶν Ἑλλήνων χρείας),[4] have stimulated debate about how far the work should be read as part of a broader anti-Christian agenda.[5] It has received less attention as an example of spiritual autobiography.

In this last respect, its most striking aspect is the apparent extent to which its concerns overlap with those of hagiography. Like many pagan texts, including hagiographies, it makes rich use of Homeric allusions.[6] At an early stage, the author compares himself and Marcella to Odysseus giving advice to Penelope on the eve of his departure.[7] Apart from their general connotations of heroism, these epic allusions, as Helene Whittaker notes,[8] transform the physical journey into a familiar Neoplatonic metaphor of spiritual progress. This allegorical narrative frame is further enhanced by the description of life with Marcella as one containing all the elements of a drama.[9] To this extent, the *Letter* fulfils the defining characteristic of the hagiographical: namely a realism which locates spiritual truths in literal details. But an equally important point of contact is Porphyry's elucidation of an ideal of sanctity via his own example.

---

[3]   A. Zimmern, Introduction to ibid. (tr.) *Porphyry the Philosopher to his Wife Marcella* (1910), p. 12.

[4]   Porphyry, *Ad Marcellam* 4, ed. and tr. Edouard des Places, *De Vita Pythagorae*; *Ad Marcellam* (Paris, 1982).

[5]   Helene Whittaker, 'The Purpose of Porphyry's Letter to Marcella', in *SO* 76 (2001), p. 155. The argument is plausible but impossible to prove: on the one hand, the work contains no explicit references to the faith; on the other, as I argued earlier in the case of Neoplatonic hagiographies, for it to be effective in an anti-Christian role, we should perhaps not expect them (see pp. 31–2).

[6]   For philosophical uses of Homer amongst pagan Neoplatonists, see Robert Lamberton, *Homer the Theologian: Neoplatonist Allegorical Reading and the Growth of the Epic Tradition* (Berkeley, 1986), pp. 83–143.

[7]   Porphyry, *Letter to Marcella* 4. Edwards is right to say that the likening of Porphyry to a named Homeric character has no comparison in the *Lives* (Mark Edwards, 'Scenes from the Later Wanderings of Odysseus', in *CQ* 38 (1988), p. 520) but here we have a very clear comparison from Porphyry himself.

[8]   Whittaker, 'The Purpose of Porphyry's Letter to Marcella', p. 155.

[9]   Porphyry, *Letter to Marcella* 2.

His self-portrait contains many aspects attributed to his own master in the *Life of Plotinus*. Echoing the sentiments expressed by Plotinus when refusing a portrait, Porphyry begins the *Letter to Marcella* with a statement of bodily unattachedness to his family. Here, however, the issue does not revolve around his origins (although he makes no mention of them); instead, he reminds Marcella of his philosophical motives for entering a celibate marriage with her and for adopting her children. This purely philanthropic commitment also recalls Plotinus' treatment of orphans at Rome.[10] Elsewhere a definition of the human soul voiced by Porphyry comes very close to that attributed to Plotinus during the painting incident.[11] By uttering such fundamental Platonic tenets, and by addressing Marcella as a master addresses a disciple,[12] Porphyry places himself in a role closely analogous to that of his own teacher. To call this stance an autobiographical equivalent to hagiography perhaps does not express the similarity strongly enough. In asking Marcella 'who could be a more faithful witness to me than yourself?'[13] Porphyry appeals to his wife almost for notional third-person support for claims he makes about himself.

The *Letter to Marcella* is not Porphyry's only piece of autobiographical writing. His *Life of Plotinus* includes a number of personal statements, including a description of a physical journey to Sicily taken during his student years in Rome.[14] The passage is particularly interesting, since another third-person version of this episode appears in Eunapius' hagiography.[15] It is highly significant that although Eunapius implies that his account is based on Porphyry's own,[16] a number of important differences emerge. In the shorter account, Plotinus, having correctly detected his pupil's suicidal melancholy, recommends a trip to Sicily as a remedy. There Porphyry recovers, but at the cost of being absent when his master dies.[17] Eunapius' version is grander in style, and more deeply marked by literary allusions. The parallel between the philosopher's journey, and that of his mythical predecessor Odysseus does not escape Eunapius,[18] and

---

10   Ibid. 1–2. See Porphyry, *Life of Plotinus* 9.

11   ἐγὼ οὐχ ὁ ἁπτὸς οὗτος καὶ τῇ αἰσθήσει ὑποπτωτός, ὁ δὲ ἐπὶ πλεῖστον ἀφεστηκὼς τοῦ σώματος, ὁ ἀχρώματος καὶ ἀσχημάτιστος, καὶ χερσὶ μὲν οὐδαμῶς ἐπαφητός, διανοίᾳ δὲ μόνῃ κρατητός· ibid. 8 (p. 110).

12   Ibid. 6.

13   Ibid. 3.

14   Porphyry, *Life of Plotinus* 11.

15   Eunapius, *Lives* 456.

16   'As he himself says', Eunapius, *Lives* 456 (tr. Wright, p. 355).

17   Porphyry, *Life of Plotinus* 11.

18   The parallel is thoroughly Neoplatonic, and is allegorically exploited by Plotinus at *Enneads* 1.6.8.17–28 (tr. A.H. Armstrong, vol. 1, pp. 257–9). For Numenius' probable

occurs on two levels. Geographically, both involve Sicily; spiritually, they could
be regarded as concerning related themes. Just as Odysseus' encounter with the
Sirens was commonly interpreted as an allegory of the various temptations which
man in his earthly state had to resist, so too is Porphyry's journey an occasion to
confront the lure of suicide.

How can the divergence between the two accounts be explained? It cannot,
of course, be disproved that Eunapius simply invented an alternative version
of the story, although it would be hard to understand his motivation since, in
doing so, he would have exposed himself unnecessarily to the charge of misusing
or misreading the *Life of Plotinus*, a text he elsewhere praises highly.[19] A more
satisfactory explanation is offered by Edwards who suggests that Eunapius'
source was not the short passage in the *Life of Plotinus*; rather, the memoir
(ὑπόμνημα) by Porphyry on which Eunapius claims to have based his own
account was a longer, now inextant work.[20] Edwards also suggests that through
inattentiveness Eunapius conflated the short reference to the physical journey in
the *Life of Plotinus* with a metaphorical language of spiritual progress borrowed
from Homer and reused in the memoir. One consequence of this would be the
transposition to Sicily of spiritual developments which had already been worked
through in Italy.[21]

An important assumption appears to underpin Edwards's argument: namely
that symbolic and metaphorical aspects are more typical of hagiography than
of autobiography. But another possible way to view the divergence suggests a
much closer relationship between the two forms of writing. The crucial question
is why, in positing the existence of a lost autobiographical source for Eunapius'
account, we should not also attribute to it precisely those poetic features assumed
by Edwards to be characteristic of his hagiographer: namely the conflation of
literal and metaphorical language and the use of Homeric imagery? Although
we can only speculate about the contents of a lost text, we have already seen
how Porphyry demonstrates precisely these tendencies in the *Letter to Marcella*.
In view of this, it would hardly be surprising if, in describing a much more
melancholic spiritual journey involving Sicily, Porphyry exploited the obvious
overlap between figurative and literal language offered by Homer's *Odyssey*. In

---

earlier interpretation of the passage, see Lamberton, *Homer the Theologian*, p. 53. Edwards
observes the varied ends to which the theme was deployed by Neoplatonic writers: 'Scenes
from the Later Wanderings of Odysseus'.

[19]   Porphyry had done such a good job in his biography that Eunapius could afford to
describe Plotinus' life quickly: *Lives* 455.

[20]   Ibid., p. 519; Richard Goulet, 'Variations romanesques sur la mélancholie de
Porphyre', in *Hermes* 110 (1982), p. 444.

[21]   Edwards, 'Scenes from the Later Wanderings of Odysseus', p. 520.

doing so, he would, after all, have been following the example already set by Plato in his partly autobiographical *Seventh Letter*.[22] A further advantage of this interpretation is that we would no longer be obliged to impute to Eunapius inattentive reading of a text whose contents are a matter of speculation.

Nonetheless, the counter-argument must surely be that this reading leaves the narrative conflict unresolved. If Eunapius indeed interpreted the memoir competently, does this not mean that Porphyry produced two different versions of the story, including contradictory locations for his recovery? Not necessarily. Porphyry's account of his melancholy in the *Life of Plotinus* is very short; understandably, since his own mental state was not the primary focus of the passage but rather his master's extraordinary insight into character.[23] Such brevity does not allow Porphyry any notion of progress – be it spiritual or physical – of the type on which we might expect a personal memoir to dwell. As for the specific question of whether or not Plotinus came to Sicily, it may be that the saving influence was a memory of the philosopher, in the same way that the memory of Porphyry's teachings are meant to serve Marcella just as well as her husband's physical presence.[24] This difference too need not necessarily be due to inattentiveness on Eunapius' part: it is possible that he believed these implications to be obvious to readers familiar with the original work.

If correct, this interpretation provides not only further evidence of the literary overlap between first and third person spiritual writing. It also suggests that, at least for a fortunate few, this overlap was rooted in a social context, namely personal contact with holy men. Such contact was what enabled them to detect deeper spiritual meanings at work in their own lives. Porphyry's interpreter Eunapius provides another good example of this. Towards the end of the *lives*, purportedly following Plutarch's example,[25] he weaves his own story into the narrative, and devotes a brief passage to his arrival as a young man in Athens, where he went to study under the legendary Prohaeresius. The passage has attracted attention from historians examining the philosophical schools of late antiquity.[26] But what we might term the narrative's romantic quality,

---

[22] Plato, *Letter* 7 345D–E. I am not concerned about the (in)authenticity of the letters. The important point is that they were regarded as genuine by Neoplatonists: Wallis, *Neoplatonism*, pp. 18–24.

[23] Porphyry, *Life of Plotinus* 11.

[24] Idem, *Ad Marcellam* 10 (tr. E. des Places, p. 111). An almost identical sentiment is voiced by Julian concerning his absence from Sallustius: *Oration VIII*, 247 C–D (tr. Wright, vol. 2, p. 185).

[25] Eunapius, *Lives* 454.

[26] Alan D. Booth, 'On the date of Eunapius' coming to Athens', in *AHB* 1 (1987); David Frederick Buck, 'Prohaeresius' recruitment of students', in *LCM* 12.5 (1987); David

which includes the typically hagiographical tendency to conflate the literal and metaphorical, has been less frequently noted. The incident's importance is established from the outset, as Eunapius refers the reader back to the earlier chapter on the life of the 'divine Prohaeresius'; now we are to find out more, from the personal testimony of an eye-witness, who had 'the very great privilege' to share 'an intimate friendship' with him. By the time the adolescent Eunapius arrives in Athens, the 87-year-old Prohaeresius presents a picturesque figure, young in spirit, with a head of hair like sea-foam, so that the author 'regarded him as an ageless and immortal being, and heeded him as he might some god'. After this dramatic description, the focus switches back to the author. With cultural associations incomparably rich for author and reader, the physical arrival at the Piraeus cannot but be pregnant with significance. The fact that it was night-time probably adds to this effect. We have already discussed the sombre significance Marinus would accord to Proclus' crepuscular arrival at Athens some decades later (see p. 60). It may be that Eunapius too had not just a personal, but a more general cultural point in mind; he does not hesitate to remind readers of the decline of a city in which 'battles were being fought to win only one or two pupils'.[27] The city and its inhabitants soon form a backdrop integral to his own story. The picturesque contrast between Eunapius' slim financial means, and his intellectual wealth ('he had most of the works of the ancient writers by heart, his sole possession'),[28] finds a parallel in the poverty narratives recounted a few pages later to praise the young Prohaeresius, and his classmate Hephaestion.[29]

The dramatic quality of this arrival is vastly enhanced by the dangerous fever Eunapius had caught during the journey. Like many narrow survivors[30] he was no doubt inclined to see the hand of providence at work in his life. His account

---

Frederick Buck, 'Eunapius of Sardis', Oxford DPhil. thesis (1977), pp. 13–23 also focuses on the practical questions. The portrait's literary function is mentioned only briefly by Buck, 'Eunapius' *Lives of the Sophists*: a Literary Study', p. 153.

[27]   Eunapius, *Lives* 485 (tr. Wright, p. 479). For the physical decline of Athens, Buck, 'Eunapius of Sardis', p. 19.

[28]   Ibid., pp. 13–15.

[29]   Eunapius, *Lives* 487. Eunapius' romantic portrayal of his student days has interesting parallels in Libanius' *Autobiography (Oration 1)*, ed. and tr. Albert Francis Norman (Oxford, 1965): note especially his devotion to his teacher and studies (8–9), a life-threatening affliction (12), desperation to see Athens, and living conditions in a tiny room (16). For a general discussion of student travel in late antiquity, see Edward J. Watts, 'Student Travel to Intellectual Centers: what was the Attraction?' in L. Ellis and F.L. Kidner (eds), *Travel, Communication and Geography in Late Antiquity* (San Fransisco, 2004), pp. 13–24.

[30]   Good contemporaneous examples include Libanius' experience of being struck by thunder: *Oratio* 1, 9 (tr. A.F. Norman, p. 7); Jerome's feverish and life-changing dream in which Christ rebuked him because *Ciceronianus es, non Christianus*: *Letter* 22.30; Gregory

of the recovery confirms this feeling: the proximity of death; the rumours which swept the city; the 'grandiloquent' Homeric word applied to the moment the medicine cleared his stomach and set him on the road to recovery;[31] the balanced, alliterative formula describing the beginning of his friendship with the doctor who saved him.[32] Above all, the heart-warming philanthropy of his master Prohaeresius, who claims to have grieved for the dying boy as for a son, though he had yet to meet him, and whom he subsequently entrusts to the care of his star student. As in the case of Plotinus' intervention to save Porphyry, Prohaeresius' attention to the young Eunapius merely manifests his exceptional philanthropy. But for Eunapius personally, it is, of course, like intellectual encounters between other great philosophers,[33] a spiritual credential, and one acceptable precisely because it can be advanced without loss of humility. The fragile, precious link forged between the old and young man acquires, for Eunapius, the quality of a miracle. That his relationship with Prohaeresius comes to constitute a core personal truth is shown by an alternative synopsis of the same episode later in the work, in which the pseudo-filial bond replaces all other elements.[34]

A significant proportion of late antique autobiographical material comes from hagiographers who were also the disciples of holy men; the same is equally true amongst Christians. Palladius not only reports the spiritual intensity of his travels around the Egyptian desert;[35] pretending to refer to someone else, he closes his work with an assessment of his own spiritual progress.[36] Cyril of Scythopolis considered himself blessed to have known Sabas, one of the two main subjects of his *History*;[37] it is Sabas and his own master Euthymius who appear to him in a dream and bless him with spiritual oil to help him overcome

---

of Nazianzus' decision to devote himself to God having survived a shipwreck: *De Vita Sua*, 124–99, ed. and tr. Christoph Junck, *Gregor von Nazianz: De Vita Sua* (Heidelberg, 1974).

[31] 'ἀπελυμάνη', Eunapius, *Lives* 486. Wright (p. 483, footnote 1) identifies the source of this 'grandiloquent' word as *Iliad* i.313.

[32] 'καὶ τότε ἀκριβῶς ὁ σωθεὶς τῷ σώσαντι'.

[33] Eunapius, *Lives* 460. Other dramatic encounters recorded by Eunapius include Julian and Maximus (ibid. 475), Chrysanthius and Aedesius, (ibid. 500). All of these incidents recall that between Plotinus and Ammonius Saccas: Porphyry, *Life of Plotinus* 3.

[34] 'The author, who had attained at this time to about his sixteenth year, arrived at Athens and was enrolled among his own pupils, and Prohaeresius loved him like his own son', Eunapius, *Lives* 493 (tr. Wright, p. 513).

[35] E.g. his description of the community at Nitria, Palladius, *Lausiac History*, 7.5: 'about the ninth hour one can stand and hear the divine psalmody issuing forth from each cell and imagine one is high above in paradise'.

[36] Ibid. 71.1–6.

[37] Cyril, *Lives* 180.8–181.18.

his writer's block.[38] The family of Theodoret had a long and intensive history of personal involvement with a number of local holy men such as Peter the Galatian who had once cured his mother of an eye disease;[39] indeed, since Theodoret himself had only been conceived with the help of Macedonius' prayers following a long period of infertility for his parents, he could credit the holy man with his very existence.[40] More recently, he had achieved a sort of surrogate celebrity as the only person allowed into the cell of the hermit Limnaeus.[41] Hilarius' *Life of Honoratus* celebrated a saint who had personally rescued him from sin and brought him to the monastic life.[42] All of these authors could regard their own destinies as interwoven with those of the holy men concerned; this was, in large part, their motivation for writing. As Eunapius reminds us immediately after recording his master's philanthropy, 'all that happened to Prohaeresius was under the direction of some divine providence';[43] as one who had narrowly escaped death to become a virtual son to the great man, Eunapius could confidently confirm that providence was also at work in his own, albeit lesser, life.

Nonetheless, although it is possible to observe profound connections between first and third person spiritual writing in our period, there is one very important difference: autobiography never contains, as hagiography by definition must contain, a direct assertion of its subject's sanctity. The author may draw certain comparisons between his own condition and those of figures in myth or Scripture, may see spiritual truths in the literal details of his experience, may assert the hand of God in his life; he may imply that he had a high opinion of his own spiritual achievements, or indeed a low one, but he will never openly describe himself as holy. Even in a case like that of Porphyry, the most reverential statements are reserved for the writer's master.

The reason for this difference potentially has fundamental implications for the use we make of spiritual autobiography and, by extension, for the whole project of using it as a source for religious experience. The problem is reminiscent of that identified in Gibbon's observation that, though Bernard of Clairvaux described other people's miracles, he never mentions his own.[44] One view would

---

[38]　Ibid., pp. 84–5.

[39]　Theodoret, *History* 9.5–8.

[40]　Ibid. 13.16–18.

[41]　Ibid. 22.3.

[42]　Hilarius, *Life of Honoratus* 5.23–4.

[43]　Eunapius, *Lives* 486 (tr. Wright, p. 483).

[44]　'It may seem somewhat remarkable that Bernard of Clairvaux, who records so many miracles of his friend St. Malachi, never takes any notice of his own, which, in their turn, however, are carefully related by his companions and disciples. In the long series of ecclesiastical history, does there exist a single instance of a saint asserting that he himself possessed the gift

be to see the saint's perspective as too private and too remote to be represented in writing, even of an autobiographical kind. This view comes close to what we might call the late antique theory of the holy man: namely as someone defined by a privileged and hidden insight into reality. But it also suggests that the autobiographical writings we possess from the period, although written by spiritually-minded people such as disciples, are not, because they cannot be, a source for the perspective of holy men themselves. This perspective therefore becomes invisible.

A second view would be to see this difference as evidence of the hagiographer's reputed tendency towards exaggeration. Saints' lives always seemed more distinctive in the third person; indeed, sanctity itself was fundamentally a social construct, a judgement which, at least in its fullest expression, was formed in the minds of others. According to this view, although we may treat hagiography as a source for certain religious views and forms of experience characteristic of the period, it is pointless to search for a first-person perspective which corresponds directly to claims made in hagiography. The holy man's perspective is a chimera.

A third view is that spiritual autobiographies do not directly assert their subjects' sanctity only because literary decorum prevents it, and it is essentially in this respect that they differ from hagiographies. A number of late antique autobiographies have been interpreted along these lines. Neil McLynn has analysed the personal writings of Gregory of Nazianzus as the portraits of a 'self-made holy man',[45] and Stephanos Efthymiadis has described them as 'autohagiography'.[46] In a similar vein, Stefan Rebenich has convincingly exposed Jerome's 'brilliant showmanship as an ascetic champion'[47] communicated through personal letters to prominent supporters in Rome. As should be clear from our analysis of the *Life of Plotinus* and the *Letter to Marcella*, a very similar argument could be made about Porphyry.

On the face of it, texts of this third sort, in which the first and third person perspectives overlap so clearly, might seem to provide precisely the necessary correspondence for speculation into the holy man's inner life. In fact, they pose a deeper problem. In most spiritual traditions humility is an important virtue, and one often reflected in a reticence to lead. As we have seen, this general principle

---

of miracles?' Edward Gibbon, *The History of the Decline and Fall of the Roman Empire* ed. J.B. Bury (7 vols, London: Methuen and Co, 1897), vol. 1, p. 30, footnote 82.

[45]   McLynn, 'A Self-Made Holy Man: The Case of Gregory Nazianzen', pp. 463–83.

[46]   Efthymiadis, 'Two Gregories and Three Genres', p. 246.

[47]   'His brilliant showmanship as an ascetic champion who had started his impressive career in the wilderness of Chalcis has been so successful that, for more than 1,600 years, scholars have been deceived by the picture of the learned ascetic in his barren cell in the *solitudo Syriae Chalcidis*', Rebenich, *Jerome*, p. 20.

achieved a maximal expression in the Christian motif of the *fama* effect (see pp. 105–6). For autobiography to echo those very elements by which sanctity was established in hagiography, such as analogies with earlier heroic figures, or a symbol-laden external life, surely risked undermining humility as a necessary element of sanctity. Although not overtly hostile, the analyses of Gregory and Jerome by McLynn and Rebenich respectively certainly veer towards scepticism. There is nothing illegitimate about this approach. But however implicitly we impute them, any motivations which are more mundane than saintly risk invoking questions of sincerity. Nor is this problem necessarily overcome by authors like Hilarius who emphasize their own sinfulness and lowliness: such statements could also be interpreted as born of a false humility and designed to fulfil precisely the expectation that saints were humble. Indeed, at the limit, any point of contact identified between hagiography and autobiography potentially comes at the price of conceding a certain incompatibility between the hagiographical theory of sanctity as humble and unselfconscious and the historical reality of spiritual leadership. The more ground we concede on this front, the greater the risk of diminishing the central contention of the current project, namely that there was a greater continuity between these things than has usually been recognized.

Of course, with a form of writing as diverse as late antique spiritual autobiography, different texts are bound to present different problems. The important point in the immediate context, however, is a general one: we cannot assume the transition from third to first-person spiritual narrative to be a straightforward move from an image of sanctity to something more primitive, authentic, and closer to its source. Part of the reason has to do with circularity: just as we may ask what self-conception lay behind a hagiographical portrait, we may equally ask what notions of sanctity, perhaps sometimes encountered through written hagiography, influenced a holy man's self-perception. But more fundamentally, it is because we cannot presume to find in autobiography a direct account of an inner life. It is an established dictum of modern theory, voiced amongst others by Jean-Paul Sartre and Jacques Derrida, that individuals have no privileged access to the truth of their past lives, that they are bound to misremember and/or idealize them, and that, consequently, the very project of autobiography is highly problematic, if not impossible.[48] Any autobiographical statement can, potentially, be treated as merely an image projected by the writer; such images do not necessarily bring us any closer to a holy man's inner life than the judgements of a hagiographer or a part of hagiography (such as Severinus'

---

[48]   Schramm, 'Augustinus' *Confessiones* und die (Un)-Möglichkeit der Autobiographie', pp. 173–5.

self-portrait in the *Letter to Paschasius*) which we have good reason to trace back to the holy man himself.

In this sense, rather than offering solutions to the problems of hagiography, spiritual autobiography is best recognized as a form of writing which poses closely analogous challenges and invites similar questions: to what extent were such works committed to truthfulness? What was the nature of the reality they attempted to represent and what techniques did they use? What reasons do we have for positing in these works evidence of a spiritual life prior to the literary act? Given that these questions have been asked of both hagiographies and autobiographies, it is somewhat surprising how little comparative work they have generated. But to compare these two forms of writing should not just be an exercise in identifying direct mutual influence (although this is certainly possible and occasionally detectable). Rather, if, as previously argued, the hagiographical was a set of attitudes manifested in a particular type of writing, but with roots extending far beyond it into spiritual practices and attitudes, then we may treat autobiography as an opportunity to reflect on them from an alternative perspective. At least in the first instance, the 'first-person perspective on sanctity' should be interpreted thus: not as the holy man's inner life directly, but as the way in which some people wrote and thought about their own lives in a world in which sanctity was considered a human possibility and holy men an aspect of reality.

Augustine's *Confessions*: The Problem of Truthfulness

No late antique author describes his own life, and particularly his intellectual and spiritual life, with a depth and detail comparable to Augustine in his *Confessions*. It is probably also true that no other author from the period writes so extensively about the problem of truthfulness. These factors alone are enough to determine the pivotal role Augustine will play in the remainder of our discussion on autobiography. But to discuss Augustine's own commitment to truthfulness and historicity is to revisit the oldest, and most heavily debated, issue surrounding the *Confessions*. Indeed, as E. Feldman has observed,[49] the doubts raised by Boissier and Harnack about Augustine's truthfulness effectively mark the beginning of modern scholarship on the work. As far as possible, the discussion that follows will be framed within the terms of this long-standing debate and will in turn attempt to contribute to it.

---

[49] E. Feldmann, 'Confessiones' in Cornelius P. Mayer et al. (eds), *Augustinus-Lexikon* (Basel, 1986–94), pp. 1135–6.

In origin, the question involves not just the *Confessions* in isolation, but their relationship to the so-called 'Cassiciacum dialogues' (*De Beata Vita, Contra Academicos, De Ordine* and *Soliloquia*) written near Milan around a decade earlier, and shortly after he had resigned his post as rhetorician. The first three of these works purport to contain transcripts of theological and philosophical discussions led by Augustine during a scholarly country retreat featuring a mixed group of his students, friends, and family, including his mother Monica. The dialogues are interspersed with a certain amount of scene setting, character portrait, and recent personal reminiscences including, for example, of the picturesque rural atmosphere in which the debates took place. A major concern of scholars since the 1880's has been the apparent incompatibility of these documents with Augustine's account of the same period in the *Confessions*. In the later work, Augustine depicts this period as one in which, after the dramatic conversion at Milan, he gave up his job as rhetorician and turned to Christianity after a period of intense (but unsatisfactory) involvement with Platonism. But the Cassiciacum dialogues make no mention of a dramatic conversion, instead attributing his premature retirement more obliquely to a chest pain (*pectoris dolor*).[50] Furthermore, the general intellectual mood of the Cassiciacum dialogues, far from being one in which Platonism had been replaced by a more committed Christianity, has traditionally been seen as arguing, much more optimistically, for the basic compatibility of the two belief systems.[51]

On the basis of such differences, many scholars have concluded that the *Confessions*, for all their apparent declarations of truthfulness,[52] in fact contain a good deal of invention: Augustine's conversion was either a fiction, contrived for ideological purposes,[53] or, at least, it contained elements of exaggeration. Such arguments have not always implied hostility. As we shall shortly see, some scholars, such as Courcelle and J.J. O'Meara, suggested that, although the external events were fictitious, they were an inevitable and understandable way of representing the rapidly changing inner convictions he genuinely felt

---

[50]   Augustine, *Contra Academicos* 2.2.2, ed. Pius Knöll, CSEL 63 (Vienna/Leipzig, 1922); *De Beata Vita* 1.4, ed. Pius Knöll, CSEL 63 (Vienna/Leipzig, 1922); *De Ordine* 1.2.5, ed. J. Doignon (Paris, 1997). For a list, and an analysis of these, and all other autobiographical material written before the *Confessions*, see Pierre Courcelle, 'Les Premières Confessions d'Augustin', *Recherches* (Paris, 1950), pp. 269–90.

[51]   E.g. Madec, 'L'historicité des *Dialogues* de Cassiciacum', pp. 228–9.

[52]   E.g. Augustine, *Confessions* 10.3.3 (tr. Burton, p. 216): 'Those whose ears have been opened to me by love will believe me.'

[53]   A view most famously advanced by Prosper Alfaric, who maintained that Augustine as bishop wanted to conceal an earlier conversion to Neoplatonism: *L'Evolution intellectuelle de Saint Augustin*, I. *Du Manichéisme au Néoplatonisme* (Paris, 1918).

at the time.[54] But whatever his motivations, once Augustine's commitment to truthfulness had been seen as less than literal, other famous episodes in the work, such as the theft of pears in Book 4, could also be regarded as ideologically motivated, and scrutinized accordingly. Since the 1960's, a similarly spirited debate has revolved around the structure of the *Confessions*, which, some scholars have argued, reflects not just the straightforward progression of the author's life, but symbolically represents the Neoplatonic concept of the soul's fall from, and return to God.[55]

Although the *Confessions* have generated a scholarly literature not always closely related to that on hagiography, it is clear that the tendencies of the linguistic turn have had a similar impact on both. Most important is the basic assumption of an innate opposition between the text's literary/intellectual content on the one hand, and its factual content on the other. As long as this dichotomy is accepted in principle then any research into the former will sustain belief in the lesser importance to Augustine of the latter, even if only implicitly, and even if judgement is suspended.[56] The proof of this tendency is that, whilst ideological intent is sometimes used as an argument for undermining the historicity of a particular detail, the possibility that a detail might be true

---

[54]   Pierre Courcelle *Les Confessions de Saint Augustin dans la tradition littéraire* (Paris, 1963), esp. p. 181. *Affabulation* was the only way Augustine could express such deeply held convictions. Unlike Alfaric, Courcelle did not believe Augustine was concealing earlier convictions; he clearly demonstrated the thoroughly Christian, Milanese origin of Augustine's Neoplatonism. For his place in the debate's history, see O'Donnell, *Commentary* 1, pp. xx ff. Works broadly in this tradition include J.J. O'Meara, 'Elements of Fiction in Augustine's *Confessions*', in Joanne McWilliam (ed.), *Augustine: From Rhetor to Theologian* (Waterloo, Ontario, 1992), pp. 77–95. O'Meara emphasizes the inevitability of fictitiousness in any description (p. 78). See also Paula Frederiksen, 'Paul and Augustine Conversion Narratives, Orthodox Traditions and the Retrospective Self', in *JTS* 37.1 (1986); Leo Ferrari, 'Saint Augustine's Conversion Scene: the End of a Modern Debate?' in *Studia Patristica* 22 (1989); Annemaré Kotzé, *Augustine's* Confessions: *Communicative Purpose and Audience* (Leiden, 2004), p. 67. Gerald Bonner, by contrast, defends the incident's historicity: 'Augustine's Conversion: Historical Fact or Literary Device?' in P. Merino and J.M. Torrecilla (eds), *Augustinus*: *Charisteria Augustiniana* (Madrid, 1993), pp. 112–14. It is interesting, however, that part of this defence involves suggesting that the moment was only one of a number of significant spiritual conversions.

[55]   A view expressed most famously by Robert J. O'Connell, *St. Augustine's Confessions*: *the Odyssey of the Soul* (Cambridge Mass, 1969). An excellent review of the debate is provided by Ronnie J. Rombs, *Saint Augustine and the Fall of the Soul*: *Beyond O'Connell and his Critics* (Washington, 2006), p. 7ff.

[56]   Although Conybeare appears to take a middle position on the question of historicity the implication of phrases like 'the cumbersome construction (of) this staged realism' is obvious: *The Irrational Augustine*, p. 58.

seems very rarely, if ever, to be used as an argument against a particular literary interpretation.[57] Though the discussion which follows takes the side, broadly speaking, of those who have defended Augustine's historicty, its fundamental intention is not to compare specific details contained within the *Confessions* and the Cassiciacum dialogues respectively (although the contention that this incompatibility is more apparent than real is one consequence of the argument). Rather, as in the earlier discussion of hagiography, it seeks to challenge the text/ life dichotomy so central to the linguistic turn by highlighting Augustine's commitment to truthfulness, by reflecting on the *Confessions* as an instantiation of his attitudes and, ultimately, by considering the broader spiritual lifestyle of which the written text was one product.

Augustine: Truthfulness as a Value

Our discussion of hagiography began by considering the statements of literary intent made by authors of this genre, often within their prologues (see pp. 25–34). In the case of Augustine's *Confessions*, we may justly consider his title the greatest clue as to how he regarded his own literary activity. Although he never provides an explicit definition of the term 'confession', a picture of its meaning gradually develops throughout the work. Firstly, it is obvious that it involves both praise and repentance: *confessio laudis* and *confessio peccati*.[58] But, as Jean-Claude Fredouille rightly observes, more important still is that, as an address to God, confession implies 'un autre univers de pensée' pervading every page of the text: 'je confesse que j'ai volé les poires' is critically, and always, different from the more neutral 'je dit que' or even 'j'avoue que j'ai volé les poires'.[59] That the work also has a human

---

[57]　An excellent example: Danuta Shanzer, 'Pears before Swine: Augustine, *Confessions* 2.4.9' in *REA* 42 (1996), p. 48. She asks why was Augustine so ready to forego the double meaning of *malum* (= 'evil' or 'apple')? That the answer may be a simple commitment to truthfulness is never considered. In keeping with this, the question of historicity is asked (p. 45), but allowed to go unanswered. Similarly, the reasons Leo Ferrari finds for the choice of a pear tree, whilst different from Shanzer's, do not include the possibility that it simply was a pear theft: 'The Pear-Theft in Augustine's "*Confessions*"', *REA* 16 (1970), pp. 241–2.

[58]　*Enarrationes in Psalmos* 144.13, eds Hildegund Müller and Clemens Weidmann, CSEL 93, 94 (2 vols, Vienna, 2003–2004): 'Confessio enim non peccatorum tantum dicitur, sed et laudis.'

[59]　Jean-Claude Fredouille, 'Les *Confessions* d'Augustin', in Marie-Françoise Baslez, Philippe Hoffmann, Laurent Pernot (eds), *L'invention de l'autobiographie* (Paris, 1993), p. 173.

audience is of course recognized,[60] but it is never allowed to replace the sense of an ever present God.[61] As a result, falsification would be pointless because God already knows everything that Augustine confesses.[62] On the face of it, then, Augustine's decision to 'confess' his life story would seem to imply an uncompromising commitment to truthfulness.

It is clear, however, that this stance is not, fundamentally, an assertion of knowledge; rather, it describes a very complex epistemic relationship with his own life story. The epistemic aspect of confession has perhaps not been emphasized strongly enough.[63] For example, Robert O'Connell, despite his observation that the Christian life involves 'turning the un-knower into a knower',[64] makes only summary mention of the pervasive theme of moral blindness. But, quoting Psalms, 'knowledge and understanding' are the first things Augustine prays for in the *Confessions*.[65] The epistemic aspect of confession is again emphasized at the beginning of the non-narrative section. Chapter 10 begins with a repetition of Augustine's earlier prayer, this time, however, with a small but crucial adjustment: 'May I know you, my Knower; may I know you, *even as I also am known*' (my italics).[66]

---

[60] The question of the work's intended human audience (and, by extension, of its genre and the circumstances surrounding its composition), is too massive to explore here. The most complete and recent study of the *Confessions'* audience, Kotzé, *Augustine's Confessions: Communicative Purpose and Audience*, argues that, whilst the main audience were the Manichees, it included other Christians as well – (p. 67). In my view, Gillian Clark summarizes the problem best: the book is 'overdetermined: there were too many reasons for writing it', including as a refutation of hostile rumours, as therapy, to tell his life story to friends and admirers, and to show the grace of God at work: *Augustine: the* Confessions (Bristol, 2005), pp. 40–41. The main point is none of this replaces, nor even really affects, the nature of the divine address.

[61] E.g. 'If my reader is one whom you have called … let them not laugh at me as they read my account … let them love you not less, but more', Augustine, *Confessions* 2.7.15 (tr. Burton, p. 40); 'It is my purpose, in making my confession in my heart, to do what is true before you, and in making my confession in writing, to do what is true before many witnesses', ibid. 10.1.1 (tr. Burton, p. 215).

[62] Not to confess, for Augustine, means only self-deception: 'I would be hiding you from me, not me from you', ibid. 10.2.2 (tr. Burton, p. 215).

[63] There are exceptions, e.g. Lawrence Rothfield, 'Autobiography and Perspective in the *Confessions* of St. Augustine' in *Comparative Literature* 33.3 (1981), pp. 209–23. Augustine's epistemic emphasis echoes that expressed early in his *Soliloquies* (1.2.7): *Deum et animam scire cupio*.

[64] O'Connell, *St. Augustine's Confessions: the Odyssey of the Soul*, p. 27.

[65] Augustine, *Confessions* 1.1.1 (tr. Burton, p. 5).

[66] Ibid. 10.1.1 (tr. Burton, p. 215).

The pregnant position of this appeal is a major clue to the nature of confession: it concerns, for Augustine, the structure of human knowledge, the metaphysical means which render it possible. By invoking God's knowledge in conjunction with his prayer, Augustine shows that real human knowledge can be gained only through a process of dialogue with the Creator. This is already evident in the list of philosophical questions which constitute so much of the work's first book.[67] It is not the case that they represent illegitimate areas of enquiry; but, even as he poses them, Augustine also declares his inability to resolve many, allowing them instead to accumulate unanswered. Therefore, whilst his stance legitimizes philosophical speculation in a certain sense, he rigorously distinguishes such speculation from the activity of confession, as becomes clear when he considers the traditional philosophical question of the human soul's pre-existence:

> Tell me this: Did my childhood itself follow on from some previous time in my life, already dead when my childhood began? Was that stage of my life the time that I spent in my mother's womb? I have been told something of that time, and I know how women look when they are expecting; but what came even before that, O God my Sweetness? Did I exist, in some form and in some place? There is no one else who can tell me this; my father and my mother cannot tell me, and I cannot rely on the experiences of others, or on my own memory. Or do you laugh at me (Ps. 2.4, Ps. 37.13 [Ps. 36.13], Wisdom 4.18) when I ask such questions, and bid me praise you and confess myself before you for what I do know?[68]

Although the term is never explicitly defined, this passage comes very close to how Augustine seems to conceptualize the activity after which the work is named: confession is a declaration of what the Christian knows. Through confession, a Christian's knowledge is assumed to increase, by virtue of contact with its only effective source.[69] It is also highly personal since its reflects God's active involvement in each believer's life: 'You, O Lord ... bring it about that by some hidden instinct ... every consultor hears what it is right that he should hear,

---

[67]   E.g. 'But all that you fill you fill with your whole being? Or, as nothing can contain your whole being, does each thing contain a part of you? If so, is it the same part that each contains? Or does each individual thing contain an individual part of you, the larger ones containing parts of you and the smaller ones smaller parts? In that case, are some parts of you larger and some parts smaller? Or is it that you are wholly present in all places, and no one thing contains your whole being?' Ibid. 1.3.3 (tr. Burton, p. 6).

[68]   'Did I exist, in some form or in some place? There is no-one else who can tell me this ... do you laugh at me (Ps. 2.4, Ps. 3713, Wisdom 4.18) when I ask such questions, and bid me praise you and confess myself before you for what I do know?' Ibid. 1.6.9 (tr. Burton, p. 10).

[69]   'There is no other teacher of truth beside you', ibid. 5.6.10 (tr. Burton, p. 93).

according to his soul's hidden deservings.'[70] This distinguishes it, amongst other things, from the *praesumptio* of the Platonists, who, according to Augustine,[71] wrongly rely on their own intellectual powers. In this sense, confession can rightly be described as a uniquely Christian response to the point at which knowledge and ignorance meet at any particular time.[72] Dependent on, and a function of, divine knowledge, it is man's side of the dialogue with his Creator. It is always appropriate, and permanently changing. It involves, on the one hand, an admission of ignorance; on the other, a recognition that everything the confessor knows is received from God, unchosen but individually tailored.[73] To extend O'Connell's expression, the confessor becomes both 'knower' and 'knowing un-knower'.[74] Confession is the forum in which knowledge is acquired, and where the nature of knowledge is recognized.

What are the implications of this for the content of the *Confessions*? As mentioned above, that Augustine's stance includes a basic ethic of truthfulness is not necessarily denied by those who have argued that the *Confessions* in general, and the conversion scene in particular, are not wholly literal accounts. But what did Augustine think truthfulness meant? The arguments which have emerged over recent decades concerning classical notions of historical truthfulness – namely that they were more complex and less literal than one might initially assume – have affected Augustinian scholarship no less than that on hagiography (see p. 36). For example, Leo Ferrari has argued that Augustine, following the tradition of many classical historians, would have found it only

---

[70]   Ibid. 7.7.10 (tr. Burton, p. 144).

[71]   Ibid. 7.20.26 (tr. Burton, p. 155). On the specific point of intellectual autonomy, there is a case for arguing that Augustine's distinction involved something of a caricature of Platonic tradition. The philosophical importance of divine assistance was evident to Iamblichus, *On the Pythagorean Life* 1(1) (tr. Clark, p. 1) quoting Plato, *Timaeus* 27C (tr. Bury, p. 49): 'all men who possess even a small share of good sense call upon God always at the outset of every undertaking, be it small or great'. To a neutral observer, would the guidance Monica was said to receive at *Confessions* 6.13.23 sound very different from the sign of Socrates? Plato, *Apologia* 31D, 33C, 40A–C ed. E.A. Duke et al. in *Platonis Opera 1*, Scriptorium Classicorum Bibliotheca Oxoniensis (Oxford, 1995).

[72]   As implied by the following: 'I confess, therefore, what I know of myself; and I confess also what I do not know, for what I do know, I know because you enlighten me, and what I do not know, I do not know only so long as it takes for *my darkness to be like the noon-day in your sight*' [Is. 58.10, Ps. 90.8], Augustine, *Confessions* 10.5.7 (tr. Burton, p. 219).

[73]   'Let him who understands this confess to you, and let him that does not understand confess it to you also', Ibid. 11.31.41 (tr. Burton, p. 286).

[74]   I am grateful to Peter Heather for this observation.

natural to engage in a certain licence in order to capture the gist of an incident.[75] Indeed, this sort of argument seems stronger when applied to Augustine than to many hagiographers; we may expect the author of the *Confessions*, as a man who was not merely educated but a former career rhetorician, to have had a grasp of literary expectations and techniques which went far beyond a general intellectual and cultural heritage. Furthermore, one could argue that these techniques, far from being unsuited to the highly religious agenda of the *Confessions*, was precisely the forum in which they were most valuable because Augustine was trying to communicate convictions and experiences which transcended the concrete details of his exterior life. This, for example, is the essence of Courcelle's influential claim that the child's voice through which Augustine was purportedly converted was a necessary poetic device, for 'il est difficile de parler des choses de l'au-delà sans images ni affabulation'.[76]

As with hagiography, then, the definition of Augustine's notion of truthfulness revolves around the relationship between the literal and the spiritual. Augustine's clearest statements about these two types of information occurs not in the highly personal *Confessions* but elsewhere in theoretical works about the nature of the Bible. Perhaps more than any other late antique theologian, Augustine was concerned by the question of Scripture's literal truthfulness and insisted on the historical accuracy of all the events it recorded. The best known expression of this position is probably in his debate with Jerome in which he rejects the possibility that the Bible could contain even 'one polite lie'.[77] In claiming this, he was not arguing anti-allegorically; rather, what his conviction expressed was the crucial idea that Scripture's meaning – and this included any deeper, hidden messages – resided not only in its words but in the original deeds those words later recorded.[78]

---

[75]   Leo Ferrari distinguishes between Augustine's commitment to 'Truth' and to 'truth': 'Truth and Augustine's conversion scene' in J.C. Schnaubelt and F.van Fleteren (eds), *Augustine: 'Second founder of the faith'*, (New York, 1990), p. 14. In another essay, he explains Augustine's commitment to detail in terms of the three grades of historical *veritas* identified by Asclepiades of Myrlea: 'Saint Augustine's Conversion Scene: the End of a Modern Debate?' *Studia Patristica* 22 (1989), p. 244.

[76]   Courcelle, *Les Confessions de Saint Augustin*, p. 181.

[77]   Augustine, *Epistula* 28, ed. A. Goldbacher, CSEL 34 (Vienna, 1895; repr. New York, 1961), tr. Wilfrid Parsons, *Saint Augustine: Letters*, vol. 2 (Washington DC, 1953), p. 96. See J.N.D. Kelly, *Jerome: his Life, Writings and Controversies* (London, 1975), pp. 217–20 and 263–72, for discussion of their debates.

[78]   The ability of biblical events to contain allegorical meanings is insisted upon, for example, at *De Mendacio* 26, ed. J. Zycha, CSEL 41 (Vienna, 1900); *De Genesi ad Litteram* 8.4.8, 9.12.30, 11.34.45, 11.39.52, ed. and tr., Paul Agaësse and Armand Solignac (Paris, 1972); at *Letter* 102.6 (tr. W. Parsons, p. 172): 'Human power is wont to express itself by

Although Augustine's literalist attitude tends to be expressed in contexts of biblical exegesis, there are good reasons to believe that it also had an application where his own life, and his manner of recording it, were concerned. The Bible, after all, was not a text remote from everyday life; rather, it had a very general function in teaching people 'to distinguish between things perceptible to the intellect and things perceptible to the senses'.[79] It seems extremely likely that Augustine would have regarded one of its central messages – namely that God communicated deep spiritual meanings through events – as equally applicable to the small, recent and local worlds in which his life had taken place as it had been to the momentous episodes of a sacred past. It was not just the Bible that spoke to people but the entire created order.[80] For this reason, we must challenge the sort of argument advanced by Courcelle which equates Augustine's profoundly metaphysical hierarchy with a less than literal ethic towards his own life story. It is misleading to assume that by attempting to record his relationship with God, the primary challenge facing Augustine was to find suitable words and images for the ineffable. A more accurate description would be that it was to detect and interpret the messages already communicated by God through concrete events. From Augustine's literalist viewpoint, the wonderful truth was that sacred history rendered *affabulation* unnecessary.

Indeed, to follow his biblical theology further, it might also be dangerous. The Holy Spirit did not merely conceal meanings within events as they happened. Even where meanings were unclear to the initial human protagonists and recorders of events, he might eventually reveal them at some future time, thus simultaneously acting as both creative and interpretative allegorist.[81] As Williams has rightly stressed, this was, amongst other things, the very nature

---

words, but divine power by deeds'; and whilst commenting on Paul's analysis of the Exodus story (1 Cor. 10, 1–11) at *On the Profit of Believing* 8. It is important to note that Augustine's defence of biblical historicity did not entirely exclude the possibility that some allegorical truth resided in language alone. Apparently absurd surface meanings serve as a trope for indicating this: *De Doctrina Christiana* 3.87ff, ed. and tr. R.P.H. Green (Oxford, 1995). For general discussions, see Markus, *Signs and Meanings*, p. 6ff and Armand Strubel, '"Allegoria in factis" et "allegoria in verbis" in *Poétique* 21 (1975), esp. pp. 343–7 (including for the later systematization of these categories by Bede). As Strubel observes, these categories were later systematized by Bede as *allegoria in verbis* and *allegoria in factis*: '"Allegoria in factis" et "allegoria in verbis"', p. 347ff.

[79] Augustine, *Confessions* 13.18.22 (tr. Burton, p. 335).

[80] 'The created order speaks to all, but is only understood by those who hear its outward voice and compare it with the truth within themselves', Augustine, *Confessions* 10.6.10 (tr. Burton, p. 221).

[81] Augustine, *On Christian Doctrine* 3.84–5.

of biblical prefiguration.[82] For example, the Hebrews of the Exodus knew they were blessed but, unlike their Christian successors, did not realize that the events through which they lived already prefigured the immeasurable blessing of Christ's incarnation.[83] Similarly, as Augustine makes explicit in his analysis of Genesis,[84] whilst some meanings may have been clear to Moses as he wrote, others might be concealed within events only to be revealed to a particular reader centuries later. But if this highly personal process, by which 'every consultor hears what it is right for him to hear' applied to biblical exegesis, there is no reason to see why it would not apply to life more generally. As explained in *De Magistro*, Christ in his role as True Teacher guides believers in all language learning and linguistic comprehension.[85] In so far as the *Confessions* would be read by others, it is hard to see why a general ethic of truthfulness would not also have had to extend to the literal truth.

If Augustine's notions of truthfulness can be linked to a certain conception of Scripture, what did they owe to the classical rhetorical tradition? The form of education provided for the elite in antiquity was so deeply embedded in the culture that it is very hard to speak of any person who had undergone it as ever operating entirely outside it. We can say, however, that just as Augustine had been a sophisticated exponent of this system, he was by the time of the *Confessions* a sophisticated and explicit critic of it. Revealingly, one important objection he levels against at least some secular literature, such as the stories of Aeneas and Medea, is the fanciful and untrue nature of the stories it contains.[86] In the *Soliloquies*, Augustine does introduce a conceptual distinction between two kinds of falsehood: deliberate deception on the one hand, and types of lie (such as in poems and jokes etc.) which give pleasure and which the audience accepts.[87] But it is interesting that he does not seem to consider this category of acceptable fiction when discussing Apuleius in the later *City of God*: the story of his transformation into an ass, comments Augustine, was either a lie or

---

[82]　Williams, *Authorised Lives*, esp. pp. 11–16.

[83]　*Contra Faustum Manichaeum* 12.39, ed. J. Zycha, CSEL 25.1 (Vienna, 1891).

[84]　'What hindrance is it if I take (God's words) to mean something other than Moses took them to mean?' Augustine, *Confessions* 12.18.17 (tr. Burton, p. 304).

[85]　Augustine, *De Magistro* 11.38, 14.46, ed. Günther Wiegel, CSEL 77 (Vienna, 1961); *Retractationum Libri Duo*, Prologue 2, ed. Pius Knöll, CSEL 36 (Vienna, 1902), Prologue 2, tr. Mary Inez Bogan, *The Retractations* (Washington DC, 1968), p. 4: 'There is no other teacher of truth beside you', Augustine, *Confessions* 5.6.10 (tr. Burton, p. 93). For a full discussion of the theme, see Gareth B. Matthews, 'Augustine on the Teacher Within' in William E. Mann (ed.), *Augustine's Confessions: Critical Essays* (Oxford, 2006), esp. p. 32.

[86]　For denial of the historicity of mythical characters: Aeneas at Augustine, *Confessions* 1.13.22; Medea at ibid. 3.6.11. A similar point is made by Athanasius, *Life of Antony* 75.2.

[87]　Augustine, *Soliloquies* 2.16.

sufficiently unusual to be deserving of disbelief.[88] As we have seen, this sceptical stance contrasts markedly by his extremely enthusiastic response to the *Life of Antony* which included great excitement about the text's well attested, literal truthfulness (see p. 40).

No-one, I think, would deny that Augustine's *Confessions*, like any autobiography, reflected the unique character and situation of its author, and this would certainly have included the sort of education he had acquired at school, as well as the effects of hindsight which separated him from the events he described. For this reason, it would be unprofitable and impossible to attempt to defend every individual detail of Augustine's *Confessions* on the basis of his general ethic of truthfulness. Nonetheless, the general ethic must be recognized, and it makes more sense to understand it within the context of his own overt statements about writing and about the nature of biblical truth, than to associate it with secular forms of literature about which he says much less and is broadly sceptical. The ethic that informs his writing, then, seems broadly similar to that expressed by (especially Christian) hagiographers (see p. 39); the principal difference is that he is somewhat more explicit in his views and in his reasons for holding them.

The literal truthfulness of Scripture; the allegorical potential of events and not just words; the applicability of biblical exegetics to his personal experience – these are all crucial aspects of Augustine's thought, and have already been described effectively, especially by Markus and Williams.[89] In combination, these views took Augustine one very small, and very logical step away from an extremely significant conviction: namely that the world was full of signs provided by God, who guided Christians in their interpretation of them. But what did this conviction equate to in the *Confessions* themselves? And how did it affect his stance towards not just remembered, but also immediate experience? Markus' arguments, drawn from theological treatises such as *De Doctrina Christiana*, are mainly theoretical and do not extend to a direct examination of Augustine's religious experiences. Williams, by contrast, applies the theory mainly to a single incident: namely Augustine's conversion in the Milan garden, an episode of paramount importance which we shall discuss extensively later. To understand how the value of truthfulness pervades the *Confessions* more broadly, we shall first examine two other well known episodes: the pear theft in Book 2 and the

---

[88]   Augustine, *De Civitate Dei* 18.18., eds Bernhard Dombart and Alfons Kalb, (5th edition, 2 vols, Stuttgart: Teubner, 1981).

[89]   'I am suggesting ... that habits of reading the biblical text had profound repercussions on the way Augustine read his world', Markus, *Signs and Meanings*, p. 29. In particular, he is right to highlight Augustine's insistence that figurative meanings were contained within literal events, ibid., p. 5.

departure from Carthage in Book 5. Both passages yield an important insight into Augustine's conviction that profound spiritual meanings resided in literal details. No less than in the case of third person hagiography, the *Confessions* take on the task of communicating this basic truth about reality.

Literal Truthfulness and Spiritual Meaning: The Pear Tree Incident (*Confessions* 2.4.9–10.18) and the Departure from Carthage (*Confessions* 5.8.14–15)

Throughout the long history of scholarship into Augustine's theft of pears as an adolescent, most research has concerned the incident's precise ideological meaning. It is, without doubt, a highly arresting vignette. In a text where moral change in any direction is usually treated subtly, the incident follows a period of fairly unambiguous moral decline. For the first eight chapters of Book 2, the author leaves no doubt that this moral decline was sexually focused. Against this backdrop, the raid on the orchard is presented as a moral nadir. The act was entirely futile: the boys were not hungry and ended up throwing most of the fruit to pigs. As Courcelle showed, what emerges is a brilliantly argued application of the principle that 'la gravité d'une faute réside non dans l'objet, mais dans l'intention'.[90]

Augustine seems to be fairly explicit about the moral status of the deed: it was worse than the crimes of Catiline whose cruellest acts could be said to have had the function, however twisted, of keeping his men practised in crime.[91] There has been much speculation amongst scholars about the meaning and relative significance of this classical parallel. In particular, was Augustine implicitly inviting a further comparison with the fruit theft in the Garden of Eden? The suggestion rests not only on the scene's physical setting but also on its moral message: since the act was entirely futile, it could only be explained as a wilful rebellion against God, evil for the sake of evil, or, following the Platonic schema, absolute non-existence.[92] The parallel has not been universally accepted.

---

[90]   Pierre Courcelle, 'Le jeune Augustin, second Catilina', *Revue des études anciennes* 73 (1971), p. 150. A view echoed by, amongst others, Scott MacDonald, 'Petit Larceny, the Beginning of all Sin: Augustine's Theft of the Pears' in W.E. Mann, *Augustine's* Confessions: *Critical Essays* (Oxford, 2006), pp. 48–9.

[91]   Augustine, *Confessions* 2.5.11, recalling Sallust, *Bellum Catilinae* 16.3, ed. A.T. Davis (London, 1967): 'scilicet, ne per otium torpescerent manus aut animus, gratuito potius malus atque crudelis erat'.

[92]   'But you, my theft ... Are you indeed anything at all, that I can address you in this way', Augustine, *Confessions* 2.6.12 (tr. Burton, p. 38).

Courcelle claimed that, if this was Augustine's intention, he would have depicted a theft of apples rather than of pears, mirroring the biblical story more closely and allowing a fortuitous play of words on *malum* (evil) and *mālum* (apple).[93] James J. O'Donnell, by contrast, regarded this objection as 'absurd', arguing that the analogy was clear enough anyway.[94] Revisiting the choice of fruit, Danuta Shanzer located further suggestive parallels in Horace and other Latin authors.[95]

This debate reveals much about the way in which modern scholars treat the relationship between the ideological and the literal. It is not merely that the extent of the episode's historicity is contested; rather, whatever literal truthfulness the passage contains is treated primarily as a function of its particular ideological significance, not as a moral obligation in its own right. Though ingenious, Shanzer's elaborate explanation for the fruit barely considers the straightforward possibility that Augustine chose pears because that was how he remembered the incident and felt obliged to record it accurately. Similarly, by assuming that apples were required, Courcelle effectively implies that an author wishing to draw this analogy would have no qualms about changing the literal truth of such a point of detail. O'Donnell is right to suggest that the parallel is clear enough with pears.

In any autobiography, there is undoubtedly a need for rigorous selectivity: only a tiny fraction of the mass of memory can be described. It is extremely likely, therefore, that Augustine recorded only those incidents he felt to contain the greatest spiritual and symbolic potential: the pear theft was one example. In fact, it is precisely the sense of profound spiritual significance in the literal which the passage strives hard to create as it recounts an incident which, on the face of it, was extremely mundane. Augustine's emphasis on the banal is, of course, entirely continuous with his biblically-inspired view of the Bible as an accurate record of spiritually pregnant but real events. As we have seen, the truthful recording of such events in the more recent past constituted the form of realism pursued by hagiographers; there is no reason to suppose that the same transcendental attitudes exerted any less of an influence on Augustine as he described his own life.

It is not merely that, in the search for the ideological meaning of the pear theft, the literal level of truthfulness has been understated; rather, its own ideological significance has also been overlooked. What has also been missed is how far the modern debate about the incident's meaning is anticipated by the text itself and, in a sense, contained within it. Augustine is fully aware that the

93   Courcelle, 'Le jeune Augustin, second Catilina', pp. 141–2.
94   James J. O'Donnell, *Commentary* vol. 2, p. 127.
95   Shanzer, 'Pears before Swine', pp. 45–55.

pear theft and, indeed, the rest of his adolescent behaviour, can be interpreted in different ways. Recalling the theme of the Prodigal Son introduced in the first book,[96] Augustine claims that the years in question saw him 'straying further and further from you'.[97] Given his age, this description may sound excessively harsh; after all, this seems to have been the attitude of his father who was far more concerned about his schooling than anything else.[98] His mother too, whilst frowning on his sexual adventures, also regarded his secular education as important and, revealingly, thought it might lead him deeper into Christian faith.[99] But Augustine's unconventionally harsh self-criticism stems from a recognition that the sin was more than the sum of any particular deeds; to sin habitually was to blind oneself to the workings of God that constantly surround us. Monica's warnings therefore 'seemed to me just women's words ... but they came from you, though in my ignorance I thought that you were silent, and it was my mother talking'.[100] Indeed the theme of spiritual ignorance is emphasized throughout the episode: on the one hand, '*the unseen Enemy* (*inimicus invisibilis*) was mocking me',[101] on the other, 'your anger was heavy upon me, *though I did not know it*'[102] (*et nesciebam*). Augustine clearly failed to see that his bad habits concealed a raging eschatological conflict, in which 'a dark cloud came between me and the clear skies of your truth'. The crisis was not only ethical, but also strongly epistemic in character.

The pear theft episode is constructed in such a way as to match this theme of moral ignorance with a profound indeterminacy. Augustine's extraordinary ethical judgement of the incident as absolute evil contrasts markedly with its banality and the fact that it was regarded at the time as 'fun and games'.[103] But there is a strong contrast too between the Catilinarian and the Eden comparisons and each works in an entirely different way: the former is overt, systematic and even includes possible linguistic echoes;[104] the latter is entirely implicit. Whilst the Catilinarian model appears to dominate, therefore, it does not contain the deepest message of the story. Ultimately, after all, it operates negatively, by

---

[96] Augustine, *Confessions* 1.18.28.

[97] Ibid. 2.2.2 (tr. Burton, p. 31).

[98] Ibid. 2.3.5.

[99] 'My mother thought ... that the usual course of studies would not only be no hindrance to my reaching you, but might even be a help', ibid. 2.3.8 (tr. Burton, p. 35).

[100] Ibid. 2.3.7 (tr. Burton, p. 34).

[101] Ibid. 2.3.8 (tr. Burton, p. 35).

[102] Ibid. 2.2.2 (tr. Burton, p. 31).

[103] Ibid. 2.9.17 (tr. Burton, p. 41).

[104] E.g. Augustine's friends, like Catiline's conspirators, are *adulescentuli*: Sallust, *The Catiline Conspiracy* 14.5, 18.4. See O'Donnell, *Commentary* vol. 2, pp. 129, 134.

informing us of the ways that Augustine's crimes were *not* like Catiline's, but worse. Augustine chooses to dwell on only one possible way of understanding the incident, namely through one of the core texts of Roman moralistic education; by doing so, he suggests that it is on this level that he himself has understood it.

The more oblique presentation of the Eden parallel plays a different rôle. Perhaps it contributes to the necessary sense of authenticity: by remaining unconfirmed, it appears unforced, and delegates the privilege of discovery to the reader. Perhaps the avoidance of an overt biblical comparison relates to the nature of the crime: in ethical, if not in temporal terms, it is a sin without precedent, the cause of original sin, itself spontaneous, explicable only as a perverse imitation of God himself.[105] An overt parallel could have undermined these connotations. But the primary reason for the silence concerns his spiritual status at the time, and ours as readers. What is provided is an instantiation in contemporary fact of the biblical idea discussed above: namely that spiritual meanings surround us in unexpected places, in apparently innocuous details. Given Christ's role as Inner Teacher, any failure to comprehend them necessarily implied, for Augustine, a spiritual deficiency.[106] By leaving unsaid the most obvious and significant level of meaning, Augustine both invites us to interpret and makes a corresponding statement of his own earlier ignorance: 'If my reader is one whom you have called ... let them not laugh at me as they read my account ... let them love you not less, but more.'[107]

The episode therefore exposes the wide range of ways in which relatively mundane events can be perceived spiritually. The most socially common way would be as a teenage peccadillo; the initially banal description makes this clear. But Augustine subsequently shows why this interpretation would be mistaken.[108] It could also be regarded as a case of theft, a breach of one of the Ten Commandments. But this would be only a partial, too legalistic, truth and obscure the act's essential pointlessness. When considering the question of intention, we could look to precedents in Roman history, and identify a cruelty that went beyond Catiline's. But if we are alert, we will see the deed for what it really was: pure, spontaneous evil, rebellion against God, absolute non-existence. To understand sin of this kind, and to learn to avoid it, we need not look in history books, or imagine dramatic eschatological events; we need only

---

[105] Augustine, *Confessions* 2.6.14.

[106] Matthews, 'Augustine on the Teacher Within', pp. 35, 41–2.

[107] Augustine, *Confessions* 2.7.15 (tr. Burton, p. 40). The possibility of such experiences, as well as the reasons why they vary from person to person, are discussed at *On Christian Doctrine*, Preface 16–19.

[108] 'Woe to you, river of human custom!' Augustine, *Confessions* 1.16.25 (tr. Burton, p. 21).

observe the world which permanently surrounds us, interpret it correctly, and see beyond its casual, deceptive surface. It was this critical spiritual capacity that Augustine's teenage sins had nullified. In suggesting, but omitting to confirm the Eden parallel, Augustine represents not only the spiritual significance of literal events, but also the variable epistemic condition of humankind in perceiving and interpreting them.

When Augustine leaves Carthage for Rome in Book 5, he appears to have come a long way since his teenage years. A successful professor of rhetoric, he has also largely extricated himself from an earlier involvement with Manichaeism. Furthermore, his motives for moving to Rome appear entirely respectable; it was not about the better wages, he claims, but simply a desire to teach quieter, more serious students.[109] But there is a deceptiveness in this respectability. His rant against the loutish students at Carthage culminates in the familiar theme of moral ignorance: 'the more these students did things your Law will never permit ... the more wretched they were ... they were being punished ... by the very blindness with which they did them'. But the complaint seems ironic: nothing reveals moral blindness more clearly than seeing faults in others sooner than in oneself. This may be the intended tone of his haughty pronouncement on his Carthaginian students: 'I now endured as a teacher the sort of behaviour I had rejected in myself.' The hypocrisy of Augustine's respectability is soon revealed by the heartless manner in which he leaves his mother on the African shore.

The literary model for this episode is clearly Aeneas' abandonment of Dido in Book 4 of the *Aeneid* – the same sea-route, an intimate man-woman relationship, a flurry of feminine grief. Furthermore, Augustine would later feel, as Aeneas had felt, that his journey was divinely sanctioned. The principal ideological aspects of this parallel are already widely known, thanks in part to an excellent article by Camille Bennett. But as Bennett shows, the Christian moral only becomes clear when the differences between the two stories are considered. There is no divine conflict in Augustine's story, no need for human tragedy. Unlike Dido, Monica does not throw herself onto a pyre, but returns, unclimactically, 'back to her usual life'.[110] Although her pleas for Augustine to stay are ignored, God is tending 'to her true wish' by bringing her son to Italy where he will eventually become a committed Christian. God's providence is invisibly controlling the entire situation for the benefit of all involved – an unseen arrangement much more loving and wonderful than the bitter destinies imposed by pagan gods. And such divine care clearly does not reflect Augustine's merit. In many ways, he is less deserving than Aeneas whose apparent cruelty sprang from an awareness

---

[109]   Ibid. 5.8.14.
[110]   Ibid. 5.8.15 (tr. Burton, p. 98).

of divine duty. Acting from purely human motivations, Augustine was ignorant of any such plan, and therefore had no excuse. The proof of God's omnipotence in this situation is that the selfishness of Augustine's motives is not a hindrance, but actually becomes a tool in his plan: 'At Carthage you wielded the stick that drove me out, and at Rome you set out the enticements that drew me on. This you did through human agency ... '[111]

One aspect of Bennett's argument is that Augustine himself may have been consciously influenced by Virgil's *Aeneid* both during this specific incident and in his life more generally.[112] Although the suggestion is made only in passing, it touches on an extremely significant point to which we shall later return. Nonetheless, it is important to recognize that premeditated imitation is not the core of Augustine's own message in this passage; rather, he emphasizes his own ignorance. An educated man who as a schoolboy memorized the wanderings of Aeneas and wept for Dido;[113] now a professor of rhetoric, for whom classic literature was a tool of the trade – to him of all people the moral relevance of the epic parallel should have been obvious. In fact, Augustine is no more capable of recognizing it than his hysterical mother, and both are blind to the gentle hand of God in the episode. However, what does not seem to have been recognized by Bennett and others[114] is that Augustine actively disguises his awareness of this deeper meaning. Here, as in the pear tree incident, there are no overt comparisons to the hypotext, no Virgilian verbal echoes of the type we might expect. The only archetype registered comes, again, from a less obvious, unexpected source: Monica's torments indicate 'the remnant of Eve':[115] a valid point, but one which continues to suggest an Augustine capable only of identifying faults in others.

The dynamic of the Virgilian universe is divine conflict: the gods and their human allies are split into camps. Furthermore, as Aeneas' departure shows, some of the human characters in the story are conscious of this conflict. The theology of Augustine's monotheistic universe is entirely different. There is no conflict, simply an invisible control, and the suffering has an essentially epistemic character springing from human ignorance of this control. The worldview on

---

[111]   Ibid. 5.8.14 (tr. Burton, p. 97).

[112]   According to her, a 'deliberate ... literary re-enactment it was at the time ... Augustine's allusions reflect ... a life shaped by imitation of the epic'. Camille Bennett, 'The Conversion of Vergil: The Aeneid in Augustine's *Confessions*', *REAug* 34 (1988), p. 61 and footnote 28. As its relegation to a footnote suggests, the point is not developed.

[113]   Augustine, *Confessions*, 1.13.20–21.

[114]   E.g. Sabine MacCormack, who merely notes that 'it was the story, and not merely the emotive vocabulary of the *Aeneid*, that left a sediment in the *Confessions*', *The Shadow of Poetry* (Berkeley, 1998), p. 97. The observation is correct, but unexplained.

[115]   Augustine, *Confessions* 5.8.15 (tr. Burton, p. 98).

which the passage rests is no different from that which applied to the pear tree incident: Augustine represents not just spiritual meaning but, starting with himself, the potential failure of humans to grasp it. To prove the point, he depicts a situation containing two entirely different meanings and shows how easily its surface details can deceive. What from one point of view echoes with symbolism is, from another, quite mundane. The journey from Carthage to Rome, for all its epic associations, was one of the most heavily-trafficked sea-lanes of the ancient Mediterranean; we may assume that tears on its dockside were a frequent occurrence. In a similar way, the busy shipping lanes of the English Channel might recall the Norman Conquest or D-Day, but could equally mean nothing more evocative than a daytrip for cheap alcohol. By emphasizing this shallower, literal level of association Augustine encourages us to scrutinize the surface of our world, to try and detect the silent workings of a God of whom, for all his learning, he was entirely ignorant.

Augustine in the Garden (*Confessions* 8.12.28–8.12.30)

The two close readings exemplify Augustine's belief that the profoundest spiritual meanings could reside in literal information; in this sense, they are consistent with his views of biblical history. There is every reason to suspect the same principles to have been equally relevant in the case of his conversion, which he almost certainly regarded as the most important episode in his life. As in these other cases, our analysis must attempt to describe the relationship between the literal and spiritual contents of the event. But the conversion scene differs in one important respect: whereas in the two episodes described above, Augustine remained ignorant of the event's deeper meaning, the conversion is the moment where he correctly and personally interprets God's message. Just as he previously had to represent his ignorance, he now had to explain why he was able to overcome it:

> I threw myself down at random on the ground (it happened to be beneath a fig tree) (*ego sub quadam fici arbore stravi me nescio quomodo*) and gave my tears free rein ... I felt myself held by those iniquities, and cried miserably: 'How long, how long, will this "tomorrow, tomorrow" continue? Why not "now"? Why do I not put an end to my shameful conduct from this hour forward?' ('*Quamdiu, quamdiu, "cras et cras"? Quare non modo? Quare non hac hora finis turpitudinis meae?*')
>
> Behold, suddenly I heard a voice from the house next door; the sound, as it might be, of a boy or a girl, repeating in a sing-song voice a refrain unknown to

me: 'Pick it up and read it, pick it up and read it.' Immediately my countenance was changed, and I began to ponder most intensely (*statimque ... intentissimus cogitare coepi*) whether children were in the habit of singing a chant of this sort as part of a game of some kind, but I had no recollection of having heard it anywhere (*nec occurrebat omnino audisse me uspiam*). I checked my outburst of tears and arose, taking this to be nothing other than a God-sent command that I should open the Bible and read the first chapter I found, whatever it might be.[116]

One very striking aspect of Augustine's conversion is that it poses no overt challenge to natural laws. In this respect, it differs from St Paul's conversion, to which it has often been compared.[117] There is no need to follow the sceptical outlook of Courcelle, who regarded the child's voice as a symbolic projection of the author's interior convictions. Instead, we may agree with Frederick J. Crosson that Augustine never questions the fact that real children were playing next door[118] – a position which, as we have argued above, is much more consistent with his general religious outlook. With this in mind, the reader can hardly avoid the impression that, on another day, Augustine might have heard the voice subconsciously, and ignored a noise in the background buzz of everyday life. It is certainly not the case God chose to speak on that day in a way he had not previously. A decade earlier, he had preached through Monica the same message of sexual continence, but Augustine had misread it as 'women's words' (see p. 134). Even the author's failure to recognize the song may indicate only that he had never before listened properly.

But listen he does: and Augustine is content to depict his spiritual state as an important factor in the conversion. Just as moral blindness had previously prevented him from hearing God's word, the right kind of spiritual progress now gives him clarity. The chapter leading to the garden scene describes this state in detail as one of dilemma. Edging towards a commitment to a new life, he was held back at the final stage by lingering temptation and memories of carnal pleasure.[119] He imagines this condition in quantitative terms: 'It was now much less than half my being that listened (to temptation).'[120] The attitudes which underpin this spiritual state are thoroughly Christian in nature: unprecedented emotion,[121] fear

---

[116] Augustine, *Confessions* 8.12.28–9 (tr. Burton), pp. 182–3.

[117] 'Suddenly a light from heaven flashed around him', Acts 9.25.

[118] Frederick J. Crosson, 'Structure and meaning in St. Augustine's *Confessions*', in Gareth B. Matthews (ed.), *The Augustinian Tradition* (Berkeley, 1999), p. 32.

[119] Augustine, *Confessions* 8.11.25.

[120] Ibid. 8.11.26 (tr. Burton, p. 180).

[121] Ibid. 8.11.27.

and shame,[122] 'a mighty storm of tears'.[123] In brief, a state of profound suffering (like, for example, the last hours of Christ), which culminate in words which appear very much his own, spontaneous, and uttered without artifice. It is in this state of submission and unaffected humility that Christ is most able to teach us. That Augustine had finally achieved this is partly reflected by the fact his words end in a series of questions, demanding, of course, answers. The commitment Augustine describes is not, therefore, fundamentally a question of willpower; even though the questions asked concern his own conduct, they recognize ultimate dependence on God's response. The significance of this perhaps only becomes clear when compared to the equivalent assumptions of classical philosophy: Augustine's state is the very opposite of a gradually and privately won *ataraxia*. The illusion of this state had already been exposed during his Platonist days, when he could 'patter away about these (divine) matters as if quite learned in them', and yet 'did not weep'[124] – an entirely different language from the desperate *cri de coeur* which now registers his readiness for full Christian conversion.

As with a significant number of hagiographical miracles, the conversion is defined as much by a certain epistemic stance as by a particular phenomenal threshold; this is an important truth of Augustine's own theology. Another aspect of the story which chimes deeply with his world view is the profound relationship it posits between the Bible and the wider phenomenal world. The life-changing teaching lies within the Bible, but it is an event in his immediate environment that makes him open the Bible in the first place. The reference to Antony points in the same direction: biblical words had inspired the saint, but through a real life experience.[125] The two modes of observation are structurally similar and mutually complementary. Whilst the Bible trains us to look at the world in the right way, events in the world help us to see biblical passages not as canonical quotations, but as living instructions communicated to us personally. The story illustrates the idea that the Bible, far from being remote from everyday life, is an immediately applicable paradigm of it.

The range of implications which flow from Augustine's moment of clarity is vast. For him and his circle, it clearly felt like peeping through a keyhole and glimpsing an unexpected landscape. Alypius, another tortured figure struggling with spiritual problems of his own, read the next passage ('*Welcome the weak in faith*' [Rom.14.1]) and, associating it with himself, also made a deeper Christian commitment. In keeping with the belief that biblical exegesis is ultimately a

---

[122]   Ibid. 8.11.25.

[123]   Ibid. 8.12.28 (tr. Burton, p. 181).

[124]   Ibid. 7.20.26 (tr. Burton, p. 155).

[125]   'In the middle of the Gospel reading, (he) had taken heed of what was being read as if it were addressed to himself', ibid. 8.12.29 (tr. Burton, p. 183).

matter of God-guided, but deeply individual conscience, it is Alypius himself who spontaneously offers this interpretation, and Augustine, whilst treating it benignly, neither confirms nor contests its validity.[126] But it is to Monica that a special role in the episode is accorded. After years of 'pitiable tears and groans'[127] God had not only fulfilled, but exceeded her prayers for her son's spiritual health. She had always discouraged loose sexual behaviour; now Augustine was finally ready to commit to a life of celibacy. The whole turbulent mother/son relationship now falls into place, hinting at deeper mysteries: God is shown to '*do more than we ask or understand*' (Rom. 14.1)[128]

If we accept that Augustine recorded his conversion in a general spirit of truthfulness, the question remains what, exactly, it tells us about the events themselves. The problem, again, is similar to that we encountered in the case of hagiographical narratives. The contention that such stories offered a richer historicity than is often assumed lay not merely in the desire of hagiographers to relate the truth, but also in the possibility of explaining their narratives as extensions and products of particular spiritual habits. In the same way, Augustine's account will seem more historically plausible if we can explain how and why the events occurred in the way he describes. We must, in other words, consider not just the stance of Augustine the author towards his past, which has been the overwhelming focus of scholarship to date, but a more neglected area: namely the relationship between the events of that day and the life he had led hitherto.

A very real possibility, I would suggest, is that the event gained the status it did because Augustine on some level expected it, following the principle (observed already in antiquity)[129] that those most eager for signs were most likely to experience them. Expectation, of course, is greatly enhanced by known models. Ever since St Paul, dramatic, divinely controlled conversion had loomed large in the Christian imagination, and it is significant that Augustine had been reading Paul just before entering the garden. As Philip Rousseau has

---

[126] As Gareth B. Matthews observes, man's ultimate dependence on Christ, as the teacher within, mean that all humans are, effectively, on their own in the world: 'Augustine on the Teacher Within', p. 35.

[127] Augustine, *Confessions* 8.12.30 (tr. Burton, p. 184).

[128] Ibid.

[129] Tacitus' account of a military disturbance on the German frontier, for example, brilliantly captures this phenomenon of mass, self-perpetuating superstition: 'so pliable to superstition are minds once unbalanced', – *Annales* 1, 28.1–2, eds Karl Halm, Georg Andresen and Erich Köstermann, *Tacitus* vol. 1, Bibliotheca Teubneriana (Leipzig, 1936). Translation by J. Jackson in *Tacitus: Annals I–III*, Loeb Classical Library (London/New York, 1931, reprinted 1992), p. 291.

observed,[130] more recent models of Christian conversion were also fresh in Augustine's mind: Marius Victorinus, whose example, the author admits, 'was the very thing that I was sighing for';[131] Ponticianus and his circle, in turn deeply touched by reading the *Life of Antony*.[132] In Williams's view, it was this last model which proved definitive: although as an educated man Augustine was closer to Marius Victorinus in background than he was to Antony, the opaque and mysterious nature of the aristocrat's conversion (which occurred 'suddenly and unexpectedly') made him an impossible model to follow.[133] The nature of his conversion makes it impossible to quantify the relative importance of these models and sentiments at the time. What we should appreciate, however, is that the conversion was not an alternative source of conviction. It provided no new information, it made him read a passage with which he was already familiar in a text he knew well and had been reading only moments before; the life he wished to lead was already fixed in his mind before he entered the garden. Although it does not necessarily follow from this that the episode itself was largely symbolic, we may nonetheless concur with Courcelle that the conversion was the product of 'longs débats intérieurs qui l'ont précédée'.[134]

Of course, the role of expectation only goes so far; it cannot of itself explain all the phenomena which contributed to the conversion, such as the highly symbolic fig tree, the fortuitous proximity of Scripture and, of course, the mysterious child's voice. A still greater problem facing an explanation based on expectation, however, is not the improbability of all the necessary components being present at the right time; after all, strange things do happen, and their uncanny coincidence can just as well be treated as part of the reason Augustine felt spoken to. Rather, it is to reconcile Augustine's expectations with his need to believe in the authentic, uncontrived nature of the events themselves for if these had been in doubt then it would have risked undermining its epiphanic potential.

The problem of authenticity has already been discussed in the context of the *fama* effect (see pp. 105–6). It was a concern recognized by Augustine who, even at the time of writing the *Confessions* conceded the temptation of asking God

---

[130]   The growth of asceticism amongst Westerners 'was heavily dependent on the availability of a religious literature', Philip Rousseau, *Ascetics, Authority and the Church in the Age of Jerome and Cassian* (Oxford, 1978), p. 93.

[131]   Augustine, *Confessions* 8.5.10 (tr. Burton, p. 168).

[132]   Ibid. 8.6.15.

[133]   Williams, *Authorised Lives*, pp. 157–64.

[134]   Pierre Courcelle, '"*Tolle, lege*", fiction littéraire et réalité' in *Recherches* (Paris, 1950), p. 201. This position is supported by Gillian Clark, *Augustine: the* Confessions (Bristol, 2005), p. 69.

for signs,[135] a sin akin putting the Lord to the test.[136] We might regard it as the ethical equivalent of relating the past untruthfully since both challenged God's autonomy over events. It is understandable therefore that his account stresses the incident's random, mundane nature: 'I threw myself down at random on the ground (it happened to be beneath a fig tree)' (*ego sub quadam fici arbore stravi me nescio quomodo*).[137] According to Williams, this use of indefinite pronouns and statements of uncertainty (both common throughout the *Confessions*) is one of a number of devices which indicate an ultimate agnosticism about the significance of his religious experiences.[138] In my view, it is more likely to have been an instance of the spontaneity principle, a way of reassuring the reader (and perhaps himself) that his own relationship with the events of that day was fundamentally naïve and unpremeditated. It is for this same reason that he insists on never having heard the child's song before. Rather than judgements made in retrospect, these may well have been the very criteria which allowed Augustine to take the incident seriously at the time. At least in this sense, his conversion, *pace* Williams,[139] indeed had its closest parallel in that of Marius Victorinus: the 'sudden and unexpected' nature of this great man's conversion was probably part of what made it seem religiously authentic, and therefore an appealing model. In the same way, the great significance he attributed to his encounters with the *Hortensius*[140] and Platonic books[141] owed much to the sudden, unexpected impact they had on him. If such spontaneity was a necessary aspect of conversion, it is hardly surprising that Augustine too should have required it when his own time came.

By arguing this, it is not necessary to go as far as to suggest that Augustine as an actor had absolutely no influence on the phenomena themselves; it is crucial to recognize, however, that any such influence must have been subtle enough not to disturb his absolute need for spontaneity. The description of his reaction to the child's voice contains at least hints of the sort of influence expectation could plausibly have exerted on the episode. The reaction is instantaneous,

---

[135] 'How many devices (the Enemy) deploys to get me to seek a sign from you!' *Confessions* 10.35.56 (tr. Burton, p. 249).

[136] Exodus 17.2, Deuteronomy 6.16, Psalms 78.18, Isaiah 7.10–12, Matthew 4.7, Luke 4.12, Acts 15.10, I Corinthians 10.9.

[137] Ibid. 8.12.28. Augustine's frequent use of indefinites has been noticed by J.J. O'Meara, 'Augustine's *Confessions*: Elements of Fiction', pp. 90–91. O'Meara plausibly argues that the device enhances emotion and sometimes takes on the quality of an incantation.

[138] Williams, *Authorised Lives*, p. 215.

[139] Ibid., pp. 157–8.

[140] Augustine, *Confessions* 3.4.7.

[141] Ibid. 7.9.13.

but the ablative phrase describing it demands attention: '*statimque mutato vultu intentissimus cogitare coepi*' (my italics).[142] Firstly, it leaves the question of agency ambiguous: who or what caused his face to change so suddenly? Secondly, it is interesting that, in the very moment which describes his mental turmoil, Augustine should consider his own external appearance, just as he remembered that of the fig tree or the wall; he was already conscious of himself as part of the picture. The description suggests a certain intellectual hastiness, an interpretation already present. This hastiness was not a question of speed *per se*; after all, Augustine claims to have pondered 'most intensely whether children were in the habit of singing a chant of this sort'.[143] Revealingly, however, the moment of certainty, and the resumption of tears, come from something much weaker than a fact, or even than the concrete belief they did not sing such songs; merely from his failure to recall 'having heard it anywhere'. Beyond this, no steps were taken to verify the incident's status. The only such step, in other words, was internal; one would be right, therefore, to suspect that what went on internally contains the real solution to the event's external appearance.

To put it another way, even if Augustine did not shape events actively, he could still have subtly moulded the whole episode through omission. Just how true this was is shown by one hitherto virtually unnoticed element of the episode which is perhaps so obvious that it is easy to ignore.[144] Augustine does not look over the wall. In terms of the author's psychology, the importance of this cannot be emphasized too strongly. For to anyone engaged in any other belief system, to anyone interested in the child's voice for any other reason, this (or some equivalent, such as going next door) would surely have been the most obvious act demanded by the situation.

There is a theological answer to the question of why he did not: Augustine was not interested in the child that produced the voice, only in the divine message it transmitted. As was shown by his ideas about biblical history, God was capable of communicating through any means, and in that sense the child's identity (age, gender etc.) was irrelevant. As long as he was genuinely being guided by God in his interpretation, there was no further need for, or indeed possibility of, verifying the incident. But this answer is incomplete. For, if Augustine was already certain that God had spoken, then the act of looking over the wall would not have constituted an attempt at verification in any case; he could have done so merely out of a benign, even pious curiosity; a proselytizing desire, perhaps, to

---

[142]   Augustine, *Confessions* 8.12.29 (ed. O'Donnell, vol. 1, p. 101).

[143]   Ibid. (tr. Burton, pp. 182–3).

[144]   The only exception seems to be Nicholas Wolterstoff who notes in passing that Augustine could have hurdled the wall to talk to the child: 'God's Speaking and Augustine's Conversion' in Mann (ed.), *Augustine's* Confessions: *Critical Essays* (Oxford, 2006), p. 166.

share with the child the importance of the moment in which he or she had just played an unwitting part. Anyone doubting the wall's significance should reflect that, from a strictly philosophical viewpoint, the same message could have been delivered through a visible child playing as Augustine passed in the street, but can we really imagine him attributing to these circumstances the same significance?

A more complex reason lies behind the omission. The child's voice could more easily be interpreted as a message from God if he did not look over the wall, and this *despite* the fact that, from a strictly philosophical perspective, the material details of the event in no way should have undermined its epiphanic potential. And from a historical viewpoint, this is perhaps what is most remarkable about the incident: that this very special moment in this very special place was not to be dwelt on; that the desired conclusion, once leapt to, had to be seized immediately and whole before any complicating details could threaten it. The rapid return indoors may have felt at the time, and been later remembered as, an excited rush; but it could have been as much an escape from the epiphany's extreme fragility.

On this reading, the wall played a crucial role in allowing the incident to acquire and retain the desired significance. It did this in a number of ways. Partly it was protective: by shielding the child, it suppressed all extraneous information; it ensured that the voice arose from an unknown. For a man like Augustine, as for many hagiographers (see p. 69), the tendency would always be to identify the unknown with a deeper kind of mystery. Since Augustine also took the idea of God speaking through people very seriously,[145] the complete suppression of the child's human identity made it much easier to identify him or her as such a vessel. More generally, the wall gave the whole episode an allegorical form which resembled his deepest, most general notions of reality. Suddenly, on one side was the sensible world; on the other, the simpler, divine realities that transcended it, and revealed themselves only occasionally, spontaneously, and in moments of genuine mystery. This does not necessarily mean, however, that the wall, or anything else that day, were symbols of a merely literary character. Rather, it may have been a mundane but perfectly positioned historical fact out of which Augustine, equipped with the necessary philosophical assumptions and *Interpretationswille*,[146] was able to mould a real event which he could regard as significant, and yet authentically beyond his control or understanding.

---

[145]   E.g. Augustine, *Confessions* 2.3.7, where Augustine claims God was talking through his mother. See also *On the Happy Life* 4.27; *On Order* 1.5.13, 1.10.28 (ed. J. Doignon, pp. 102, 140). For a general discussion, see Wolterstoff, 'God's Speaking and Augustine's Conversion', pp. 161–74.

[146]   To use Auerbach's phrase, 'Figura', p. 451.

Chapter 4
A Late Antique Spiritual Lifestyle?

Augustine at Cassiciacum

The reading of Augustine's *Confessions* offered in the previous chapter, which places expectation rather than retrospect at the heart of his conversion, confers a twofold advantage: it both preserves his strict commitment to truthfulness and also explains the incident's particular details with a specificity and hermeneutical sensitivity otherwise reserved for essentially literary interpretations. But beyond that day and beyond that garden, much remains to be answered. If a certain world view lent itself to certain spiritual experiences, if it made possible a certain way of life, then we should surely expect it to extend beyond a single incident. But if there were other events of this kind in which Augustine interpreted the world around him from a spiritual perspective, why did he not record them? If we cannot answer this question, then Augustine's spiritual outlook on the day of his conversion looks less like a way of life than a dispositional (and, at worst, one off) mood.

But there is another problem: doesn't the attribution of intense spiritual expectations to Augustine diminish him? To wait and ask for signs, to leap to spiritual conclusions, to use one's own conscience as the only ultimate yardstick of their validity – all this might easily suggest a rather superstitious, socially isolated, even delusional figure. Since such an eccentric outlook would seem hard to reconcile with the immense critical standards manifested in his writings it would, amongst other things, hardly serve the cause of historical plausibility. To be truly convincing, we need to show that Augustine's conversion was just one expression of a way of a life which adhered to a certain normality, not only in the sense that it was sustainable over time, but also in the sense that it fitted with the needs of others, and was, perhaps, shared by them.

It is with this in mind that we now turn to the Cassiciacum dialogues. As with the *Confessions* to which they have often been compared, considerable scholarly energy has been directed towards the historicity of these documents. Although they too contain assurances of truthfulness (such as the claim that a *notarius* was employed to record the conversations as they occurred[1]), it has

---

[1] Augustine, *Against the Academics* 1.1.4; *On Order* 1.2.5. Augustine also writes to his dedicatee Zenobius that there was 'no cause nor occasion for pretence' since everyone at Cassiciacum knew one another and Zenobius: *On Order* 2.10.28 (tr. J.J. O'Meara, pp. 306–7).

been somewhat easier to dismiss them in so far as, unlike the *Confessions*, they are not addressed to God,[2] but dedicated to prominent patrons: Romanianus, Zenobius and Manlius Theodorus.[3] This, combined with their strict literary form, has been seen by some as a source of historical doubt: like any *littérateur*, was Augustine really 'being himself' or was he adopting a role and fulfilling certain expectations? The question of historicity has sometimes come down to small, untestable details: was the *notarius* real or a literary conceit?[4] Do we believe that discussion continued throughout the night?[5] Are elements of the scene setting (such as changes in the weather) meant literally or allegorically?[6] Were the uncannily wise interventions of Augustine's uneducated mother genuine, or do they represent the case for Christian inclusivity?[7] Although grey areas may exist, the conclusion to any one of these enquiries can have a marginal effect on our view of the whole corpus: were the dialogues (more or less) genuine records, or (more or less) literary fictions?

In recent years a number of scholars have challenged the traditional view of the Cassiciacum dialogues as representations of an optimistic Christian Platonism,[8] and stressed instead elements of disillusionment with classical philosophy, and a correspondingly strong sense of the limitations of human reason compared

---

It is significant that, in his *Retractationes*, Augustine, whilst regretting some things, made no statement of regret about the historicity of any of the dialogues, and implies that things were recorded truthfully.

[2]   J.J. O'Meara dismisses all assurances to truthfulness in the dialogues as 'worthless': 'The Historicity of Augustine's early Dialogues', in *Studies in Augustine and Eriugena* (Washington, 1992), f. 7, p. 316. If we do accept that the dialogues involved a less ethically demanding mode, it is misleading to follow Courcelle in calling their autobiographical component (and that of other texts) *'premières confessions'*: Courcelle, 'Les premières *Confessions* de saint Augustin'.

[3]   For Augustine's relationship with his patrons, see Catherine Conybeare, *The Irrational Augustine* (Oxford, 2006), pp. 14–27.

[4]   An argument first made by Alfred Gudeman, 'Sind die Dialoge Augustins historisch?' in *Silvae Monacenses* (Munich, 1926), pp. 16–27; J.J. O'Meara, 'The Historicity of Augustine's early Dialogues', in *Studies in Augustine and Eriugena* (Washington, 1992), p. 18. The most forceful opposition to this view is made by Madec, 'L'historicité des *Dialogues* de Cassiciacum', pp. 217, 230.

[5]   Which J.J. O'Meara disputes: ibid., pp. 20–21.

[6]   McWilliam, 'The Cassiciacum Autobiography', *Studia Patristica* 18.4 (1990), p. 37. For Conybeare, the scene setting is a part of the dialogues' theatricality: *The Irrational Augustine*, pp. 44, 96.

[7]   Ibid., pp. 63–6.

[8]   Such as we find expressed, for example, by J.J. O'Meara, 'Augustine's *Confessions*: Elements of Fiction', p. 82.

to the power of Christian faith.[9] These considerations certainly minimize the ideological distance between the Cassiciacum dialogues and the *Confessions*, and suggest no more than different stages on the same intellectual journey. But this has done little to resolve the problem of historicity, partly because certain issues, such as the apparent conflict between the different accounts of his conversion, cannot be so easily dismissed. There is also a feeling in some quarters, perhaps, that the question of historicity is somewhat exhausted and unproductive, and that it is wiser simply to suspend judgement on the issue.[10]

Unlike recent important work by Conybeare which concentrates on the ideology of the dialogues, the analysis which follows focuses more narrowly on those narrative passages in which Augustine describes the occasion of the house party, and the events and personal interactions which took place during it. Their content will be analysed in such a way as to suggest a new area of textual compatibility with the *Confessions*. The reason for doing so is not simply to challenge one of the oldest arguments for doubting the historicity of the one or other source; more importantly, it aims to reveal a more general and, more normal way of life consistent with, and explicative of, Augustine's experience in the Milan garden. The dialogues supply this broader context in two ways. Firstly, they record events and discussions which occurred shortly after the conversion, thus extending the period of time under investigation. Secondly, they depict Augustine not alone but surrounded by friends and family and thus provide an initial opportunity to ask whether his attitudes were unusual and personal, or if they chimed with the needs and attitudes of others.

One crucial aspect of the Cassiciacum dialogues can only be understood if we treat them not just as texts but as the record of an event: namely how much

---

[9]   Courcelle's argument that Augustine's Neoplatonism came chiefly through his contact with Ambrose's Milanese Christianity already went a long way to reconciling the two bodies of work. Recent works which depict the Cassiciacum dialogues' commitment to philosophy as more nuanced include Dennis E. Trout, 'Augustine at Cassiciacum: *Otium Honestum* and the Social Dimensions of Conversion', *VC* 42 (1988), esp. p. 132ff.; McWilliam, 'The Cassiciacum Autobiography'; Carol Harrison, 'Augustine of Hippo's Cassiciacum *Confessions*: Towards a Reassessment of the 390's', *AS* 31.2 (2000); Conybeare, *The Irrational Augustine*, esp. p .2.

[10]   'We are hovering in a liminal space between writing and speaking, between fiction and reportage': Conybeare, *The Irrational Augustine*, p. 30. Similarly Gillian Clark on the *Confessions*: *Augustine: the* Confessions (Bristol, 2005), p. vii. When she claims to 'historicise' the work, she refers only to placing the work in its context, and not in assessing the accuracy of its claims. A short summary of Augustine's early life, based on the *Confessions* (pp. 8–32) precedes much longer sections about the text's nature. Only occasionally do questions of historicity re-emerge (eg. pp. 67–9), and then she pointedly reserves judgement.

expectation Augustine and his party brought to the experience.[11] In a broad sense, this was true of the whole practice of *otium* as a recognized intellectual endeavour stretching back centuries and enshrined in national literature.[12] It had an additional poignancy for fourth-century Christians who experimented with how to integrate this practice into that of ascetic retreat.[13] Undoubtedly, these various connotations applied at Cassiciacum. The texts' dialogic form is only the most obvious vestige of a frequently noted Ciceronian heritage;[14] Augustine was also keen to point out the religious nature of some of the disputations.[15] But these expectations did not just relate to the scope and nature of the activity; rather, they had a major personal component: 'Experience shows that when men of little importance apply themselves to great matters, these matters lend greatness to them'.[16] As argued earlier, expectations of this type were enhanced by known models: Manlius Theodorus was chosen as the addressee of *On the Happy Life* because, as a retiree from public affairs, he had shown how to play 'the role of a great man, of a real man' (*magni ... hominis personam atque ... veri hominis*).[17] The party had much to live up to.

There are a number of ways in which these considerations impact on the question of historicity. Firstly, the more we recognize the power of cultural and intellectual expectation at Cassiciacum, the less necessary it becomes to attribute any generic features to the act of literary production.[18] The most prominent example of this is the dialogic form which J.J. O'Meara[19] regarded as

---

[11]   A thorough analysis of Cassiciacum along these lines seems to be original. Trout is unusual in having at least posed the question of what Augustine expected from the retreat: 'Augustine at Cassiciacum: *Otium Honestum* and the Social Dimensions of Conversion', p. 136.

[12]   Good general introductions to this tradition and to the Christian response to it include Jacques Fontaine, 'Valeurs antiques et valeurs chrétiennes dans la spiritualité des grands propriétaires à la fin du IVe siècle occidental' in *Etudes sur la poésie latine tardive d'Ausone à Prudence* (Paris, 1980); Trout, 'Augustine at Cassiciacum: *Otium Honestum* and the Social Dimensions of Conversion', pp. 132–46.

[13]   See Rousseau, *Ascetics, Authority and the Church in the Age of Jerome and Cassian*, p. 94; Leyser, *Authority and Asceticism*, pp. 34, 144.

[14]   E.g. J.J. O'Meara, 'The Historicity of Augustine's early Dialogues', pp. 16–17; Conybeare, *The Irrational Augustine*, p. 3ff.

[15]   Augustine, *On the Happy Life* 1.5.

[16]   *Contra Academicos* 1.2.6, tr. John J. O'Meara, *Against the Academics* (Westminster, Maryland, 1951), p. 42.

[17]   Augustine, *On the Happy Life* 2.16, tr. Ludwig Schopp (London, 1939), p. 64. That the senator's example may have influenced the group is suggested by Trout, 'Augustine at Cassiciacum: *Otium Honestum* and the Social Dimensions of Conversion', p. 135.

[18]   As J.J. O'Meara assumes: 'The Historicity of Augustine's early Dialogues', pp. 16, 19.

[19]   Ibid., p. 16ff.

an artificial literary construct and, therefore, a reason for doubting the works' historicity. In a subtler vein, Conybeare argues that this form allows for a kind of 'staged realism ... in acute suspense between the real and the imaginary'.[20] It is, of course, a question of balance: it would be foolish to deny that an element of redaction into a readable form took place, just as J.J. O'Meara and Conybeare do not deny that the works are loosely based on some sort of event.[21] What needs to be challenged, however, is the deep and widespread assumption that literary genre and historicity necessarily constitute an oppositional dichotomy. A more satisfactory explanation is that a certain mode of expression was expected and used because it was considered appropriate to a very recognizable cultural situation. This view is supported by Augustine's admission that this particular form of discussion was a discipline he imposed on the group,[22] and one which caused a certain 'carefuleness of expression'.[23] To draw a contemporary parallel, it is common for scholars of a particular academic discipline to communicate to one another using a vocabulary and conventions equally attested in their writings. This mode of linguistic expression is neither surprising, nor is it considered artificial just because they may talk to their friends and families in a different register.

The controversial presence of a *notarius* should probably be treated in the same way: not as a further artifice of the genre,[24] but as an entirely plausible arrangement, explained by the group's desire to carry out an activity, and not

---

[20]   Conybeare, *The Irrational Augustine*, p. 49. See also pp. 30, 59–63. Although Conybeare sees the dialogue form as less restrictive than O'Meara she still maintains that its use is determined by a certain intellectual function – namely, it aims at a certain ambiguity.

[21]   J.J. O'Meara, 'The Historicity of Augustine's early Dialogues', pp. 22–3; ibid., *The Young Augustine* (London, 1954), p. 193. Conybeare thinks, for example, that the roster of characters may be real: *The Irrational Augustine*, p. 48. By contrast, even those supportive of the dialogues' historicity have conceded a certain editorial rewriting: André Mandouze, *Saint Augustin. L'aventure de la raison et de la grâce* (Paris, 1968), pp. 130–31; J. Doignon, Introduction to *Augustine: De Beata Vita* (*La vie heureuse*) (Paris, 1997), pp. 22–3.

[22]   Augustine, *Against the Academics* 1.3.8; *On Order* 1.10.30.

[23]   'nonnulla loquendi cura': ibid. 1.2.5.

[24]   As J.J. O'Meara assumes: 'The Historicity of Augustine's early Dialogues', pp. 17–18. This aspect of O'Meara's argument seems to me particularly weak. It may or may not be the case that assurances of note taking in Plato's *Epinomis* and other works are fictitious, but the argument that the reference to the *notarius* follows in this line would be only really convincing if we could show that Augustine recognized earlier such assurances as a literary conceit – something O'Meara does not consider. Furthermore, to defend his argument on the basis that 'record taking was very common in the fourth century AD' is very strange – why does this make the *notarius* a 'plausible fiction' and not, quite simply, plausible? The more common sense position is argued by B.L. Meulenbroek, 'The Historical Character of

merely produce a text, in the correct way.[25] But the deeper historical significance of the *notarius* is not just that it makes the texts more accurate as records; rather, the participants' awareness of his very presence has a concrete impact on their conversation and behaviour, such as by making the young men compete with one another.[26] It is partly because their words are constantly and irrevocably becoming text that the many narrative expectations characteristic of the situation remain constantly present. If, to adapt Conybeare's phrase, this staged reality is a 'cumbersome construction',[27] if it indeed hovers between fiction and reportage,[28] then this may be true in a second sense: namely that the dialogues are not a derivative version of the group's intellectual activity, but that the activity itself bore the heavy imprint of textual influences and expectations. Indeed, these expectations become, in a sense, the primary reality against which the conversation must be measured; the question 'are we fulfilling them?' can never be evaded. At one point, having floundered in his reasoning, Licentius asks for the record to be altered.[29] His objection is not that the *notarius* has recorded inaccurately, but nor is it merely a statement of regret ('I should not have said that'). Rather, the urgent indicative ('non dixi, inquit exclamans'[30]) is almost a denial that an ideal has momentarily been betrayed.

We should not think of this ideal as purely cultural at Cassiciacum: there was a sense of proximity not just to recognized intellectual norms, but to profound spiritual truths; the feeling of participation was extremely personal. The problems discussed were not the only objects of thought: rather like a hagiographer observing the soul from a distance, Augustine scrutinized his companions' states of minds intensively as they talked; the possibility that God was talking, or could be talking, through and to members of the party was tantalizingly shared.[31] How highly-charged this religious atmosphere could be is

---

Augustine's Cassiciacum dialogues', *Mnemosyne* 13.3 (1947); Mandouze, *Saint Augustin. L'aventure de la raison et de la grâce*, pp. 130–31.

[25]   As argued in particular by Madec, 'L'historicité des *Dialogues* de Cassiciacum', who convincingly contends that this and other formal qualities belonged to the *règles du jeu* of a classical retreat, p. 230.

[26]   Augustine, *Against the Academics* 1.3.8; *On Order* 1.10.29–30.

[27]   Conybeare, *The Irrational Augustine*, p. 58.

[28]   Ibid., p. 30.

[29]   Augustine, *On the Happy Life* 2.15.

[30]   Ibid.

[31]   Sometimes this may seem like a very general point about human comprehension, eg. Augustine, *On the Happy Life* 4.35 (tr. Schopp, p. 83): 'this hidden sun pours into our innermost eyes that beaming light. He is all the truth that we speak.' Much more personal, however are the direct and individual attributions of divine *inflammatio* to Monica: *On Order* 2.1.1, p. 27; *On the Happy Life* 4.35. Her special ability is confirmed at *Confessions*

further revealed by a fascinating passage in *On Order*.[32] As dawn broke after a late night discussion about God's ordering of the universe, Licentius claims to have been suddenly overcome by a feeling of disinterest in the poetic arts to which he had given too much attention, and by a corresponding enthusiasm for the much greater beauty of Philosophy. After tearfully sharing the emotion of the moment with the group, Licentius declares himself amazed by 'how reluctantly' (*tam aegre*)[33] he has been drawn away from poetic trifles, and 'borne above to things great and marvellous. In very truth, is this not a conversion to God?'

Conybeare is right to identify the general similarity between this event and Augustine's conversion in the Milan garden.[34] But these similarities are worth elaborating in depth. The event takes place in an atmosphere of high emotional religiosity, and one tearfully shared by the group. Also important are expectations. On a general level, it is probable that some of the same conversion models which had informed Augustine (as well, perhaps, as Augustine's own) now impacted on Licentius. More immediately, the Psalm sung in celebration ('O Lord God of Hosts, convert us'[35]), was one Licentius had been singing incessantly the previous day. There is both an internal and an external component: the dawn furnishes an allegorical atmosphere,[36] but like Augustine in the garden, Licentius has to believe that his dramatic mood change was beyond his control.

So Augustine's garden conversion was not entirely unique. But the historical importance of Licentius' conversion is not merely in revealing what elements constituted such an event; it also gives us, against the backdrop of the house party, some sense of the context that enabled them to occur. Licentius' conversion was merely one of the most deeply felt moments, but the hand of God was detected in many other places.

Rather than simply listing these events, it is best to analyse them philosophically as products of the world view which they exemplify. We do not have to content ourselves with general observations about the subjectivity of religious experience; rather, we should recognize how far Augustine's world view

---

6.13.23 (pp. 28–9). Still more powerful is the case of the boys. Imagine the intensity of introspection unleashed in the young Trygetius upon being told, during a philosophical discussion, that he was *nearly* the herald of God! – *On Order*, 1.5.13. Licentius is clearly caught by the mood: when considering the possibility of divine inspiration he admits, 'Aut fortasse ... aliquid mecum est', *On Order* 1.10.28.

[32] Ibid. 1.8.21.
[33] Ibid. 1.8.23.
[34] Conybeare, *The Irrational Augustine*, p. 98.
[35] Psalms 79.8.
[36] McWilliam, 'The Cassiciacum Autobiography', p. 37ff; Conybeare, *The Irrational Augustine*, p. 96, foonote 7.

and that of his charges made such subjectivity both respectable and inevitable. After an introduction, *On Order* begins with Augustine and his companions waking to hear the strange sound of running water on the stones outside, mysteriously rising and falling in volume;[37] Licentius observes that there must be a hidden order governing everything, of which human beings catch only occasional glimpses.[38] Within human life, such order had a narrative form; the very fact that the group woke to hear the water at all, enabling the discussion to take place, could be regarded as a glimpse of such an order.[39] Since nothing belonged outside this order, any event could, according to Licentius' extreme expression of these instincts, become a candidate for some sort of spiritual interpretation.

Licentius' conversion, which occurred at dawn shortly after this conversation, can legitimately be regarded as an expression of this world view. Scholars have been right to identify the allegorical pregnancy of the dawn, but wrong to assume that this necessarily constitutes a literary device on Augustine's part. If, for us as readers, 'it is hard to resist a symbolic reading of this timing,'[40] it probably struck Licentius (with all his expectations and sensitivities) that way too. The same may be true of the early morning cockerel fight: why should we not treat it is as a real event, whose spiritual significance was equally irresistible to witnesses?[41] What strikes one most of all about such events is not just their plausibility, but also how much the identification and interpretation of them was consistent with perfectly normal observational and conversational habits. At the most minimal level, there were mere humorous comparisons: don't think you can get away with a Tuscan argument just because you're on a farm![42] Other analogies were more ambiguous: when the rich birthday meal is compared to a rich spiritual feast,[43] when the bright weather inspires the group to brighten up their minds,[44] are these mere pleasantries or do they have a genuine spiritual meaning? The difficulty in answering this question is precisely the point: Augustine's perception and discussion of events, like those of most people, are

---

[37]   Augustine, *On Order* 1.3.6.

[38]   Ibid. 1.2.5 (pp. 88–90).

[39]   Ibid. 1.5.14 (p. 104).

[40]   Conybeare, *The Irrational Augustine*, p. 96, footnote 7.

[41]   As a symbol of hope: *On Order* 1.8.25. The symbolic potential (but not the historical plausibility) of the event is recognized by J. McWilliam, 'The Cassiciacum Autobiography', p. 37ff.

[42]   Augustine, *Against the Academics* 3.4.9.

[43]   Augustine, *On the Happy Life* 2.9.

[44]   Augustine, *Against the Academics* 2.4.10.

full of metaphors of many different kinds;[45] what marked him and his party out was the relatively high frequency with which he detected in such metaphors not only personal ingenuity but deeper spiritual truths. Cassiciacum reveals, therefore, that those of a certain mindset were bound to encounter spiritually significant events because, in their eyes, so many otherwise ordinary events could be perceived as spiritually significant.

Augustine's world view leant itself to interpretation in one further way. No less than the hagiographers with whom he shared a basic transcendental world view, Augustine was constantly confronted with the ambiguity of the phenomenal world, whose relationship to higher realities could variously be regarded as one either of opposition or of dependence (see pp. 45–6). Where the spiritual interpretation of individual phenomena was under consideration, this fundamental philosophical problem represented an opportunity of sorts: events could symbolize either aspect of the relationship. In philosophical terms, the problem Licentius encountered whilst praying on the toilet was analogous to that faced by, for example, Neoplatonic philosophers when describing their subjects' physical appearances. The day before the conversion, the question had been whether it was an inappropriate place for prayer (as Monica complained), or merely a matter of complete indifference: Licentius was sure God would hear his voice even if an enemy locked him in![46] On the next day, and from a different viewpoint, it had become an appropriate symbol of the physical depths (specifically, those of the human body) from which God rescues us.[47] Precisely in its distance from God it had become symbolic of that distance.[48] The mood had changed from humorous to intense, and within this vision of the world a new, indeed, opposing, interpretation of the event could easily be found to suit it.

Despite the heavy weight of expectation behind it, the external aspect of Licentius' conversion is clearly less prominent and less extraordinary than that

---

[45]   The most celebrated expression of this observation is the classic work of George Lakoff and Mark Johnson, *Metaphors We Live By* (Chicago, 1980). One of their central contentions, which is highly applicable here, is that metaphors are not merely linguistic phenomena, but condition the way humans structure their conceptual system of the world: ibid., p. 145.

[46]   Augustine, *On Order* 1.8.22.

[47]   'From what indeed do you think we pray to be converted to God ... if not from a certain uncleanness of the body and its stains?' Augustine, *On Order* 1.8.23, tr. Robert P. Russell (London, 1939), p. 260.

[48]   Similarly, Monica's burial in Italy rather than in Africa with her husband at *Confessions* 9.11.28 (tr. Burton, p. 206): her acceptance of this ('nothing is far from God') effectively expressed the awareness of the fundamental opposition between this world and the next: space is spiritually irrelevant. But, in a curious way, the location of her burial place becomes symbolic of that very irrelevance, and of her acceptance of it.

of Augustine in the Milan garden. Nonetheless, the young man is still bold in attributing major spiritual significance to a strong internal feeling. Part of the legitimacy for this claim rested on his recognition that the origin of an individual's thoughts, no less than the external phenomena around him, were ultimately mysterious;[49] to put it in the words of the *Confessions*, God knows us better than we know ourselves.[50] Seen from this perspective, even thoughts could become candidates for spiritual interpretation. Most famously, the group is united in treating Monica's thoughts as divinely inspired in this way.

The Cassiciacum dialogues thus suggest that Augustine's conversion took place within a very wide, and very rich, field of spiritual experience, and one entirely compatible with certain aspects of a world view he shared with others. But with this in mind, the most relevant question is not how such experiences could be justified, but how they could be delimited. For Augustine was aware of the risk that spiritual interpretations could be mistaken, overhasty and indiscriminate. Later, in *On Christian Doctrine*, he would address this problem in relation to biblical exegesis.[51] But, as with other issues, there is no reason to think that the problems posed by sensible reality were any different, except in so far as biblical history offered the advantage that its constituent events, at least, were already contained within, and delimited by, the sacred text.

Thus a major part of the way of life to which both the Cassiciacum dialogues and the *Confessions* attest is a process of spiritual discrimination. There was an urgent and immediate need to distinguish God's intention from the individual's own will, by identifying events definitively outside the latter's control, events that could fulfil the strict requirement of the spontaneity principle. We have seen how, in the garden, it was crucial to the validity of Augustine's interpretation that he had never before heard the child's song.[52] This is why Licentius' definition of conversion ('to uplift oneself wholeheartedly by virtue and temperance from the excess of vices'[53]) is an incomplete description: Augustine did not just need an accumulation of the necessary convictions, but a narrative sense in which

---

49   Augustine, *On Order* 1.5.14.

50   A thought expressed by Augustine at *Confessions* 1.6.9, 10.1.1, 10.5.7, 11.31.41.

51   *On Christian Doctrine* 2.18–20. For a discussion of how Augustine attempted to limit biblical exegesis, see Philip Rollinson, *Classical Theories of Allegory and Christian Culture* (London, 1981), pp. 44–8.

52   This applied to Neoplatonists as well as Christians, and for similar philosophical reasons. On the way to the city, part of the reason the reader can be sure that Proclus' sudden thirst near the Socrateum was an omen was precisely because 'he had not yet learned or heard that honours were paid to Socrates anywhere'. Marinus, *Life of Proclus* 10 (tr. Edwards, p. 71). See pp. 59–60.

53   Augustine, *On Order* 1.8.23 (tr. Russell, p. 260).

something had happened *to* him. Crucially, however, Licentius' description does not fully apply even to his own case. In the absence of external phenomena, the strength and strangeness of internal convictions needed to display an equivalent authenticity. How could one know if a certain thought came from God? How could one know if the voice of Reason one heard was coming from inside or outside (the question with which Augustine opened the *Soliloquia*)?[54] Monica, when faced with this problem, relied on a taste 'not explicable in words'[55] – this inexplicability, the fact it tasted like nothing else, was crucial to its authenticity. Similarly Licentius: however intense the spiritual expectations he brought to Cassiciacum, he still needed to believe that he had been drawn away from poetry 'reluctantly': by something, in other words, definitively beyond his control.

Memory, as well as its counterpart, forgetting, also had a major role to play in spiritual discrimination. The same mind that could look back over years and identify the pear tree incident, or the voyage to Italy, as symbolically significant, was also (and necessarily) capable of judging, and forgetting, many other less spiritually rich incidents, including, perhaps, ones whose authenticity had felt less than definitive at the time.[56] But the recognition of memory's role in no way negates the crucial contention about expectation. Not only were the two faculties subject to the same philosophical prejudices, they were also capable of working together in very practical ways.

Indeed, Augustine himself describes the mutual co-operation of memory and expectation in his description of poetry recitation at *Confessions* 11.28.38; he made it clear that these theoretical principles applied to any experience of time, from the individual syllables of a poem, to the living of a human life, or even the whole generation of humanity.[57] Continuing with this metaphor, we may add a further comment. A polished poetry recitation will convey a feeling of unexpectedness, though, paradoxically, this may be achieved precisely through practice and subsequent familiarity. We have argued that familiarity and practice were crucial to sustaining the authentic, biblically-rooted identity of the monastic community on the 'desert' island of Lérins (see p. 102). A similar point can be applied to the spiritual life led by Augustine. As with the rehearsal of a performance, the ability to forget mistakes was also the ability to continue practising. The long build-up to Augustine's conversion did not consist merely in

---

[54]   'ait mihi subito sive ego ispe sive alius quis, extrinsecus sive intrinsecus, nescio; nam hoc ipsum est quod magnopere scire molior', Augustine, *Soliloquies* 1.1 (ed. G. Watson, p. 22).

[55]   Augustine, *Confessions* 6.13.23 (tr. Burton, pp. 28–9).

[56]   A view close to that of Bonner, 'Augustine's Conversion: Historical Fact or Literary Device?', pp. 112–14.

[57]   Augustine, *Confessions* 11.28.38.

introspection;[58] rather, it was the summit of a mountain of comparable spiritual experiences hinted at elsewhere both in the *Confessions* and Cassiciacum dialogues. The 'definite landmark' he had long wished for may well have been imagined as a sign of this sort.[59] By the time it finally arrived, Augustine hints at the frustration caused by such waiting.[60] It is important to recognize, therefore, that the impressive constellation of phenomena which constituted the episode was possible only through enormous patience. That such patience should prove tireless was partly because (to borrow Karl Popper's terminology) there was no conceivable alternative principle capable of refuting his expectations; no number of less successful occasions could have falsified the hypothesis that God did speak through events, and would eventually speak to him personally and definitively in this way.[61] At most, any lack of success merely indicated the temporary un-preparedness of his soul, and could, in time, be forgotten.

The Cassiciacum dialogues support this picture by revealing not only how wide the field was from which spiritual experiences were drawn, but also how naturally they could be hierarchized. As we stated above, spiritual scrutiny of the world involved the use of quite normal observational and conversational habits. Just as our regular use of metaphors and the like involve varying degrees of complexity and commitment, so too did the party's corresponding spiritual scrutiny yield different grades of experience. The mere peaceful feeling of sitting in the meadow beneath the group's favourite tree probably contributed something to the atmosphere; Augustine's excitement at feeling the boys grasp a complex point was no doubt more intense;[62] Licentius' conversion, or the symbolic cock-fight, obviously represented some of the most memorable moments of the retreat.

Amongst those who have stressed the subjective nature of personal narrative, there has, perhaps, been a tendency to focus excessively on the effects of hindsight. But as Alisdair MacIntyre argues, 'we all live out narratives in our lives and … we understand our own lives in terms of the narratives we live out'.[63] In

---

[58]   *Pace* Courcelle, "'*Tolle, lege*', fiction littéraire et réalité' in *Recherches* (Paris, 1950), p. 201; Gillian Clark, *Augustine: the* Confessions (Bristol, 2005), p. 69.

[59]   Augustine, *Confessions* 5.14.25 (tr. Burton, p. 105).

[60]   'I was postponing from day to day the decision to despise my worldly hope and follow you alone on the grounds that no certain landmark had emerged': Ibid. 8.7.18 (tr. Burton, p. 174).

[61]   For a summary of his views, see Karl Popper, *Science: Conjectures and Refutations* in M. Curd, J.A. Cover (eds), *Philosophy of Science: the Central Issues* (New York, 1988), pp. 3–10.

[62]   Augustine, *On Order* 1.3.8.

[63]   Alisdair MacIntyre, *After Virtue*, pp. 211,214. A similar (if differently motivated) argument about the centrality of narrative to human experience is provided by the

this sense, memory can be seen as a perfectly compatible extension of practices regularly and immediately brought to bear on personal experience. Focusing like other scholars on Augustine's retrospective position, Paula Frederiksen argued that conversion accounts are likely to accord to culturally recognized models.[64] We may extend her point into the realm of expectation: both Cassiciacum and the *Confessions* also show just how much the scrutiny and hierarchization of spiritual experience contained a social component. This was clearly true on a general cultural and intellectual level. Spiritual experience was guided by agreed religious and philosophical symbols. A young Neoplatonist might have had equally good philosophical reasons to treat the instruction *tolle, lege* as spiritually significant, but he would have reached for other sacred texts; he may have been struck not by the fig tree, but by another feature of the garden with a different symbolic significance.

But spiritual scrutiny involved a more immediate social component, and this component was a major element in making it not just philosophically justifiable, but a practical and sustainable way of life. Even before his conversion, Augustine had been living in a small, spiritually-committed community.[65] Significant moments, such as the group's discovery of the *Life of Antony*, were heavily shaped by consensus.[66] To extend the method of thought experiment employed above, would Augustine have attributed to his conversion the same significance had his mother and Alypius not also treated it with such immediate excitement? Shared tears immediately supported Augustine's interpretation, just as they sometimes did at Cassiciacum.[67] The spiritual aspirations and expectations brought to the house party were able to reach a high level of personal intensiveness partly by virtue of being collective, shared, and mutual: an observation which is both psychologically persuasive and thoroughly in keeping with Augustine's sense of Christian community.[68] Monica's *inflammatio*, so important in making the case

---

philosopher Daniel C. Dennett, *Consciousness Explained* (Boston/London, 1991), p. 418: 'Our tales are spun, but for the most part we don't spin them; they spin us.'

[64] Frederiksen, 'Paul and Augustine Conversion Narratives, Orthodox Traditions and the Retrospective Self', p. 33.

[65] Augustine, *Confessions* 6.14.24.

[66] Ibid. 8.6.14–15 (pp. 171–3). Ponticianus, who introduced them to the work had had a similar experience; his initial reaction to the work was instantly reflected by his companion who resolved to 'stand by him and share with him in this great reward and great service'.

[67] Augustine, *Against the Academics* 2.7.18.

[68] 'R: Why do you want those people whom you love either to live at all or to live with you? A: So that we may together, with one mind, seek to know our souls and God. For in that way anyone who is the first to discover something can easily lead the others to that same point.' *Soliloquies* 1.12.20 (tr. G. Watson, p. 53).

for Christian inclusivity, is made more plausible by an enthusiastic consensus.[69] This social explanation does not detract from Augustine's firm conviction that the ultimate spiritual yardstick was internal: as long as God spoke through people – and this is a theme also emphasized in the *Confessions*[70] – then the two sources of support would run together. Augustine did not need to be socially isolated to hear the voice of God.

How crucial such mutual support was is indicated by one central difference between the two conversions which has not yet been mentioned: unlike his own, Augustine treats that of Licentius with a benign, but measured, enthusiasm.[71] The nature of spiritual experience meant that, under scrutiny, any individual event could be significant, but could equally be controversial. This was particularly true of conversion whose ultimate Pauline model imposed strong and unusually rigid narrative expectations: it had to be a definitive, and unique moment within each Christian life. As a result, it required an especially judicious response. Licentius was sincere but young and enthusiastic[72] and the event lacked the definitive autonomy of the child's voice. How could Augustine be sure whether or not it was a genuine conversion? He needed to wait and see. Perhaps, at this stage, he was not yet sure whether his own conversion met these strict criteria: with consensus and conscience still forming, he was not yet ready to declare his position publicly. This would at least partly explain why the Cassiciacum dialogues describe the physical circumstances of his conversion more obliquely. As for Licentius, he received, around a decade after Cassiciacum, a letter from Paulinus of Nola, still urging him to 'break loose from delay and the confining bonds of the world'.[73] Perhaps Augustine's reservations about his conversion had been right; perhaps, alternatively, it was his failure to provide unambiguous validation that prevented that day from becoming the definitive turning point.

Although the events covered by the Cassiciacum dialogues and the *Confessions* differ, they should not be seen as contradictory accounts. Rather, they represent different grades of the same type of experience; the way of life

---

[69] 'Nihil verius, nihil divinius dici potuit': Augustine, *On the Happy Life* 4.27; *On Order* 1.11.32.

[70] Such as Monica's special taste: *Confessions* 6.13.23. See Wolterstoff, 'God's Speaking and Augustine's Conversion', pp. 161–74.

[71] Augustine, *On Order* 1.8.24. For this measured enthusiasm, see Conybeare, *The Irrational Augustine*, pp. 97–8.

[72] A similarly cautious line is taken by Augustine when discussing the case of a particular girl still too young to know if she really wants to become a nun, and whose expressed wishes may yet prove to be 'the light whim of a chatterer': *Letter 254* (tr. Parsons, vol. 5, p. 246).

[73] Paulinus of Nola, *Epistula* 8.3, ed. W.A. Hartel, CSEL 29 (Vienna, 1894, reprinted 1999), tr. P.G. Walsh, *Letters of Saint Paulinus of Nola* (London:, 1967), vol. 1, p. 78.

more closely revealed during the house party is precisely the sort of fertile soil capable of yielding moments such as Augustine's conversion.

Despite the exceptional expectations surrounding conversion as an idea, it is this regular, lower level of spiritual scrutiny, that tells us more about Augustine's way of life, and about that of his entourage. We should not think of Licentius' conversion as a failure simply because it did not culminate in a definitive conclusion. Even if it had, the Cassiciacum dialogues, written as they were after Augustine's conversion, show that the need for spiritual scrutiny was never satisfied, even after the most dramatic incidents. This shows us why Augustine's way of life, once embarked upon, proved so sustainable. What lay at its heart, and what confession corresponded to, was the belief that human life was, and had to remain, mysterious. The conclusion of any gain in knowledge was always further mystery. Even the message of the Milan garden was, ultimately, that God 'can do more than we ask or understand'.[74] The *Confessions* clearly contain the sense that a narrative whole exists, but equally the sense that knowledge of this whole lies with God alone. Seen from this perspective, mystery did not dissuade belief but encouraged it. Whether ultimately remembered or not, Licentius' conversion, like almost all spiritually pregnant incidents, would be felt, analysed in terms of certain beliefs, and then used to justify further searching of the same type.

Augustine, in other words, was not merely an interpreter, but an actor whose behaviour sustained his vision of the world. This point is of interest not least when addressing the debate about the text's structure. Many scholars have noted the parallelism between Augustine's physical journeys, especially from Africa to Italy and back, and the exile and return of his soul. The parallel seems too striking and obvious to ignore, yet any account of the *Confessions* which delineates too precise a relationship may be attacked as artificial, not least because of the improbability of deliberate retrospective distortion for allegorical purposes. An indication of this dilemma can be found in a paper by Leo Ferrari: unable to overlook the comparison, yet unsure of its meaning and wary of exaggerating its importance, his subsequent middle position ends up merely non-committal.[75]

One possible solution is to recognize the uncertainty in the secondary literature as nothing other than a projection and consequence of Augustine's own world view, an outlook profoundly tolerant of mystery. Part of the reason Augustine is able both to suggest the comparison, and to leave its significance

---

[74]   Augustine, *Confessions* 8.12.10 (tr. Burton, p. 184).

[75]   Simply calling the prodigal son parallel 'a general similarity' hardly resolves the problem: Leo Ferrari, 'The theme of the Prodigal Son in Augustine's *Confessions*', in *RA* 12 (1977), p. 105. His analysis of garden imagery is vulnerable to the same criticism: 'Truth and Augustine's Conversion Scene', in C. Schnaubelt and F. Van Fleteren (eds), *Collecteana Augustiniana* (New York, 1990), p. 144.

unconfirmed has to do with the habit of delegating interpretative responsibility to the reader. But it is entirely in keeping with his mindset that the suspicion of his journey's spiritual significance was felt not merely in hindsight, but was one that, from time to time, informed and motivated him even as he underwent it, as he tried to give spiritual significance to his external life at the time. In this sense, Bennett's point about imitating known epic paradigms may be particularly valid (see p. 137).

For someone keen to scrutinize their life in the way Augustine did, it was inevitable that the literal and metaphorical meanings of exile would soon overlap. As we have seen, the same analogy is implicit in many hagiographies (see pp. 49–50). Like all such metaphors, its force derived from both its positive and negative aspects; the symbolism could work in two opposing ways. At times, he may have used his physical travels as a symbolic means of focusing on the changing state of his soul; at others, the Plotinian reflection that we 'cannot get there by foot or in a carriage' may have drawn his attention from present circumstances to his more real, more urgent spiritual condition.[76] In any case, the fact that the metaphor no longer lay in words he had merely read, but was, in a sense, encapsulated by his own experience, made its spiritual significance more poignant, in just the same way that, according to Augustine, personal familiarity with snakes facilitates interpretation of biblical imagery about them.[77] The two meanings could exist side by side, uncertainly and indefinitely, precisely because Augustine's outlook never required their relationship to be clearly defined. In fact, the reverse is true. Convictions were more able to thrive in the absence of precision, where correspondences were suspected but still mysterious. One paradoxical (and somewhat perverse) consequence of a belief system where the greatest truths were assumed to be unknown[78] was the tendency not to resolve definitively things identified as sacred, but rather a desire to perpetuate the mystery surrounding them: 'Toute chose sacrée et qui veut demeurer sacrée s'enveloppe de mystère.'[79] The well-known, tantalizing sense that the *Confessions* contain some structural key capable of unlocking their mysteries is

---

[76] *Confessions* 10.26.37 (tr. Burton, p. 238) echoes these sentiments: 'we go *backward and forward* (Job 23.8), but do not find you in any place'. For a general discussion of the metaphor, see Gillian Clark, 'Pilgrims and Foreigners: Augustine – Travelling Home' in L. Ellis and F.L. Kidner (eds), *Travel, Communication and Geography in Late Antiquity* (San Fransisco, 2004).

[77] Augustine, *On Christian Doctrine* 2.60.

[78] Ibid. 2.6.7.1–8.

[79] 'All things which are sacred and want to remain sacred wrap themselves in mystery': Stéphane Mallarmé, 'Hérésies artistiques: l'art pour tous' in *Oeuvres complètes* (ed. H. Mondor, G. Jean-Aubry), p. 257.

not, as O'Donnell rightly states, an indication that such a key exists, but nor is it pure illusion as he implies;[80] rather, it reflects a precisely analogous suspicion brought by Augustine to his own experience, to which his behaviour regularly contributed, and which he could not help but pass on to the reader. Any scholar attempting to explain the apparent structural relationship between the interior and exterior journeys recorded in the *Confessions* should recognize that the same Augustine who suggested the connection would automatically have rejected any proposed resolution to it as (at best) incomplete.

It is sometimes said that the *Confessions* are not a conventional autobiography but concern 'inner history'.[81] Our analysis has suggested that this description is somewhat simplistic. This is not merely because the work records events – and this includes external events – truthfully. It is also because the external reality in which Augustine sincerely sought meaning was itself moulded by the expectations and analysis 'always already' brought to it. As long as allegory was applicable to much more than literature, his internal and external history cannot be fully separated. It has rightly been said that allegory is a term used to describe both an interpretative and a creative process.[82] This notional distinction is valid, but for people like Augustine, each allegorical practice would continually and irresistibly encourage the other.

Beyond Augustine

But how many people were like Augustine? A thinker of exceptional insight who, amongst other things, produced an autobiography of extraordinary literary character – in what sense was the spiritual lifestyle to which the *Confessions* attest relevant to the world beyond him and his entourage? The question is important, not only in any attempt to make a broader statement about the spiritual life of late antiquity, but also in terms of the philosophical assumptions which underpin the lifestyle in question. The greater the common ground between Augustine's spiritual lifestyle and that of other people, the more convincing the argument that its character was not merely personal, but was a natural consequence of the period's basic philosophical assumptions.

There are at least two other late antique autobiographers who deserve close comparison with Augustine: namely the emperor Julian and Gregory of

---

[80]   As O'Donnell implies, *Commentary* vol. 1, p. xxiii.

[81]   E.g. Rousseau, *Ascetics, Authority and the Church in the Age of Jerome and Cassian*, p. 92. In a similar vein Gillian Clark calls them 'spiritual autobiography': *Augustine: the Confessions* (Bristol, 2005), p. 39.

[82]   Rollinson, *Classical Theories of Allegory and Christian Culture*, p. ix.

Nazianzus. Since both figures have generated their own substantial scholarly literatures and debates, the following discussion can be only preliminary, a limited observation of some common ground intended to bring further light on the lifestyle in question. That the autobiographical statements of these figures have attracted little comparative study is somewhat surprising, not least because they were fellow students at Athens. They have also rarely been compared extensively with Augustine. Gregory wrote a range of works explicitly about himself in the form of orations and poems, the most important of which is simply entitled *Concerning his Own Life* (περί τόν ἑαυτοῦ βίον). Julian produced no single autobiographical work but left a series of personal statements scattered through, amongst others, public and private letters, panegyrics, polemical works and hymns; the autobiographical character of many of his writings was already recognized by the Byzantine historian Zosimus.[83] It is striking that, despite their very diverse form, these writings contain important thematic similarities to those of Augustine: memories, relations with the divine, religious experiences and self-conception all feature strongly. The differences too are not without interest. That the works differ from those of Augustine in form makes it harder to attribute similarities to mere literary convention. Julian's militant paganism, which constitutes such an important theological difference, allows the historian to consider the deeper psychological consequences of a general philosophical transcendentalism.

It is also striking that, despite the separateness of the literature they have generated, the central question raised by scholars about the autobiographical writings of Gregory and Julian have often resembled those posed in relation to Augustine. Do they reveal anything about their private, inner lives, or is any autobiographical value compromised, either by the occasional and often propagandistic nature of their writings,[84] or by the rigidities of accepted form?[85] As with Augustine's *Confessions* and other late antique texts, recent years have seen the growth of a scholarship much more comfortable when describing the

---

[83] Zosimus, *Historia Nova* 3.2.4, ed. and tr. François Paschoud, *Histoire Nouvelle* (3 vols, Paris, 1971–89).

[84] Monique Alexandre, 'Fragments autobiographiques dans l'œuvre de Julien', in Marie-Françoise Baslez, Philippe Hoffmann and Laurent Pernot (eds), *L'invention de l'autobiographie d'Hésiode à Saint Augustin* (Paris, 1993), pp. 289–93; Philip Rousseau, 'Retrospect: the "essential" Gregory', in Børtnes and Hägg (eds), *Gregory of Nazianzus: Images and Reflections*, pp. 283–95; Rayond Van Dam, 'Self-Presentation in the Will of Gregory Nazianzus', *Journal of Theological Studies* 46 (1995), esp. p. 140.

[85] As argued in the case of Gregory by Martin Hinterberger: *Autobiographische Traditionen in Byzanz* (Vienna, 1999), pp. 68–9, and Brian E. Daley: *Gregory of Nazianzus* (London/New York, 2006), p. 2.

intellectual content and context of these writings than anything as personal as life and experience construed more broadly. For example, despite its title, Rowland Smith's important study, *Julian's Gods: Religion and Philosophy in the Thought and Action of Julian the Apostate* (London, 1995), has far more to say about the emperor's thought than it does about his actions.

In what ways did the thought of Gregory and Julian impact on their actions, their experience, their self-understanding? This is not the place for an exhaustive discussion of their world views, an innately complex task deserving of much more extended studies. The element of their thought of most relevance to our discussion is the relationship between spiritual truths and events in the sensible world. Whilst Gregory of Nazianzus does not produce a theoretical statement of this idea comparable to the sophisticated position of Augustine, he nonetheless demonstrates a basic Christian intuition in the truthfulness of the Bible as a historical record and in God's continuing and concrete intervention in the world. This contrasts markedly with pagan myths, which he attacks amongst other things for their lack of truthfulness.[86] Undoubtedly, this instinct manifests itself on a personal level. In mortal danger during a sea storm, a pivotal moment in his life, Gregory's prayer for salvation includes reminding God of his miracles in the biblical past.[87] Even if this memory is treated with suspicion, it contains within it the implicit belief that divine intervention in the sensible world was, and remains, a real possibility. Although he concedes that the verse form in which he chooses to write implies a certain playfulness,[88] he also insists that his fundamental aim is to tell the truth and to refute the falsehoods of detractors.[89]

The theoretical basis of Julian's personal statements is somewhat more complex. An important recurrent topic in his writings is the nature and function of myth. His views on this subject are typical of pagan Neoplatonism, though he speculates about it more explicitly than most other writers in this tradition. Myths are the vehicles for higher meanings allegorically concealed within them;[90] they communicate certain spiritual truths to those not yet ready to grasp them philosophically.[91] Their apparently incongruous elements, which may superficially be regarded as offensive to the gods, are didactically useful in that they encourage the hearer's epistemic autonomy.[92] By interpreting myth in this way, Julian defends

---

[86] Gregory of Nazianzus, *Concerning his own Life* 1240–49.

[87] Ibid. 186–92.

[88] Ibid. 7.

[89] Ibid. 40–50.

[90] Julian, *Hymn to the Mother of the Gods* 170B; *Oration VII: To the Cynic Heracleios* 216C; *Against the Galilaeans* 94A.

[91] Julian, *Oration VII* 206C–208C.

[92] Ibid. 217C–D; 222C–D.

not only his view of the gods and the universe, but also the value of the classical cultural and literary tradition. Nowhere is this clearer than in his polemical *Against the Galileans*, where he rebuts Christian detractors of pagan myth, and tries to turn their arguments against the Bible's own narrative contents.[93]

On the face of it, Julian's preoccupation with myth may seem to indicate a definitive distance in his thought between the world of events on the one hand and transcendental truths on the other; after all, it is often the incongruity, the lack of literal truthfulness of the former (elements we might perhaps be tempted to term their 'textuality') that points to the presence of the latter. On this reading, Julian contrasts markedly with Christians generally, and with Augustine especially, whose belief in sacred history underlines the symbolic capacity not just of texts, but of historical events.

But such a sharp distinction would be misleading. Julian does not explore the connection between literal and spiritual truth with the same theological precision as Augustine; rather, he allows the boundary to blur. But by doing so, he produces some surprisingly similar results. One of Julian's most factual and autobiographical passages, a potted history of himself and the rest of the house of Constantine, is related in the form of myth in order to illustrate the register's didactic function.[94] Conversely, he generally places a great emphasis on historical information,[95] and sometimes adopts a believing stance towards traditional stories whose historicity may seem inessential. In the face of non-literal interpretations, he vigorously defends against 'over-wise persons' (τινες τῶν λίαν σοφῶν) the factual truthfulness of the sacred story of the arrival of the goddess Cybele in Rome.[96] Similarly, his attitude towards the historicity of Homer's stories is, at least, ambiguous. He does declare Homer's narrative of the Aloadae fictitious, but this is in the specifically polemical context of exposing the absurdity of Christian belief in the Bible's historicity.[97] Elsewhere he uses Homer as evidence of the reality of divine intervention: apparently treating the historical existence of the Homeric heroes as a given, he claims that, just as the gods helped those distant figures, so too they may help men today.[98] There is no reason to think that the only form such interventions could take were phenomena of the most dramatic and extraordinary kind: for a practising theurgist, sacred objects

---

[93]   Julian, *Against the Galilaeans* 135B.

[94]   Julian, *Oration VII* 227C–234C.

[95]   Walter Emil Kaegi, 'The Emperor Julian's Assessment of the Significance and Function of History', *Proceedings of the American Philosophical Association* 108 (1964), pp. 29–38.

[96]   Julian, *Hymn to the Mother of the Gods* 161B (tr. Wright, vol. 1, p. 449).

[97]   Julian, *Against the Galilaeans* 135A–B.

[98]   Julian, *Oration VIII: To Sallust* 250A–B.

– statues, altars, fires etc.[99] – were all symbols of the divine every bit as present and alive as the Christian Eucharist. Apples, for example, were one of a number of foods which were taboo in the cult of Cybele and Attis, and should not be eaten because they are the 'sacred and golden ... symbols of secret and mystical rewards' and 'are worthy to be reverenced and worshipped for the sake of their archetypes'.[100] Just as for Augustine, it is not merely texts that are full of signs and meanings, but Julian's entire physical world. Indeed, in his attack on the Christians, Julian maintains explicitly that the truth reveals itself not through speech alone, but through clear signs and omens.[101]

It is against this intellectual backdrop that we must place statements by Julian and Gregory about their own spiritual experiences. Two representative passages offer a good basis for discussion: first, the account by Julian in his *Letter to the Athenians* of how he was raised to the imperial office by his troops in Gaul in defiance of the Emperor Constantius; second, Gregory's version in *On Concerning His Own Life* of his attempted departure from Constantinople after the machinations of his former protegé Maximus the Cynic had become public:[102]

> For one day, they (*the legions*) halted, and till that time *I knew nothing whatever of what they had determined* (ἄχρις ἧς οὐδὲν ᾔδειν ἐγὼ τῶν βεβουλευμένων αὐτοῖς); I call to witness Zeus, Helios, Ares, Athene, and all the other gods that no such suspicion even my entered my mind until that very evening. It was already late, when about sunset the news was brought to me, and *suddenly the palace was surrounded* (καὶ αὐτίκα τὰ βασίλεια περιείληπτο) and they all began to shout aloud, while I was still considering what I ought to do and feeling by no means confident. My wife was still alive and *it happened* (ἔτυχον), that in order to rest alone, I had gone to the upper room near hers. Then from there through an opening in the wall *I prayed to Zeus* (προσεκύνησα τὸν Δία). And when the shouting grew louder still and all was in a tumult in the palace *I entreated the god to give me a sign* (ἠτέομεν τὸν θεὸν δοῦναι τέρας) and thereupon he showed me a sign and bade me yield and not oppose myself to the will of the army. Nevertheless even after these tokens had been vouchsafed to me *I did not yield without reluctance but resisted as long as I could* (οὐκ εἶξα ἑτοίμως, ἀλλ' ἀντέσχον εἰς ὅσον ἠδυνάμην), and would not accept

99   Rowland Smith, *Julian's Gods*, pp. 101–2, 106, 111.

100   Julian, *Hymn to the Mother of the God*, 176 A (tr. Wright, vol. 1, p. 491). For an analysis of Julian's understanding of this taboo, see Britt-Mari Näsström, *O Mother of the Gods and Men: Some Aspects of the Religious Thoughts in Emperor Julian's Discourse on the Mother of the Gods* (Lund, 1990), pp. 91–2.

101   Julian, *Against the Galilaeans*, 358E.

102   A very useful overview of Gregory's life if given by Carolinne White in *Gregory of Nazianzus: Autobiographical Poems*, pp. xi–xxiii.

the salutation or the diadem. But since I could not single-handed control so many, and moreover the gods, who willed that this should happen, spurred on the soldiers and gradually softened my resolution, somewhere about the third hour *some soldier or other* (οὐκ οἶδα οὕτινός μοι στρατιώτου δόντος) gave me the collar and I put it on my head and returned to the palace, as the gods know groaning in my heart. And yet surely it was my duty to feel confidence and to trust in the god after he had shown me the sign; but I was *terribly ashamed* (ἠσχυνόμην) and ready to sink into the earth at the thought of not seeming to obey Constantius faithfully to the last.[103]

I behaved (I will not deny it) more like
a naive person than someone clever:
all at once I turned my ship around, so to speak,
but not expertly; if I had, no one would have noticed.
As it was I let out some words hinting at my departure,
Words I uttered in the pain caused by my fatherly affections.
This was what I said: "Defend the Trinity which I, your father,
Most eager to provide for you, have given my beloved children,
And remember, my dearest ones, all that I have gone through."
When the people heard these words,
And *someone who could not be restrained* (τῶν δυσκαθέκτων τινος) shouted out,
They *immediately* (εὐθὺς) erupted like a swarm of bees
Driven out by smoke, and began to shout wildly ...
They all seethed with anger and desire alike,
Anger at my enemies and desire for their shepherd.
But it is not my way to yield to violence
Or to accept an unlawful appointment:
In fact *I was unwilling* (οὐδὲ ἄσμενος) to accept even a lawful one .
I stand speechless in their midst, filled with despair,
For I do not know how to restrain their cries
Or how I can promise any one of their demands ...
Then someone, by desperation forced to speak,
(alas for the sense of hearing! I wish I had lost mine right then!)
said 'Then you will throw out the Trinity together with yourself.'
As I was afraid that a dangerous situation might ensue
I gave an oath, or rather (for I have never sworn an oath –
If I too, may boast a little in God   –
Since I was washed by the grace of the spirit),

---

[103]   Julian, *Letter to the Athenians* 284 B–D (tr. Wright, vol. 2, pp. 281–3).

> I gave my word (which was believed because of my character)
> That I would stay until some of the bishops arrived ... [104]

It is hardly surprising that the reliability of these and other passages have come under heavy suspicion, and been analysed in terms of their apologetic functions.[105] Both were pivotal and controversial moments in the life of their respective author. Despite each author's adamant insistence,[106] therefore, it is by no means unreasonable to suspect that the episodes in question may not have been entirely unpremeditated. In an exchange of letters with Oribasius presumably predating the incident mentioned above, Julian reports a recent dream foreshadowing his elevation to the emperorship; his correspondent had apparently reported to him a similar dream.[107] Similarly, Gregory's own intense unwillingness to remain in Constantinople is also questionable, and a potential alternative version is already implicit within his own. Gregory admits not only his failure to slip away quietly, but also concedes that the crowd responded to his own hints of imminent departure. What he attributes to naivety, therefore, could easily be interpreted as more calculated and intentional.[108] The evidence from both cases might well seem to confirm, either through dishonesty or retrospective idealization, the unreliability of first person testimonies.

As McLynn brilliantly shows in the case of Gregory, the self-idealization is hard to dispute.[109] Both authors make use of heroic models when defining their own lives. Every inch the pagan Neoplatonist, Julian displays not only a deep consciousness of canonical heroes such as Pythagoras, Socrates and Plato; he openly concedes the role of Alexander and Marcus Aurelius as personal inspirations and models for imitation.[110] Similarly, Gregory, who is particularly liberal in applying scriptural typologies to his acquaintances, concedes the

---

[104]   Gregory of Nazianzus, *Concerning his own Life*, 1053–1106 (extracts) (tr. White, pp. 89–93).

[105]   E.g. John Matthews, *The Roman Empire of Ammianus* (London, 1989), p. 94ff; Smith, *Julian's Gods*, p. 4.

[106]   Julian reiterates his unwillingness to be emperor in *Letter 8: To Maximus, the Philosopher* 414B and *Oration VII* 232C.

[107]   Julian, *Letter 4*, 384A–D. See Smith, *Julian's Gods*, p. 4.

[108]   As for Mclynn, 'A Self-Made Holy Man: The Case of Gregory Nazianzen', p. 476: 'Gregory's response was meanwhile to reenact the drama of withdrawal, reflection and return which he had played out so often before.'

[109]   Ibid., pp. 463–83.

[110]   Julian, *Letter to Themistius* 253A–B; *The Caesars* 317C–D. Ammianus provides further evidence of a romantic self-conception: Marcus Aurelius was his role model (*Histories* 16.1.4) and he constantly asserted that during his reign the goddess Justice had returned to earth (ibid. 22.10.6).

influence of Elijah and other biblical figures in his own life.[111] It is no surprise, therefore, that the autobiographical statements of both writers often have such a hagiographical flavour. For example, in the *Misopogon*, Julian advertises the fact that the Gallic winter provided him with the opportunity to discipline his body to withstand the rigours of a harsh physical environment – an ascetic training characteristic of a Neoplatonic sage (see p. 49);[112] Gregory refers to himself with the evocative language of spiritual exile.[113] By virtue of his first meeting with Maximus, Julian claims to have had a life-changing intellectual experience[114] of the type which gives structure to the pagan community throughout Eunapius' *Lives* (see p. 85 and p. 117) and which Porphyry celebrates in Plotinus' meeting with Ammonius Saccas.[115] As Smith observes,[116] he not only omits to share, but positively advertises to readers areas of arcane spiritual knowledge he is forbidden from disclosing.[117] Gregory, similarly, cannot decide how far he should reveal the many miracles God has performed in his life. To conceal them, he concedes, would be ungrateful; to reveal them, not free of pride.[118] But, of course, even to declare one's intention to conceal important details – as opposed to not mentioning them at all – confirms their existence and, as we have seen, such techniques of concealment and mystification have many parallels in hagiography (see p. 69).

But the question of self-idealization is complex. To equate it with a straightforward lack of personal humility would be simplistic. A striking feature of many autobiographical statements is their implicit self-doubt and ambivalence. This has been observed in the case of Augustine.[119] Even after his dramatic conversion, he warns that 'no one should be sure that one who has been able to pass from a worse state to a better is not passing also from a better state to a worse':[120] the price of wonderment is eternal vigilance. Gregory's reputation for self-promotion has perhaps meant that similar elements of reticence have

---

[111]   Gregory, *Concerning his own Life* 292 for admiration of Elijah; his father is a second Abraham: ibid. 53.

[112]   Julian, *Misopogon* 341C–D.

[113]   Gregory, *Oration 26* 14; *Oration 42* 1.

[114]   Julian, *Oration 7* 235 A–B. The reference to Maximus is elusive but a fuller version of the encounter is dramatically recorded by Eunapius: *Lives* 475.

[115]   Porphyry, *Life of Plotinus* 3.

[116]   Smith, *Julian's Gods*, p. 118.

[117]   Julian, *Oration 7* 239B; *Oration 4: Hymn to King Helios* 130C. A very similar stance is adopted by Eunapius who announces his refusal to disclose the name of the hierophant who initiated him into the cult of the Persephone and Demeter: *Lives* 475.

[118]   Gregory, *Concerning his own Life* 103–9.

[119]   J. J. O'Meara, *The Young Augustine*, pp. xxiv–xxv; Williams, *Authorised Lives*, p. 215.

[120]   Augustine, *Confessions* 10.32.48 (tr. Burton, p. 244).

received less prominence than they deserve. As we saw above, Gregory confesses his tendency towards pride.[121] He also, if not always, reserves judgement about God's hand in the events of his life, declares himself reluctant to exaggerate signs,[122] and worries about the truth or falsehood of what he says to others.[123] The range of self-statements made by Julian is similarly wide. For all his self-idealization (at one point he appears to associate himself with Plato's philosopher king[124]) he explicitly concedes his failure to live up to such models,[125] and describes himself as a humble figure from whom great things should not be expected.[126]

This is the backdrop against which we must place sometimes explicit claims by Julian and Gregory of divine guidance and religious experience. No doubt conscious of the potential accusation of wishful thinking, both authors sometimes defend the truthfulness of their spiritual claims by invoking the spontaneity principle, and this takes the form of highlighting the author's own ignorance at the time, and their completely naive and unaffected relationship with events. Gregory highlights, for example, the spontaneous way – 'an incredible fact but absolutely true' (ὃ δ'ἐστὶν οὐ πιστὸν μὲν, ἀψευδὲς δ'ἄγαν) – in which everyone joined him in prayer during the near-fatal sea storm.[127] Despite highlighting how early in life his mind had inclined towards 'something greater' than the excellent virtues taught him by his parents,[128] his ordination is given a miraculous quality through its spontaneity: 'I expected anything rather than that I should receive this amid all the vicissitudes of life.'[129] Similarly, Julian's *Hymn to King Helios* opens very personally by describing not merely the intensity of his attachment to the god, but by declaring how his interest in the life of the heavens had already developed in childhood in a way entirely independent of human intervention, and therefore suggestive of deeper spiritual truths:

> From my childhood an *extraordinary longing* (δεινὸς ... πόθος) for the rays of the god penetrated deep into my soul and from my earliest days my mind was so completely swayed by the light that illumines the heavens that not only did

---

[121]   Gregory of Nazianzus, *Concerning his own Life* 103–10.

[122]   Ibid. 1346–7.

[123]   Ibid. 1247.

[124]   Julian, *Oration VII*, 321D. His description of an encounter with Helios and subsequent earthly mission, despite his reluctance to leave the god echo the philosopher's celebrated experience at the mouth of the Cave at Plato, *Republic* 539E–540B.

[125]   Julian, *Letter to Themistius* 253B.

[126]   Ibid. 267A–B.

[127]   Gregory, *Concerning his own Life* 170.

[128]   Ibid. 95–100 (tr. White, p. 17).

[129]   Ibid. 332–3 (tr. White, p. 35).

I desire to gaze intently at the sun, but whenever I walked abroad in the night season ... I abandoned all else without exception and gave myself up to the beauties of the heavens; *nor did I understand what anyone might say to me, nor heed what I was doing myself* (οὐκέτι ξυνιεὶς οὐδὲν εἴ τις λέγοι τι πρός με οὐδὲ αὐτὸς ὅ τι πράττοιμι προσέχων) ... people went so far as to regard me as an astrologer ... and yet, I call heaven to witness, never had a book on this subject come into my hands, nor did I as yet even know what that science was ... I recognized of myself that the movement of the moon was in the opposite direction to the universe, though as yet I had met no one of those who are wise in these matters.[130]

Both Julian's acquisition of the emperorship and Gregory's failure to depart Constantinople must therefore be placed within the context of many other episodes throughout their lives in which spiritual meanings and divine plans are detected. The passages cited above at pp. 167–9 have a particular importance, however, since they purport to be not merely memories of spiritually significant episodes, but records of the specific events and thoughts which at the time made possible the detection of spiritual significance. Julian is, of course, entirely aware of the suspicions his elevation potentially invokes: he writes in part to refute them. His refutation contains two closely connected strands. First, the guarantee that his account is truthful, defended by appealing to the gods as witnesses to his testimony. The thought is close to Augustine's contention that dishonesty is futile before an omniscient God.[131] Second, the object of this guarantee: the episode's absolute spontaneity and the irrefutability of its message, even in the face of his own reluctance. The language of spontaneity, mirrored in his own passivity, infuses the passage: the palace is surrounded, he happens to be resting, the soldier who gives him the collar, far from being planted, remains anonymous. Gregory too is more object than subject: his fervent wish is to retreat into exile, and it is only his own naivety, and the subsequent uncontrollability of the crowd which immediately throw events onto a different trajectory.

These assurances of truthfulness can, of course, be questioned: they are techniques characteristic of hagiographical realism, not necessarily guarantees of historicity. As in the case of Augustine's conversion, one view would be to see in this general tendency to idealize the past grounds for doubting the historicity of these, and other, specific events recorded by each author. An opposing view – the view defended here – would be to recognize in this very tendency a historicity of a different kind: the likelihood that such an attitude towards the past corresponded to an analogous approach towards immediate experience.

---

[130]   Julian, *Hymn to King Helios* (extracts) 130C–131B (tr. Wright, vol. 1, pp. 354–5).

[131]   Augustine, *Confessions* 10.2.2. Julian makes the same point more explicitly at *Caesars* 335A.

The question, then, is how much of each episode's content can and should be interpreted in this alternative way.

First, the extent to which the events in question were expected could be seen not as a falsification of their spiritual significance, but as an important part of what made it possible and necessary for them to acquire it: the same principle of spontaneity that persuaded others was an equally crucial source of conviction for Gregory and Julian themselves; it was less their own truthfulness that was at stake than the will of God. Indeed, especially in Julian's life, a number of significant episodes could be read in this way, as events moulded by expectation rather than merely accounts coloured by retrospect. Julian's depiction of his own inspired and sudden religious conversion as a youth[132] suggests, for Smith, a certain 'literary play' on similar stories in the lives of earlier philosophers such as Socrates, Diogenes and, especially, Dio Chrysostom.[133] But however artificial we regard the latter's own conversion claims, as long as they were trusted by Julian himself, then it makes most sense to see any subsequent parallels as reflections of the emperor's sincere belief in the possibility of sudden conversion. The same could be said of the extraordinary significance he accords to his encounter with Maximus of Ephesus which resulted in his conversion to theurgic Neoplatonism.[134] This could reflect, amongst other things, a preconception about the nature and power of such intellectual encounters. Eunapius, who celebrates a number of encounters of this sort (Alypius and Iamblichus, for example, meet like two planets in their courses[135]), also reports Julian's enthusiastic reaction to his future teacher upon seeing him perform miracles: 'You have shown me the man I was in search of.'[136] Furthermore, the sign of approval given here by Zeus is only one of a number of such signs Julian claims to have received. Although he sometimes briefly mentions what they were (for example, that he was guided by bird flight),[137] he usually, as here, omits further description.[138] Nonetheless, the episode gives us an opportunity to consider what such signs actually consisted in.

Although Julian does not describe the sign, the context does provide symbolically pregnant aspects no less than in the case of Augustine's garden

---

132   Julian, *Against Heraclius* 229B–D.

133   Smith, *Julian's Gods*, p. 186.

134   Julian, *Oration VII* 235A–B.

135   Eunapius, *Lives* 460 (tr. W.C. Wright, p. 373).

136   Ibid. 475 (p. 435).

137   This is attested only by Julian's ancient editor and commentator Cyril of Alexandria: *Iuliani Imperatoris Librorum Contra Christianos Quae Supersunt* 361D, 351D, ed. C.I. Neumann (Leipzig, 1880), p. 233.

138   Julian, *Letter 58: to Libanius, Sophist and Quaestor* 399D; *Letter 2* (tr. Wright, vol. 3. p. 5).

conversion. The crowds are particularly important, because the great pressure they exerted could be felt not as an alternative source of conviction to that of God (indeed, one potentially opposed to it), but as its very vehicle. The soldiers that carry Julian on their shields were 'like men seized with a divine frenzy'.[139] Then there was the opening in the wall: presumably Julian felt that a direct and physical passage to the heavens was necessary for prayers to reach Zeus. Nonetheless, a wall separating man and God, and a narrow channel of communication between them – like Augustine's garden wall, it is an excellent physical metaphor for a transcendental universe. Whatever else the sign consisted in, this element became, in a sense, an integral part of it. It also hints that those things he considered signs did not have to be extraordinary or supernatural; perhaps one of the reasons he was able to resist this one for so long was that it was insufficiently spectacular. More important to his ultimate conviction, perhaps, was the fact that, since Julian, like Augustine, was alone at the crucial moment, no-one else was capable of immediately contradicting his interpretation. In any case, the sheer frequency of such signs does not undermine their individual plausibility so much as reveal the great quantity of phenomena to which he was prepared to accord spiritual significance.

Similar points can be made about Gregory's fudged departure from Constantinople. The provocative speech with which the incident begins could certainly be seen as grounds for doubting its spontaneity from one perspective. But from another and not incompatible one – that of his conscience – they could be regarded as precisely what made the crowd's sudden, dramatic reaction so necessary. Here also, then, the crowd is the key to the episode's meaning. A force of nature, Gregory does not overtly ascribe to them divine inspiration. Nonetheless, this status is implicit in the lone, anonymous voice in the crowd whose words somehow project themselves above the tumult such that Gregory cannot resist hearing them. Like the child beyond Augustine's garden wall, it is the anonymity of this voice, combined with its simple and penetrating message, that make it easy to interpret as the vessel of the divine will, rather than merely human opinion. The promise which Gregory immediately makes suggests that he treated it in precisely this way.

The next chapter in this incident, namely Gregory's installation in the hitherto Arian Church of the Apostles at the behest of the emperor Theodosius, is no less revealing:

> The upshot of it all was this: 'Gods hands the church', he said,
> 'through me to you and to your great efforts',

---

[139]   Julian, *Letter to the Athenians* 285C (tr. Wright, vol. 2, p. 285).

words which were unbelievable until they were fulfilled ...

... I entered the church, *I don't know how* (οὐκ οἶδ' ὅπως) .

This, too, is worth telling: for to many

It seemed that these events were miraculous;

To such people nothing seen is without significance (οἶος οὐδὲν ἀπλοῦν ἐστι τῶν ὁρωμένων),

Especially at the most critical moments.[140]

Gregory depicts the interpretation of the incident as a further point of contention between himself and the crowd: no-one can accuse him of manipulating events or people. But even in refusing to confirm divine assistance, he remains prepared to countenance it. What is particularly significant is the meagreness of the potential miracle's symbolic content, the uncertainty about what it actually consists in. The question we might be tempted to pose, therefore, is what type of incident does, or at least could, contain, spiritual significance for Gregory?

A fascinating passage in the autobiographical *Oration 26* (*About himself, on his Return from the Country*) given to his congregation after returning from a period of retreat (which he terms 'the desert') caused by the Maximus crisis, and which ends after the impostor's episcopal ambitions have been exposed:

I was walking alone, just as the sun was setting. My path led out on a promontory – for it is a habit of mine to relax from labour in this way ... I was walking, in any case, and as my feet moved along my gaze was fixed upon the sea. It was not a pleasant site, even though there are other times when it is very pleasant ... But what happened on this day? I prefer to quote the words of Scripture: 'The sea started up and was rough, because a great wind was blowing' (John 6.18). And as happens in such weather, some of the waves were raised up far out and crested for a moment, then broke and dispersed themselves quietly along the headlands, but others crashed against nearby rocks and were beaten into a frothy foam and sprayed high into the air. Then pebbles and seaweed and trumpet shells and tiny oysters were churned up and scattered about; some of then were drawn back again, as the wave receded, but the rocks themselves were unshaken, immovable – no less than if nothing had disturbed them, despite all the battering they received from the waves.

I know that I drew some profit from this for the philosophic life, and *being, as I am, the kind of person who relates everything to myself* (ὅιος ἐγὼ πάντα συντείνων πρὸς ἐμαυτόν) especially when I find myself staggered (ἰλιγιάσας) by some aspect of the situation (which was then the case), I took in what I saw as not *at*

---

[140]   Gregory of Nazianzus, *Concerning his own Life* 1311–45 (extracts) (tr. White, pp. 107–9).

all irrelevant (οὐ παρέργως). *The scene became a lesson for me!* (καί μοι τὸ θέαμα παίδευμα γίνεται). For surely, I said to myself, is not the sea our life and all our human affairs – since so much about them is salty and unstable?...

... When people undergo trials, some always seem to me to be swept away like things without weight, breathless and offering no resistance to what threatens them ... Others seem like rock, worthy of that Rock on whom we stand, and whom we worship.[141]

What Gregory has witnessed is nothing more than a particularly dramatic natural occurrence; he does not pretend otherwise. This does not stop him, however, from declaring the event staggering and from relating it to the situation faced by him and others caught up in the Maximus crisis. It is in this capacity that he not merely witnesses, but experiences this concrete and extended metaphor. It is tempting to try to establish the precise meaning of this incident and the status the author accorded to it. Was it a random event which had set off a useful train of thought in his mind or a set of truth-laden symbols divinely intended for his eyes? The question cannot be resolved: Gregory himself describes it with non-committal *litotes* (οὐ παρέργως) and it is unclear how, or by whom, it 'became a lesson' for him. But this very ambiguity is highly revealing of his spiritual lifestyle, at least as much as the dramatic events surrounding his failed departure. To interpret spiritually one's life was not, ultimately, to possess a set of critical tools with which one could detect the buried thresholds of meaning. In the absence of such criteria, the episodes during which the thresholds were purportedly crossed will always appear to us suspect and open to the distorting effects of retrospect. But in the case of Gregory, no less than that of Augustine, to focus on these moments alone risks overlooking the more mundane roots of the judgements reached and their continuity with familiar habits of observation and language. To say that Gregory found theological meaning in the 'most improbable materials'[142] is, from another viewpoint, to recognize how deeply and thoroughly he was prepared to countenance spiritual significance in the world around him. The fact he did so reverently and hesitantly, the fact there was always a need for more answers, were aspects of the very process by which his world became infused with meaning.

The particular character of Julian's acquisition of the emperorship also makes more sense once it is imagined as part of a spiritual lifestyle. What Julian's case makes particularly clear is that this lifestyle did not depend only on a cognitive

---

[141] Gregory, *Oration 26* 8-9, ed. and tr. Justin Mossay and Guy Lafontaine, *Grégoire de Nazianze: Discours 24–26*, Sources Chrétiennes 284 (Paris, 1981), tr. Brian E. Daley, *Gregory of Nazianzus* (London/New York, 2006), p. 110.

[142] Mclynn, 'A Self-Made Holy Man: The Case of Gregory Nazianzen', p. 476.

habit geared towards the detection of spiritual meaning in events; rather, it was capable of producing events which lent themselves to spiritual judgements. This lifestyle was, therefore, no less prone to subjectivity than the wilful embellishment of the past; it was, in many ways, its counterpart. One practical implication of this attitude can be seen in the *Hymn to King Helios* and *Hymn to the Mother of the Gods*. Near the end of each hymn Julian informs his correspondent of the restricted conditions under which each was written. The first was composed 'in three nights at the most, in harmony with the three-fold creative power of the god, as far as possible as it occurred to my memory';[143] the latter:

> in the short space of one night, *without having read anything on the subject beforehand, or thought it over* (οὐδὲν οὔτε προανεγνωκόσιν οὔτε σκεψαμένοις περὶ αὐτῶν). Nay, I had not even planned to speak thereof until the moment that I asked for these writing-tablets. May the goddess bear witness to the truth of my words![144]

These claims can, of course, be used to explain the quality of the works concerned.[145] But given the highly religious nature of each piece, we should probably countenance a deeper significance. For one thing, they reflect the possibility attested elsewhere by Julian of experiencing signs in the very act of writing.[146] In a related way, he gives the context of writing, namely the period of time in question, a sacred, metaphorical meaning. But more broadly, by restricting himself to a limited time period, by writing at night without plan or reference – from a stance, in other words, of faith – Julian was less excusing the works' contents than attributing them to the inspiration of the god as opposed to his own ingenuity. There is, of course, a certain paradox here: the spontaneity is forced, the product of studied and artificial strictures. But this reveals still more clearly its central importance as a value. The deeper the influence of models, the more closely anticipated and yearned for the outcome, the more urgent the need to distinguish the authentic voice of God from merely private hopes and wishes, and in doing so, have them divinely approved with absolute conviction. As with Augustine, the many signs and omens Julian reports probably reflect only a fraction of those he experienced, rejected and considered. However high or low he set the bar, however wide he allowed the field of signification to extend, it was these habits that constituted his spiritual lifestyle on a daily basis and guaranteed an occasional epiphany.

---

143 Julian, *Hymn to King Helios* 157 B–C (tr. Wright, vol. 1, p. 431).
144 Julian, *Hymn to the Mother of the Gods* 178D–179A (tr. Wright, vol. 1, p. 499).
145 E.g. Smith, *Julian's Gods*, p. 144.
146 Julian, *Letter 2* (tr. Wright, vol. 3, p. 5).

This chapter can usefully end with a word of caution. Although the cases of Gregory and Julian suggest that Augustine was far from unique in the sort of spiritual lifestyle to which he attests, it would be dangerous to draw from these cases, even collectively, a too sweeping lesson about the religious life of late antiquity. It is important to recognize the existence of autobiographies which are both religious in focus and of a very different character. One such example is Egeria's *Travels*, probably written in the early 380's.[147] As a nun who had made the long journey to Egypt and Palestine from the far West of the Empire in order to describe the sacred sites for the benefit of her spiritual 'sisters',[148] there is no reason to doubt Egeria's piety. What is extraordinary, however, is the 'assured literalism'[149] with which she expresses it. As she admits,[150] her curiosity for the biblical landscape was limitless and, as Wilkinson observes,[151] comes close to obliterating the contemporary, Roman world around her. Everywhere she goes, she interrogates local monks and clergy on the finest topological details from the route of the Exodus to the measurement of the valley adjacent to the Mount of God.[152] But, in a sense, it is for this very reason that the biblical past too only comes alive in a very restricted sense. For her voracious appetite for literal detail not merely exceeds, but entirely excludes, any allegorical speculation. This, one might argue, was not the task in hand; hermeneutics could happen at home, only a living witness could help her audience 'picture better what happened in these places when (reading) the Holy Books'.[153] Nonetheless, in an age characterized by such inventive biblical exegesis it is striking that Egeria makes no attempt to relate the mass of detail to spiritual truth, nor during her entire journey records any allegorical conversation with one of her many willing collocutors. Moreover, this is despite the frequent religious services that pepper the journey during which allegorical preaching occurs,[154] and despite the fact she finds herself intensively reconstructing events famed for their figurative meaning. If, for example, her special fascination for the Exodus reflects the

---

[147]   The generally accepted date is not undisputed. See P. Maraval's Introduction to *de itinerario* (ed. idem, p. 27ff.)

[148]   Whether her *sorores* are nuns in a formal sense is unclear. See ibid., pp. 23–7.

[149]   J. Wilkinson, 'Introduction', in idem, *Egeria's Travels to the Holy Land* (Warminster, 1981), p. 39.

[150]   'Sum satis curiosa': Egeria, *Travels* 16.3.

[151]   J. Wilkinson, 'Introduction', in idem, *Egeria's Travels to the Holy Land* (Warminster, 1981), p. 43.

[152]   Egeria, *Travels* 2.1.

[153]   Egeria, *Travels* 5.9, tr. John Wilkinson, *Egeria's Travels to the Holy Land* (Warminster, 1981), p. 98.

[154]   Ibid. 46.2–3.

theological fashion of the time, her treatment could hardly be more at odds with it. Steered willingly by monks, her entire interest is taken up tracing the exact zigzagging route of the ancient Hebrews. Revealingly, for her seventh-century commentator Valerius, this relentlessly literal approach clearly felt incomplete: when describing her journey, he could not resist inserting, as if on her behalf, an inflated spiritual language sometimes bordering on allegory.[155] But these are his words only; Egeria finds herself in the position of many 'in-the-footsteps-of' travellers: the very precision of her geographical quest is, *pace* E.D. Hunt,[156] an acceptance of the unbridgeable temporal gap that remains between her and her theme. However pious, her *peregrinatio* is purely literal; its spiritual, metaphorical sense, if suspected, is never explored, and when, after three years, it starts drawing to a close, *patria* can still mean, without ambiguity, the Western province she first set out from.[157]

Another autobiographical work which lacks the spiritual scrutiny of events characteristic of the other texts we have discussed is Libanius' *Oratio* 1. This work, at least part of which appears to have been designed for public performance,[158] is an account of the author's life and career; an attempt to expose both the good and bad fortune encountered along the way.[159] The contrast with more spiritually-minded narratives is subtle: the work is certainly neither detached nor unreligious. Libanius talks about the gods frequently: he prays, sometimes intensively; both good and bad events are attributed to them. But divine intervention comes across as slightly remote and impersonal even when, as his life progresses and his fortunes deteriorate, specific gods are invoked. Apart from a couple of dreams[160] (a phenomenon about which he is elsewhere

---

[155] The difference in tone is striking throughout, but expressions like 'ibi in corde istius Deum sitientis influit fons aque vive salientis in vitam eternam' introduce an emphasis absent from the original. Valerius, *Epistola Beatissime Egerie Laude Conscripta Fratrum Bergidensium Monachorum a Valerio Conlata* 2.8–9, ed. and tr. Manuel C. Díaz y Díaz in *Egérie: Journal de Voyage (Itinéraire) et Lettre sur la bienheureuse Egérie*, Sources Chrétiennes 296 (Paris, 1982).

[156] Who claims the gap is elided: Hunt, *Holy Land Pilgrimage*, p. 106.

[157] Egeria, *Travels* 17.1.

[158] A.F. Norman, introduction to Libanius, *Oratio* 1 (Oxford, 1965), p. xii ff. As Norman observes, the work appears to have been composed over a long period, with the later parts containing more private and personal material.

[159] Libanius presents his work as an attempt to refute the view that he is either the most, or least, fortunate of men: *Oratio* 1.1.

[160] Ibid. 1.67, 143.

sceptical),[161] and the fulfilment of the occasional personal justice,[162] the work lacks the sense we find in spiritual narratives that the world of events is full of deeper meanings to which one can and should be sensitive. Unlike in Augustine's *Confessions*, Libanius is always the main actor in his story and his emphasis gradually becomes more personal and intimate throughout the work.[163] His life is not, therefore, a spiritual journey in the sense that it leads him to general truths. The attribution of events to the gods marks the end of analysis; even if events do contain a complex message, it appears largely unknowable. Indeed, as A.F. Norman convincingly argues, Libanius' core philosophical beliefs cannot even be discerned in the work.[164]

Even a brief summary of the works of Egeria and Libanius reveal religious sensitivities very different from those expressed in the works of Augustine, Gregory and Julian. They serve, therefore, as a useful reminder that the world of late antiquity, though highly doctrinaire, was nonetheless capable of producing a wide variety of religious attitudes and modes of experience. Of course, many questions could be asked about these differences: to what extent do they stem from differences in personality and/or in the kinds of texts they intended to produce? Do Egeria and Libanius reveal the possibility of different kinds of religious outlook from that of, say, Augustine (and, indeed each other), or only differing extents of intensity on a notional continuum? Whilst answers to these questions lie beyond the scope of the current discussion, they at least remind us of an important closing consideration. Just as we argued that dramatic religious experiences needed to be understand against the wider background of a spiritual lifestyle, this lifestyle is not necessarily the whole or the only form which religious beliefs and experiences could take in late antiquity. Conversely, it is against the background of other possibilities that the ultimately personal nature of the choices made by Augustine and others stands out.

---

[161] A senator he knew 'had often been deceived by silly dreams that made promises impossible to fulfil', ibid. 239 (tr. Norman, p. 125).

[162] Ibid., e.g. 193–4.

[163] A.F. Norman, introduction to Libanius, *Oratio* 1 (Oxford, 1965), esp. p. xx.

[164] Ibid., esp. pp. xviii, xxvii.

Conclusion
Sanctity between Belief and Self-Doubt

Like much historiography, this book has been an investigation of the texts produced by a certain society, of the lives of certain people within that society, and of the relationship between these two things. It began by analysing the style and intellectual basis of hagiography, a literary genre strongly characteristic of the late antique period. It ends having described a spiritually-focused lifestyle which corresponded closely to the structures and attitudes characteristic of this genre. We have depicted the relationship between text and life as one of great fluidity, and have defined this fluidity as a particular form of historicity. This basic insight can be expressed in a number of ways. One might say, for example, that religious life and the experiences of which it was composed had a textual structure long before anyone put pen to paper; that religious ideas did not remain ideas only but had a tendency to become actualized, often symbolically, in events; or that spiritual texts were historical to the extent that art imitated life just as life imitated art.

But this last statement is an incomplete truth. From a late antique perspective, it was not art that was actualized in events, but reality. And this notion of reality, which was rooted in a radical metaphysical transcendentalism, was ultimately very different from the modern scholar's notion of historicity. This could be the only legitimate basis of any fluidity between the textual world and the world of events, since the latter was itself a realm which reflected, pointed to, and symbolized higher realities. We must, therefore, reflect on the relationship between our sense of historicity and their notion of truthfulness. On some level, they may simply be complementary. The symbolic potential of the sensible world strongly encouraged spiritually-minded writers to record its contents truthfully and, as we saw in Chapter 1, this notion of truthfulness included a respect for literal detail. Conversely, it also served as a motivation to observe its contents in ways whose closest analogues were literary.

Nonetheless, the historian can only begin to grasp the nature of the spiritual lifestyle in question by recognizing the philosophical commitments of its participants. One might summarize this lifestyle by saying that, like hagiography, it was animated by the tension between two poles: on the one hand, an extremely open system of signification, an extraordinary sense of the ubiquity of possible spiritual meaning, and the willingness to countenance its presence everywhere. One might well, on this basis, describe the lifestyle in question as highly superstitious, and therefore quite in keeping with late antiquity's traditional reputation as a religiously excessive, otherworldly period. But on the other hand, this lifestyle required another pole: namely a genuine need for certainty, a search for precise and productive symbols validated, above all, by spontaneity. Of course, this is also often a feature of hagiography. But the hagiographer had the advantage of appealing to the authority of his sources and subject. Phenomena encountered personally could be validated only by a sense of externality to oneself, even if that meant nothing more concrete than an unfamiliar 'taste' or a surprising and unwilled thought. And in this second sense, it would be somewhat misleading to describe the lifestyle in question as superstitious, at least not quite in the sense in which Bronislaw Malinowski memorably defined magic, namely as a set of practices intended to assert control over chance and accident, over the unpredictable and uncertain.[1] The techniques of spiritual scrutiny described above aimed, in a sense, at precisely the opposite of this: the discovery of, and submission to, a reality entirely and demonstrably independent of human influence. For practical purposes, the historian may well treat the hagiographical as a creative process, but it is vital to recognize that it had to feel like a purely interpretative one.

One suspects that, over time, this sense grew gradually more elusive. Certainly within Christianity, the more recognizable hagiographies became as a form, the hagiographical as a vocabulary, and holy men as an institution, the more this very tradition became a pressure, a heritage for which it was hard to find genuinely new expressions and forms, both as a form of writing and as a way of life. Already in the *Apophthegmata Patrum*, the author complains that, whilst earlier generations of monks led lives guided by the books of the prophets, the present generation simply recopies them and leaves them idle on shelves.[2] If Symeon Stylites had been vulnerable to the accusation that his ascetic practice lacked any precedent, his later Gallic imitator Vulfolaic, according to Gregory of Tours, was criticized for being too obscure to follow such an illustrious model.[3] If there was 'a decline of the holy man' from the sixth and seventh centuries

---

[1]   Bronislaw Malinowski, *Magic, Science and Religion* (repr. Bristol, 1978) esp. pp. 139–40.

[2]   *Apophthegmata Patrum* 10.191.

[3]   Gregory of Tours, *Historia Francorum* 8.15, eds Henri Omont and Gaston Collon, *Grégoire de Tours. Histoire des Francs* (Paris, 1913), tr. Lewis Thorpe, *Gregory of Tours: The History of the Franks* (Harmondsworth, 1974), p. 447.

onwards, as has been suggested,[4] we may tentatively suggest that this was one contributing factor.

But within the late antique period itself, even if we accept that the holy man was a historical, rather than simply a textual phenomenon, the problem remains: where precisely do we locate him within society? And what texts can we use to find him? Was he, fundamentally, an institution, a product and projection of the group that would come to surround him and of late antique society in general? Or, was he, in the Jamesian sense, defined by particular forms of personal experience, of beliefs about the universe and about himself? The two main types of source on which this book has focused leave these questions quite mysterious. It is to hagiographies that we owe our notion of the holy man as a recognizable institution; but these texts, whilst assuming that he does possess special insight, tend to treat his own understanding and experiences as unknowable. Autobiographical writings, by contrast, allow a much greater insight into a spiritually focused lifestyle but, as we have seen, do not obviously tally with the hagiographer's notion of the holy man as someone approaching perfection.

This problem would be less severe if it consisted only in a lack of information; it is much more serious to the historical thesis of this book if the sources present contradictory viewpoints. Nothing in hagiography seems more suggestive of this latter possibility than the *fama* effect discussed at the end of Chapter 2: the device, common in Christian hagiographies, in which holy men, by humbly attempting to flee fame, in fact accumulate it. The problem posed by the *fama* effect is not merely its miraculous nature, but that this miracle is born of a complete contradiction between the crowd's view of the holy man and the holy man's view of himself. It may seem almost logically impossible for a historian to offer an account of the device which is at once truthful on the part of the author, sincere on the part of the holy man, and historically plausible to modern eyes. Would this form of behaviour really have the social effect hagiographers claim? Could the ethic of humility which defines the holy man really be authentic?

The first question is easier and it is one to which the arguments of this book can be readily extended: the spiritual significance of the *fama* effect was comprehensible not just to readers but also to observers; not only did it demonstrate the necessary ethic of humility, but the physical travels often associated with it served as a mechanism for engaging the observer's attention. Both these things require the historical holy man to have been very close to the way in which society imagined him. But the *fama* effect may have stood for another sort of proximity; namely, that of a process which bound the holy

---

[4]　Claudia Rapp, 'Byzantine Hagiographers as Antiquarians, Seventh to Tenth Centuries', in Stephanos Efthymiadis, Claudia Rapp and Dimitris Tsougarakis (eds), *Bosphorus: Essays in Honour of Cyril Mango* (Amsterdam, 1995), pp. 31–44.

man and broader society together and in which both were engaged. It is true that, following a tendency observed by Brown, hagiographies tend to present big moments to the detriment of much longer, less dramatic processes,[5] and in many works such as the *Life of Martin*, the *fama* effect is invoked only within the confines of a particular chapter, to explain isolated incidents (usually episcopal or abbatial election).[6] In others, such as the *Life of Honoratus*,[7] it is indeed presented as a process, and one capable of explaining the spread of the holy man's reputation. However, even this latter category of text associates change purely with the scale of the groups that recognize him. For a hagiographer observing from the perspective of a long agreed consensus, increasing recognition was probably both inevitable and the only kind of process his subject's sanctity could conceivably undergo.

But to most historical observers, things must have seemed very different before a holy man's reputation had been fully established or when, perhaps, it remained controversial. We might imagine that in this more plausible, ambiguous scenario, the ideological simplicities of the *fama* effect would have no place; in fact, it is precisely there that its role as a social process makes sense. For in the absence of total consensus, the function of the process may have been not only to spread the holy man's reputation to the point where he would embrace his reluctant destiny, but the very means by which society tested not just the holy man's will but the will of God. For the many Christians willing to follow true holy men, but for precisely this reason, cautious about who fulfilled this category, these were crucial concerns. God's voice, spontaneous and definitive, was needed. Even widespread popular recognition did not on its own instantly or universally equate to divine validation. For example, despite massive popular support it was only after God condemned the dissenting party through a *sors biblica* that Martin's election as bishop could go ahead.[8]

The fact that the *fama* effect contains an elegant, paradoxical, logic does not therefore negate the possibility that it was a recognized social practice. This seems still truer when we bear in mind the tendency of texts to report only success. As with any test, there were conceivable alternative outcomes, and it is not hard to imagine what these may have been. Some holy men might flee too definitively; others might appear too keen to lead, or too lazy,[9] or their pious actions misplaced. Very occasionally, hagiographical texts allow us a glimpse of

---

[5]   Brown, 'The Rise and Function of the Holy Man', p. 81.

[6]   E.g. Sulpicius, *Life of Martin* 9.

[7]   Other texts in this category include Ferrandus' *Life of Fulgentius* and Jerome's *Life of St. Hilarion*.

[8]   Sulpicius, *Life of Martin* 9.5.

[9]   John Chrysostom, *De Compunctione* 1.6, ed. J-P. Migne, PG 47 (Paris, 1858).

these other possibilities: the initial suspicions when Honoratus left home (see p. 88); the total disappearance of a nun who deserved to be the community's *amma* but was too humble to accept the role;[10] the monk Ammonius who sheared off his left ear to avoid ordination, and was finally left alone after he threatened to cut out his tongue too.[11] Between these possible outcomes there are many conceivable grey areas – perhaps on many occasions portents were either not forthcoming or ambiguous. But because these alternative outcomes posed no threat to the method of detecting sanctity, such possibilities encouraged only patience, and could in time be forgotten just as Augustine, once spoken to on a particular day, could largely forget the frustrated silent years that preceded it.

Nonetheless, the chief problem with this explanation of the crowd's response to the holy man is when we consider its implications for the second question concerning the holy man's perspective. For the less the *fama* effect appears mysterious to us, the greater the risk that it would have appeared not just recognizable, but comprehensible and explicable to contemporaries, including to the holy man himself. This returns us promptly to the problem of sincerity: if holy men just feigned social reticence, or participated in it only by way of some accepted ritual, then its apparently profound influence over other people becomes harder to explain. In any case, it means that the hagiographical *fama* effect, which required sincere belief in the autonomy of God's message, lacked genuine historical equivalence.

The question of sincerity may seem an area beyond the natural bounds of historical scrutiny, but it has received attention from modern philosophers and literary critics, including the late Bernard Williams in his celebrated *Truth and Truthfulness* (2002). Critiquing Rousseau's view of the authentic self as something entirely autonomous, interior and discoverable only through introspection, Williams argues that it can and must involve a social component. Through social contact, we respond to the needs of others, we practise and become our convictions, we develop an authentic identity.[12] This, I would suggest, is highly relevant to the *fama* effect and to hagiography and holy men more generally. As hagiographers presented it, the *fama* effect required holy men to be entirely unaware of, and resistant towards the role society attempted to accord them, until the moment where, after divine guidance, they embraced it fully and irrevocably. Because historians find these elements individually improbable, and their combination frankly implausible, they are likely either to dismiss the

---

[10]   *Apophthegmata Patrum* 18.24.

[11]   Palladius, *Lausiac History* 11.2–3. Theodoret also relates several stories about monks refusing to exercise the functions of the priesthood: *Religious History* 3.11, 13.4, 15.4, 19.2.

[12]   Bernard Williams, *Truth and Truthfulness: an Essay in Genealogy* (Princeton, 2002), chs 5 and 8.

entire story, or to rescue its basic form by positing a certain insincerity on the holy man's part. But in invoking this latter explanation, are we not committing Rousseau's error? Are we not assuming that holy men were entirely transparent to themselves, and had a direct, clear knowledge of their identity and status?

Hagiographers themselves often express doubt about a holy man's precise identity, but do so from a stance of reverence, concerned only that they may not capture the whole truth (see p. 29). The holy man himself, it is implied, seems to possess, in one sense, a total and tranquil self-knowledge; in another (as manifested not least in the *fama* effect), a perfect humility. But this perspective, I would suggest, constitutes one of the deepest and most significant aspects of untruth in hagiography, as well as an unwitting source of truth: the holy man's perception of himself was closer to the hagiographer's own incomplete view of him than the latter realized. If Eunapius was unsure whether Chrysanthius was Socrates' reincarnation or merely his intellectual heir, it is quite probable that Chryanthius himself toyed with the same question and found the answer no easier (see p. 65). The *fama* effect may simply have been an extreme way for the holy man to address continued doubts about himself, his identity, his spiritual progress. In the absence of divine confirmation – the only possible source of certainty – these questions were projected onto the crowd which could be treated as its potential vehicle. Just as the crowd scrutinized the holy man's behaviour in the search for divine confirmation of the truth about him, the holy man looked to the crowd for the truth about himself.

This does not mean that when holy men entered a process by which they would become famous, they did so with no preconception of the result: Honoratus' attempt to live up to the example of Abraham shows this, as does the very public way his protégé Hilarius fled to the desert before the gathered crowds at his funeral, purportedly to avoid succeeding him![13] But equally emphatically, it should not imply that they began this process only in order to embrace a position of leadership, or that the process served only a tactical function in enabling them to do so. The relationship between living up to paradigms and resisting society's attentions need not imply contradiction. Gandhi, for example, rarely failed to find perfect symbols for communicating to his movement and the international media, but this does not mean he was being insincere when he complained of the pain caused by the unwanted title *Mahatma*.[14] In late antiquity as in any age, those with the strongest interest in progressing spiritually were also those keenest to test themselves and most sensitive to the results. These arguments may seem strange given that in most hagiographies, popular recognition is not enough to

---

[13]   Honoratus, *Life of Hilarius* 9.11–12.

[14]   Mohandas Karamchand Gandhi, *An Autobiography: My Story of Experiments with the Truth*, tr. Mahadev Desai (repr. Harmondsworth, 1982), p. 14.

convince the holy man of his destiny without divine confirmation. But as our autobiographies have shown, widespread social acceptance could sometimes be regarded as the vessel of God's own. Despite the impressive combination of elements which constituted his garden epiphany, the immediate validation given by Alypius and Monica doubtless firmed up Augustine's conviction in the authenticity of his conversion immeasurably. Similarly with the *fama* effect: God's approval for the ordination of Martin[15] and Ambrose[16] was indicated by a voice in the crowd.

In a sense, the *fama* effect can be seen as paradigmatic of the argument pursued throughout this book. For holy men as for other people, their identity, the person they became, had a narrative aspect. But this aspect was not only their own, existential creation; rather, it drew on narrative types in which they and others could authentically believe. The excellence and humility which collide in the *fama* effect, then, were ideals only observable in a narrative form, but which could never be definitively authenticated in this form alone. For precisely this reason it had major historical consequences. If the spiritual lifestyle this book describes proved sustainable and persuasive to its practitioners, it is because it reflected the pressures exerted by models and ideals which were both remote from, and more real than immediate circumstances. For the spiritually committed individual, the extent of one's alignment with them was a question which could neither be ignored nor resolved. The spiritual life proceeded in a permanent, but precisely directed, state of doubt. The more real the object of the spiritual search was believed to be, the more that evidence of progress would both surround the searcher and at the same time fall short of proof. The questions multiplied and provoked, making a whole way of life their only meaningful answer.

---

[15]   Sulpicius, *Life of Martin* 9.
[16]   Paulinus, *Life of Ambrose* 6.

Bibliography

Primary Sources

Ambrose of Milan, *Epistularum Liber Decimus; Epistulae extra Collectionem; Gesta Concilii Aquileiensis*, ed. Michaela Zelzer, CSEL 82.3 (Vienna: F. Tempsky, 1982), tr. J.H.W.G. Liebeschuetz, *Ambrose: Political Letters and Speeches* (Liverpool: Liverpool University Press, 2005).

Ammianus Marcellinus, *Res Gestae*, ed. Wolfgang Seyfarth (2 vols, Leipzig: Teubner, 1978), tr. John Carew Rolfe, *Ammianus Marcellinus: Histories*, Loeb Classical Library, 315 (London/New York: Harvard University Press, 1935–39; repr. 2006–).

Apophthegmata Patrum, ed. Jean-Claude Guy, *Les Apophthegmes des Pères: Collection Systématique*, Sources Chrétiennes 387, 474, 498 (3 vols, Paris: Editions du Cerf, 1993–2005).

Athanasius of Alexandria, *Vita Antonii*, ed. and tr. G.J.M. Bartelink, *Athanasius: Vie d'Antoine*, Sources Chrétiennes, 400 (Paris: Editions du Cerf 1994), tr. Robert C. Gregg, *Athanasius: the* Life of Antony *and Letter to Marcellinus* (New York: Paulist Press, 1980).

Augustine, *Confessiones*, ed. with commentary, James J. O'Donnell (Oxford: Oxford University Press, 1992), tr. Philip Burton, *Augustine: Confessions* (London: Everyman, 2001).

— *Contra Academicos*, ed. Pius Knöll, *Contra Academicos Liber Tres; De Beata Vita Liber Unus; De Ordine Liber Duo*, CSEL 63 (Vienna and Leipzig: Hölder – Pichler – Tempsky, 1922), pp. 1–81, tr. John J. O'Meara, *Against the Academics* (Westminster, Maryland: Newman, 1951).

— *Contra Faustum Manichaeum*, ed. J. Zycha, *De utilitate credendi; De duabus animabus; Contra Fortunatum; Contra Adimantum; Contra epistulam fundamenti; Contra Faustum*, CSEL 25.1 (Vienna: F. Tempsky, 1891), pp. 251–797, tr. Roland Teske, *Augustine: An Answer to Faustus, a Manichaean* (Hyde Park, NY: New City Press, 2007).

— *De Beata Vita*, ed. Pius Knöll, *Contra Academicos Liber Tres; De Beata Vita Liber Unus; De Ordine Liber Duo*, CSEL 63 (Vienna and Leipzig: Hölder – Pichler – Tempsky, 1922): 89–116, tr. Ludwig Schopp, *The Happy Life by Aurelius Augustine* (London: B. Herder, 1939).

— *De Civitate Dei*, eds Bernhard Dombart and Alfons Kalb (5th edition, 2 vols, Stuttgart: Teubner, 1981), tr. R.W. Dyson, *The City of God against the Pagans* (London: Cambridge University Press, 1998).

— *De Doctrina Christiana*, ed. and tr. R.P.H. Green (Oxford: Oxford University Press, 1995). Following Green's numbering, only book and paragraph numbers are used for reference.

— *De Genesi ad Litteram*, ed. and tr., Paul Agaësse and Armand Solignac, *Augustin: La Genèse au sens littéral* (Paris: Editions du Cerf, 1972).

— *De Magistro*, ed. Günther Wiegel, CSEL 77 (Vienna: Hölder – Pichler – Tempsky, 1961), tr. Robert P. Russell, *The Teacher* = *The Teacher, The Free Choice of the Will; Grace and Free Will* (Washington D.C.: Catholic University of America, 1968).

— *De Mendacio, De fide et symbolo; De fide et operibus; De agone christiano; De continentia; De bono coniugali; De Sancta virginitate; De bono viduitatis; De adulterinis coniugiis lib. II; De mendacio; Contra mendacium; De opere monachorum; De divinatione daemonum; De cura pro mortuis gerenda; De patientia*, ed. J. Zycha, CSEL 41 (Vienna, 1900).

— *De Ordine*, ed. J. Doignon, *Bibliothèque augustinienne* (Paris: Editions du Cerf 1997), tr. Robert P. Russell (London, 1939).

— *De Utilitate Credendi*, ed. and tr. Andreas Hoffmann, *Über den Nutzen des Glaubens* (Freiburg am Breisgau: Herder, 1992).

— *Enarrationes in Psalmos*, eds Hildegund Müller and Clemens Weidmann, CSEL 93, 94 (2 vols, Vienna: Verlag der Österreichischen Akademie der Wissenschaften, 2003–2004).

— *Epistulae*, ed. A. Goldbacher, CSEL 34, 44, 57, 58 (4 vols, Vienna: F. Tempsky, 1895–1923; repr. New York: Johnson Reprint Corp., 1961–70), tr. Wilfrid Parsons, *Saint Augustine: Letters*, vol. (5 vols, Washington DC: Catholic University of America Press, 1951–56).

— *Retractationum libri duo*, ed. Pius Knöll, CSEL 36 (Vienna: F. Tempsky, 1902), tr. Mary Inez Bogan, *The Retractations* (Washington DC: Catholic University of America Press, 1968).

— *Soliloquia*, ed. H. Fuchs, *Selbstgespräche; Von der Unsterbichkeit der Seele* (Munich: Artemis, 1986), tr. Gerard Watson, *Soliloquies and The Immortality of the Soul* (Warminster: Aris and Philips, 1990).

Boethius, *Philosophiae Consolationis Libri Quinque*, ed. Rudolf Peiper (Leipzig: Teubner, 1871), tr. S.J. Tester in S.J. Tester, Hugh Fraser Stewart and Edward Kennard Rand (trs.), *Boethius: The Theological Tractates and the Consolation of Philosophy*, Loeb Classical Library (London/New York, Harvard University Press, 1918, reprinted 1973).

Cassian, John, *De Institutis Coenobiorum; De Incarnatione contra Nestorium*, ed. M. Petschenig, CSEL 17 (Vienna: F. Tempsky, 1888; repr. Verlag der Österreichischen Akademie der Wissenschaften, 2004), tr. Boniface Ramsey, *John Cassian: The Institutes* (New York: Newman Press, 2000).

— *Collationes*, ed. M. Petschenig, CSEL 13 (Vienna: F. Tempsky, 1886, repr. Verlag der Österreichischen Akademie der Wissenschaften, 2004), tr. by Boniface Ramsey, *John Cassian: The Conferences* (New York: Paulist Press, 1997).

Constantius of Lyons, *Vita Germani*, ed. and tr. René Borius, *Constance de Lyons: Vie de Saint Germain d'Auxerre*, Sources Chrétiennes 112 (Paris: Editions du Cerf, 1965), tr. F.R. Hoare in *The Western Fathers being the lives of SS. Martin of Tours, Ambrose, Augustine of Hippo, Honoratus of Arles and Germanus of Auxerre* (London: Sheed and Ward, 1954). Following Hoare's English translation, only paragraph numbers are used, and not chapters numbers.

Cyril of Scythopolis, *Vitae*, ed. Eduard Schwartz, *Kyrillos von Skythopolis*, Texte und Untersuchungen der altchristlichen Literatur 49:2 (Leipzig: Hinrich, 1939), tr. Richard Price, *Cyril of Scythopolis: Lives of the Monks of Palestine* (Kalamazoo: Cistercian Publications, 1991).

Damascius, *Vitae Isidori Reliquiae*, ed. and tr. Polymnia Athanassiadi, *Damascius: the Philosophical History* (Athens: Apamea Cultural Association, 1999).

Diogenes Laertius, *Vitae Philosophorum*, ed. and tr. Robert Drew Hicks, *Diogenes Laertius: Lives of Eminent Philosophers*, Loeb Classical Library (Cambridge MA: Harvard University Press, 1925; repr. 1970).

Egeria, *De Itinerario*, ed. and tr. Pierre Maraval and Manuel C. Díaz y Díaz = *Egérie: Journal de Voyage (Itinéraire) et Lettre sur la bienheureuse Egérie*, Sources Chrétiennes 296 (Paris: Editions du Cerf 1982), tr. John Wilkinson, *Egeria's Travels to the Holy Land* (Warminster: Aris and Philips, 1981).

Ennodius, *Opera*, ed. Frederick Vogel, MGH AA 7 (Berlin: Weidmann, 1885; repr. 1961).

— *Life of St. Epiphanius*, tr. Genevieve Marie Cook in Roy J. Deferrari (ed.), *Early Christian Biographies: lives of: St. Cyprian, by Pontius; St. Ambrose, by Paulinus; St. Augustine, by Possidius; St. Anthony, by St. Athanusius; St. Paul the first hermit, St. Hilarion, and Malchus, by St. Jerome; St. Epiphanius, by Ennodius* (Washington D.C.: Catholic University of America Press, 1952; repr. 1964).

Eucherius, *De Laude Eremi*, ed. Salvatore Pricoco (Catania: Centro di studi sull'antico Cristianesimo, 1965), tr. Tim Vivian, Kim Vivian, Jeffrey Burton Russell in *Lives of the Jura Fathers* (Kalamazoo, Michigan: Cistercian Publications, 1999).

Eugippius, *Vita Severini*, ed. and tr. Philippe Régérat, *Eugippe: Vie de Saint Séverin*, Sources Chrétiennes 374 (Paris: Editions du Cerf, 1991), tr. Ludwig Bieler, *Eugippius: The Life of Saint Severin* (Washington D.C.: Catholic University of America Press, 1965).

Eunapius, *Fragmenta Historiarum*, ed. with tr. R.C. Blockley in *The Fragmentary Classicising Historians of the Later Roman Empire: Eunapius, Olympiodorus, Priscus and Malchus* (2 vols, Liverpool: Cairns, 1981–83).

— *Vitae Philosophorum ac Sophistarum*, ed. with tr. Wilmer Cave Wright, *Philostratus and Eunapius: Lives of the Sophsists*, Loeb Classical Library (London/New York: Harvard University Press, 1921; reprinted 1968).

Favorinus, *De Exilio*, ed. Adelmo Barigazzi, *Favorino di Arelate: Opere* (Florence: Le Monnier, 1966), tr. Tim Whitmarsh in *Greek Literature and Roman Empire: The Politics of Imitation* (Oxford: Oxford University Press, 2001).

Ferrandus, *Vita Fulgentii*, ed. Jacques-Paul Migne, *S. Fulgentii Episcopi Ruspensis Opera Omnia*, PL 65 (Paris, 1847), pp. 117–50, tr. Robert B. Eno in *Fulgentius: Selected Works* (Washington D.C.: Catholic University of America Press, 1997). Eno's numbering does not follow that of the PL. Only page numberings, and not section numberings therefore refer to Eno's edition.

Gandhi, Mohandas Karamchand, *An Autobiography: My Story of Experiments with the Truth*, originally published in Gujurati (2 vols, Ahmedabad: Navajivan Press, 1927–29); tr. Mahadev Desai (Harmondsworth: Penguin, repr. 1982).

Gerontius, *Vita Melaniae Iunioris*, ed. and tr. Denys Gorce, *Vie de Sainte Mélanie*, Sources Chrétiennes 90 (Paris: Editions du Cerf, 1962), tr. Elizabeth A. Clark, *Life of Melania the Younger* (New York: Edwin Ellen Press, 1984).

Gregory of Tours, *Historia Francorum*, eds Henri Omont and Gaston Collon, *Grégoire de Tours. Histoire des Francs* (Paris: A Picard, 1913), tr. Lewis Thorpe, *Gregory of Tours: The History of the Franks* (Harmondsworth: Penguin, 1974).

Gregory of Nazianzus, *De Vita Sua*, ed and tr. Christoph Junck, *Gregor von Nazianz: De Vita Sua* (Heidelberg: Carl Winter, 1974), tr. Carolinne White, *Gregory of Nazianzus: Autobiographical Poems* (Cambridge: Cambridge University Press, 1996).

— *Oration 26*, ed. and tr. Justin Mossay and Guy Lafontaine, *Grégoire de Nazianze: Discours 24–26*, Sources Chrétiennes 284 (Paris, Editions du Cerf, 1981), tr. Daley, Brian E., *About Himself, On his Return from the Country, Gregory of Nazianzus* (London/New York: Routledge, 2006).

Gregory of Nyssa, *De Vita Moysis*, ed. Jean Daniélou, *La Vie de Moïse* (Paris: Editions du Cerf, 1968).

Hilarius of Arles, *Vita Honorati*, ed. Samuel Cavallin, *Vita Hilarii* in *Vitae Sanctorum Honorati et Hilarii, Episcoporum Arelatensium* (Lund: Gleerup 1952), tr. F.R. Hoare in *The Western Fathers being the lives of SS. Martin of Tours, Ambrose, Augustine of Hippo, Honoratus of Arles and Germanus of Auxerre* (London: Sheed and Ward, 1954).

Historia Monachorum in Aegypto, ed. and tr. André-Jean Festugière (Brussels: Société des Bollandistes, 1961). tr. Norman Russell, *The lives of the Desert Fathers: the Historia monachorum in Aegypto* (London/Oxford/Mowbray/Kalamazoo: Cistercian Publications, 1981).

Honoratus of Marseilles, *Vita Hilarii*, ed. Samuel Cavallin, *Vitae Sanctorum Honorati et Hilarii, Episcoporum Arelatensium* (Lund: Gleerup, 1952), tr. Paul-André Jacob, *La Vie d'Hilaire d'Arles*, Sources Chrétiennes 404 (Paris: Editions du Cerf, 1995).

Iamblichus, *De Vita Pythagorica Liber*, ed. Ludwig Deubner (Leipzig: B.G. Teubner, 1937), revised Ulrich Klein (Stuttgart: Teubner, 1975), tr. Gillian Clark, *On the Pythagorean Life* (Liverpool: Liverpool University Press, 1989).

Jerome, *Epistulae*, ed. Isidore Hilberg, CSEL 54, 55, 56 (Vienna: Verlag der österreichischen Akademie der Wissenschaften, 1910–18, repr. 1996), *Vita Pauli, Vita Malchi, Vita Hilarionis*, ed. and tr. Pierre Leclerc, Edgardo Martín Morales, *Jérôme: Trois Vies de Moines (Paul, Malchus, Hilarion)*, Sources Chrétiennes 508 (Paris: Editions du Cerf, 2007).

John Chrysostom, *Comparatio Regis et Monachi*; *Adversus Oppugnatores Vitae Monasticae*; *De Compunctione*, PG 47 (Paris, 1858),tr. David G. Hunter, *John Chrysostom: A Comparison Between a King and a Monk/Against the Opponents of Monastic Life* (Lampeter: Edwin Mellen Press, 1988).

Julian, *Iuliani imperatoris quae supersunt praeter reliquias apud Cyrillum omnia*, ed. Friedrich Karl Gottlob Hertlein (2 vols, Leipzig: B.G. Teubner, 1875–76).

— *Iuliani Imperatoris Librorum Contra Christianos Quae Supersunt*, ed. C.I. Neumann (Leipzig: Teubner, 1880), tr. Wilmer Cave Wright, *The Works of the Emperor Julian* (3 vols, Cambridge M.A./London: Harvard University Press, 1913–23; repr. 1980).

Libanius, *Autobiography (Oration 1)*, ed. and tr. Albert Francis Norman (Oxford: Oxford University Press, 1965).

Life and Miracles of Thecla, ed. and tr. Gilbert Dagron, *Vie et Miracles de Sainte Thècle* (Brussels: Société des Bollandistes, 1978).

Marinus, *Vita Procli*, ed. Rita Masullo, *Marino di Neapoli, Vita di Proclo* (Naples: M. D'Auria 1985), tr. Mark Edwards in *Neoplatonic Saints: the Lives of Plotinus and Proclus by their Students* (Liverpool: Liverpool University Press, 2000.)

Miracles of Demetrius, ed. and tr. Paul Lemerle, *Les plus anciens recueils des miracles de Saint Démétrius* (2 vols, Paris: Editions du Centre National de la Recherche Scientifique, 1979).

Ovid, *Tristia* and *Ex Ponto*, ed. and tr. Arthur Leslie Wheeler, Loeb Classical Library (London/New York: Harvard University Press, 1924; repr. 1996).

Palladius, *De Gentibus Indiae et Bragmanibus*, ed. J.D.M. Derrett, in 'Palladius on the races of India and the Brahmans', *Classica and Mediaevalia* 21 (1960), pp. 64–135.

— *Historia Lausiaca*, ed. G.J.M. Bartelink. *La storia lausiaca* (Milan: Fondazione Lorenzo Valla, 1974), tr. Meyer, Robert T., *Palladius: Lausiac History*, Ancient Christian Writers 34 (New York: Paulist Press, 1964).

Paulinus of Nola, *Opera*, ed. Wilhelm August, Ritter von Hartel, CSEL 29 (2 vols, Vienna: Fl Tempsky, 1894; repr. Verlag der österreichischen Akademie der Wissenschaften, 1999), tr. Patrick Gerard Walsh, *Letters of St. Paulinus of Nola* (London: Longman's Green and Co., 1967).

Paulinus of Milan, *Vita Ambrosii*, ed. and tr. Mary Simplicia Kaniecka, *Vita sancti Ambrosii, mediolanensis episcopi, a Paulino eius notario ad beatum Augustinum conscripta* (Washington D.C.: Catholic University of America Press, 1928), tr. F.R. Hoare in *The Western Fathers being the lives of SS. Martin of Tours, Ambrose, Augustine of Hippo, Honoratus of Arles and Germanus of Auxerre* (London: Sheed and Ward, 1954). Following Hoare's English translation, only paragraph numbers are used, and not chapters numbers.

Philostratus, *De Vita Apollonii Tyanei*, ed. and tr. C.P. Jones, Loeb Classical Library (3 vols, London/New York: Harvard University Press, 2005–2006).

Plato, *Epistula 7*, ed. and tr. R.G. Bury in *Plato* vol. 9 [*Timaeus, Critias, Cleitophon, Menexenus, Epistles*] Loeb Classical Library (London/New York: Harvard University Press, 1929; repr., 1989.)

— *Respublica*, ed. with tr. P. Shorey: *Plato* vols 5 and 6, Loeb Classical Library (2 vols, London/New York: Harvard University Press, 1930; repr. 1994).

— *Symposium*, ed. W.R.M. Lamb in Plato vol. 3 [*Lysis, Symposium, Gorgias*] Loeb Classical Library (London/New York: Harvard University Press, 1925; repr. 1983), pp. 73–245, tr. Michael Joyce in Edith Hamilton and Huntingdon Cairns (eds), *Plato: The Collected Dialogues* (Princeton, 1989).

— *Politicus*, ed. and tr. Harold N. Fowler in W.R.M. Lamb, in *Plato* vol. 8 [*The Statesman, Philebus, Ion*] Loeb Classical Library (London/New York: Harvard University Press, 1925; repr. 1962), pp. 5–195.

— *Theaetetus*, ed. and tr. Harold N. Fowler in *Plato* vol. 7 [*Theaetetus, Sophist*] Loeb Classical Library (London/New York: Harvard University Press, 1921; repr., 1977).

— *Timaeus*, ed. and tr. R.G. Bury in *Plato* vol. 9 [*Timaeus, Critias, Cleitophon, Menexenus, Epistles*] Loeb Classical Library (London/New York: Harvard University Press, 1929).

Plotinus, *Enneades*, ed. and tr. A.H. Armstrong, Loeb Classical Library (7 vols, London/New York: Harvard University Press, 1966–85; repr. 1995).

Porphyry, *De Abstinentia, Porphyre: de l'abstinence*, ed. and tr. Jean Bouffartigue, Alain-Philippe Segonds, Michel Patillon (3 vols, Paris: Editions du Cerf, 1977–95), tr. Gillian Clark, *On Abstinence from Killing Animals* (London: Duckworth, 2000).

— *De Vita Plotini et Ordine Librorum Eius*, ed. and tr. A.H. Armstrong, in ibid., ed. tr., *Plotinus* vol. 1, Loeb Classical Library (London/New York: Harvard University Press 1966; repr. 1995), tr. Mark Edwards as *On the Life of Plotinus and the Arrangement of his Works* in *Neoplatonic Saints: the Lives of Plotinus and Proclus by their Students* (Liverpool: Liverpool University Press, 2000).

— *De Vita Pythagorae; Ad Marcellam*, ed. and tr. Edouard des Places (Paris: Editions du Cerf, 1982).

Regula Benedicti, ed. and tr. H. Rochais, *La Règle de Saint Benoît* (Paris: Desclée De Brouwer, 1980).

Regula Magistri, ed. and tr. Adalbert de Vogüé, Sources Chrétiennes 105–7 (3 vols, Paris: Editions du Cerf, 1964–65).

Regula Sanctorum Patrum, ed. and tr. Aadalbert de Vogüé. Sources Chrétiennes 297–8 (2 vols, Paris: Editions du Cerf, 1982).

Rutilius Namatianus, *De Reditu Suo*, ed and tr. Jules Vessereau and François Préchac, *Rutilius Namatianus: Sur son retour* (Paris: Belles-Lettres, 1961).

Sallust, *Bellum Catilinae*, ed. A.T. Davis (London: Oxford University Press, 1967).

Sallustius, *De Diis et Mundo*, ed. and tr. Arthur Darby Nock, *Sallustius: Concerning the Gods and the Universe* (Cambridge: Cambridge University Press, 1926).

Sulpicius Severus, *Vita Martini*, ed. and tr. Jacques Fontaine, *Sulpice Sévère: Vie de Saint Martin*, Sources Chrétiennes 133–5 (3 vols, Paris: Editions du Cerf, 1967–69), tr. F.R. Hoare, *Life of Martin* in *The Western Fathers being the lives of SS. Martin of Tours, Ambrose, Augustine of Hippo, Honoratus of Arles and Germanus of Auxerre* (London: Sheed and Ward, 1954).

Tacitus, *Agricola*, eds Robert Maxwell Ogilvie and Ian Archibald Richmond (Oxford: Oxford University Press, 1967), tr. Maurice Hutton, *Tacitus vol. 1: Agricola, Germania, Dialogus*, Loeb Classical Library (London: Heinemann, 1970).

— *Annales*, eds Karl Halm, Georg Andresen and Erich Köstermann, *Tacitus* vol. 1 (Leipzig: Teubner, 1936), tr. J. Jackson in *Tacitus: Annals I–III*, Loeb Classical Library (London/New York: Heinemann, 1931, reprinted 1992).

Theodoret of Cyrrhus, *Philotheos Historia*, eds Pierre Canivet and Alice Leroy-Molinghen, *Histoire des moines de Syrie: Histoire Philothée*, Sources Chrétiennes 234, 257 (2 vols, Editions du Cerf: Paris 1977–79), tr. Richard Price, *Theodoret of Cyrrhus, History of the Monks of the Syria* (Cistercian Publications: Kalamazoo, 1985).

Valerius of Bierzo, *Epistola Beatissime Egerie Laude Conscripta Fratrum Bergidensium Monachorum a Valerio Conlata*, ed. and tr. Manuel C. Díaz y Díaz in *Egérie: Journal de Voyage (Itinéraire) et Lettre sur la bienheureuse Egérie*, Sources Chrétiennes 296 (Paris: Editions du Cerf 1982).

Vitae Patrum Jurensium, ed. François Martine, *Vies des pères du Jura*, Sources Chrétiennes 142 (Paris: Editions du Cerf, 1988), tr. Tim Vivian, Kim Vivian and Jeffrey Burton Russell, *The Lives of the Jura Fathers* (Cistercian Publications: Kalamazoo, 1999).

Vita Pachomii, ed. François Halkin, *Les vies grecques de S. Pachome* (Brussels: Société des Bollandistes, 1929). Reprinted with translation by Apostolos Athanassakis, *The Life of Pachomius (Vita Prima Graeca)* (Missoula, Montana: Scholars Press, 1975).

Zosimus, *Historia Nova*, ed. and tr. François Paschoud, *Histoire Nouvelle* (3 vols, Paris: Belles-Lettres, 1971–89).

Secondary Literature

Alexandre, Monique, 'Fragments autobiographiques dans l'oeuvre de Julien', in Marie-Françoise Baslez, Philippe Hoffmann and Laurent Pernot (eds), *L'invention de l'autobiographie d'Hésiode à Saint Augustin* (Paris: Presses de l'Ecole normale supérieure, 1993), pp. 285–303.

Alfaric, Prosper, *L'Evolution intellectuelle de Saint Augustine*, I. *Du Manichéisme au Néoplatonisme* (Paris: Emile Nourry, 1918).

Anderson, Graham, *Saint, Sage and Sophist: Holy Men and their Associates in the Early Roman Empire* (London: Routledge, 1994).

Ankersmit, F.R. *The Reality Effect in the Writing of History; the Dynamics of Historiographical Topology* (Amsterdam: Koninklijke Nederlandse Akademie van Wetenschappen, 1989).

Athanassiadi, Polymnia, *Julian: An Intellectual Biography* (Oxford: Oxford University Press, 1981).

Auerbach, Erich, 'Figura' in *Archivum Romanicum: Nuova Rivista di Filologia Romanza* 22 (1938), pp. 436–89.

— *Mimesis: the Representation of Reality in Western Literature*, translated by William R. Trask (Princeton University Press: Princeton, 1953).

Babut, Ernest-Charles, *Saint Martin de Tours* (Paris: H. Champion, 1912).

Baine Harris, R. (ed.), *The Significance of Neoplatonism* (Norfolk, Virginia: International Society for Neoplatonic Studies, 1976).

Barnes, Timothy D., *Ammianus Marcellinus and Representation of Historical Reality*, (Ithaca/London: Cornell University Press, 1998).

— *Early Christian Hagiography and Roman History* (Tübingen: Mohr Siebeck, 2010).

Barnish, S.J.B., 'Ennodius' Lives of Epiphanius and Antony: Two Models of Christian Gentlemen', *Studia Patristica* 24 (1993), pp. 13–19.

Barthes, Roland, 'L'Effet de réel', *Communications* 11 (1968), pp. 84–9.

— 'Introduction to the Structural Analysis of Narratives', in *The Semiotic Challenge*, tr. Richard Howard (Oxford: Basil Blackwell, 1988), pp. 95–135.

Baslez, Marie-Françoise, Philippe Hoffmann and Laurent Pernot (eds), *L'invention de l'autobiographie d'Hésiode à Saint Augustin* (Paris: Presses de l'Ecole normale supérieure, 1993).

Bastiaensen, A.A.R., 'Jérôme hagiographe', in Guy Philippart (ed.), *Hagiographies: histoire internationale de la littérature hagiographique latine et vernaculaire en Occident des origines à 1550* (Turnhout: Brepols, 1994), pp. 97–123.

Berg, Beverly, 'Dandamis: an Early Christian Portait of Indian Asceticism', in *Classica and Mediaevalia* 31 (1970), pp. 269–305.

Bennett, Camille, 'The Conversion of Vergil: The Aeneid in Augustine's *Confessions*', *Revue des études augustiniennes* 34 (1988), pp. 47–69.

Binns, John, *Ascetics and Ambassadors of Christ: The Monasteries of Palestine 314–631* (Oxford: Oxford University Press, 1994).

Blowers, Paul M., 'The Bible and Spiritual Doctrine: some Controversies within the Early Eastern Christian Ascetic Tradition', Paul M. Blowers (ed.), *The Bible in Greek Christian Antiquity* (University of Notre Dame Press: Notre Dame, 1997), pp. 229–55.

Blowers, Paul M. (ed.), *The Bible in Greek Christian Antiquity* (University of Notre Dame Press: Notre Dame, 1997).

Blumenthal, H.J, 'Marinus' *Life of Proclus*: Neoplatonist Biography', *Byzantion* 54 (1984), pp. 469–94.

Bonner, Gerald, 'Augustine's Conversion: Historical Fact or Literary Device?' in P. Merino and J.M. Torrecilla (eds), *Augustinus: Charisteria Augustiniana. Iosepho Oroz Rota dicata* (Madrid: Editorial Augustinus, 1993), pp. 103–19.

— *St. Augustine of Hippo: Life and Controversies* (London: SCM, 1963, repr. Norwich: Cantebury Press, 2002).

Booth, Alan D., 'On the Date of Eunapius' Coming to Athens', *Ancient History Bulletin* 1 (1987), pp. 14–15.

Booth, Philip, Matthew J. Dal Santo and Peter Sarris (eds), *An Age of Saints? Power, Conflict and Dissent in Early Medieval Christianity* (Leiden: Brill, 2011).

Bordieu, Pierre, 'Marginalia – Some Additional Notes on the Gift', in Alan D. Schrift (ed.), *The Logic of the Gift: Towards an Ethic of Generosity* (London/ New York: Routledge, 1997), pp. 231 –41.

Børtnes, Jostein and Tomas Hägg (eds), *Gregory of Nazianzus: Images and Reflections* (Copenhagen, Museum Tusculanum, 2006).

Bratož, Rajko, *Severinus von Noricum und seine Zeit*: *Geschichtliche Anmerkungen* (Vienna: Oesterreichischen Akademie der Wissenschaften, 1983).

Brown, Peter, *Augustine of Hippo: a Biography* (London: Faber, 1967).

— *Authority and the Sacred: Aspects of the Christianisation of the Roman World* (Cambridge University Press, 1995)

— 'The Christian Holy Man in Late Antiquity' in *Authority and the Sacred: Aspects of the Christianisation of the Roman World* (Cambridge: Cambridge University Press, 1995).

— *Power and Persuasion in Late Antiquity: Towards a Christian Empire* (Madison, Wisconsin: University of Wisconsin Press, 1992).

— 'The Rise and Function of the Holy Man in Late Antiquity', *Journal of Roman Studies* 61 (1971), pp. 80–101, repr. in Brown, Peter, *Society and the Holy in Late Antiquity* (London: Faber and Faber, 1982).

— 'The Rise and Function of the Holy Man in Late Antiquity, 1971–1997' in *Journal of Early Christian Studies* 6.1 (1998), pp. 353–76.

— 'The Saint as Exemplar in Late Antiquity', *Representations* 2 (1983), pp. 1–25.

Brunert, Maria-Elisabeth, *Das Ideal der Wüstenaskese und seine Rezeption in Gallien bis zum Ende des 6.Jahrhunderts* (Münster: Aschendorff, 1994).

— 'Die Bedeutung der Wüste im Eremitentum', in Uwe Lindemann and Monika Schmitz-Emans (eds), *Was ist eine Wüste?: Interdisziplinäre Annäherungen an einen interkulturellen Topos* (Würzburg: Königshausen und Neumann, 2000), pp. 59–69.

Buck, David Frederick, 'Eunapius' *Lives of the Sophists*: a Literary Study', *Byzantion* 62 (1992), pp. 141–57.

— 'Prohaeresius' Recruitment of Students', *Liverpool Classical Monthly* 12.5 (1987), pp. 77–8.

Coleiro, E., 'St. Jerome's Lives of the Hermits', *Vigiliae Christianiae* 11 (1957), pp. 161–78.

Caluori, Damian, 'The Essential Functions of a Plotinian Soul', *Rhizai* 2 (2005), pp. 75–93.

— 'Reason and Necessity: The Descent of the Philosopher-Kings', in *Oxford Studies in Ancient Philosophy* 40 (Oxford: Oxford University Press, 2011), pp. 7–27.

— 'The Date of Porphyry's ΚΑΤΑ ΧΡΙΣΤΙΑΝΩΝ', in *Classical Quarterly*, New Series 17 (1967), pp. 382–4.

Cameron, Averil, *Christianity and the Rhetoric of Empire: the Development of Christian Discourse* (Berkeley, 1991).

— (ed.), *Fifty Years of Prosopography: the Later Roman Empire, Byzantium and Beyond* (Oxford: Oxford University Press, 2003).

— 'Form and Meaning: The *Vita Constantinii* and the *Vita Antonii*' in Tomas Hägg and Philip Rousseau (eds), *Greek Biography and Panegyric in Late Antiquity* (Berkeley: University of California Press, 2000), pp. 72–88.

— 'On Defining the Holy Man', in James Howard-Johnston and Paul Anthony Hayward (eds), *The Cult of Saints in Late Antiquity and the Early Middle Ages: Essays on the Contribution of Peter Brown* (Oxford: Oxford University Press, 1999), pp. 27–43.

Chadwick, Henry, *Boethius: The Consolations of Music, Logic, Theology and Philosophy* (Oxford: Oxford University Press, 1981).

Claassen, Jo-Marie, *Displaced Persons:the Literature of Exile from Cicero to Boethius* (London: Duckworth, 1999).

Clark, Elizabeth A., *History, Theory, Text: Historians and the Linguistic Turn* (Cambridge MA: Harvard University Press, 2004).

Clark, Gillian, *Augustine: the* Confessions (Cambridge: Cambridge University Press, 1993, repr. Bristol: Phoenix Press, 2005).

— 'Philosophic Lives and the Philosophic Life', in Tomas Hägg and Philip Rousseau (eds), *Greek Biography and Panegyric in Late Antiquity* (Berkeley: University of California Press, 2000), pp. 29–51.

Collingwood, Robin George, *The Idea of History* (Oxford: Oxford University Press, 1946).

Confino, Alon, *The Nation as Local Metaphor: Württemberg, Imperial Germany, and National Memory 1871–1918* (Chapel Hill: University of North Carolina Press, 1997).

Conybeare, Catherine, *The Irrational Augustine* (Oxford: Oxford University Press, 2006).

Cooper, Kate, 'The Widow as Impresario: Gender, Legendary Afterlives, and Documentary Evidence in Eugippius' *Vita Severini*' in Walter Pohl and Maximilian Diesenberger (eds), *Eugippius und Severin* (Vienna: Verlag der Österreichischen Akademie der Wissenschaften, 2001), pp. 53–63.

Courcelle, Pierre, 'Le "*Tolle, Lege*"; fiction littéraire et réalité', in Pierre Courcelle, *Recherches sur les Confessions d'Augustin* (Paris: E. de Boccard, 1950), pp. 188–202.

— 'Le jeune Augustin, second Catilina', in *Revue des études anciennes* 73 (1971), pp. 141–50.

— *Les Confessions de Saint Augustin dans la tradition littéraire: antécédents et postérité* (Paris: Etudes augustiniennes, 1963).

— 'Les premières *Confessions* de saint Augustin' in *Révue des études latines* 21–2 (1943–44), pp. 155–74.

— *Lettres grecques en Occident: de Macrobe à Cassiodore* (Paris: E. de Boccard, 1948).

Cox, Patricia, *Biography in Late Antiquity: a Quest for the Holy Man* (Berkeley: University of California Press, 1983).

— (Cox Miller, Patricia), 'Strategies of Representation in Collective Biography: Constructing the Subject as Holy' in Tomas Hägg, Philip Rousseau (eds), *Greek Biography and Panegyric in Late Antiquity* (Berkeley: University of California Press, 2000), pp. 209–54.

Crabbe, Anna, 'Literary Design in the *De Consolatione Philosophiae*' in Margaret Gibson (ed.), *Boethius: His Life, Thought and Influence* (Oxford: Oxford University Press, 1981), pp. 237–74.

Crome, Peter, *Symbol und Unzulänglichkeit der Sprache: Jamblichos, Plotin, Porphyrios, Proklos* (Munich: W. Fink, 1970).

Crosson, Frederick J., 'Structure and Meaning in St. Augustine's *Confessions*', in Gareth B. Matthews (ed.), *The Augustinian Tradition* (Berkeley: University of California Press, 1999), pp. 84–97.

Cullman, Oscar and Philippe Ménoud (eds), *Aux sources de la tradition chrétienne: Mélanges Goguel* (Neuchâtel: Delachaux et Niestlé, 1950).

Dagron, Gilbert, 'L'ombre d'un doute: l'hagiographie en question Vie–XIe siècle', *Dumbarton Oaks Papers* 46 (1992), pp. 59–68.

Daley, Brian E., *Gregory of Nazianzus* (London/New York: Routledge, 2006).

Dennett, Daniel C., *Consciousness Explained* (Boston/London: Little, Brown, 1991).

De Vogüé, Adalbert, 'Sur la patrie d'Honorat de Lérins, évêque d'Arles', in *Revue Bénédictine* 88 (1978), pp. 290–91.

Diesenberger, Maximilian, 'Topographie und Gemeinschaft in der *Vita Severini*', in Walter Pohl and Maximilian Diesenberger (eds), *Eugippius und Severin* (Vienna, 2001), pp. 77–98.

Dillon, John, 'Die Vita Pythagorica – ein "Evangelium"', in Michael von Albrecht (ed.), *Jamblich: Peri tou Pythagoreiou bio. Pythagoras: Legende –*

Lehre – Lebensgestaltung (Darmstadt: Wissenschaftliche Buchgesellschaft, 2002), pp. 295–302.

— 'Holy and not so Holy: On the Interpretation of late antique Biography', in Brian McGing and Judith Mossman (eds), *The Limits of Ancient Biography* (Swansea: Classical Press of Wales, 2006), pp. 155–67.

— '"Orthodoxy" and "Eclecticism": Middle Platonists and Neopythagoreans' in John Dillon and A.A. Long (eds), *The Question of 'Eclecticism'*, (Berkeley: University of California Press, 1988), pp. 103–25.

— and A.A. Long (eds), *The Question of 'Eclecticism'*, (Berkeley: University of California Press, 1988).

Dodds, E.R., *Pagan and Christian in an Age of Anxiety* (Cambridge: Cambridge University Press, 1965).

Dumner, Jürgen and Meinholf Vielberg (eds), *Zwischen Historiographie und Hagiographie* (Stuttgart: Steiner, 2005).

Edwards, Mark, 'Birth, Death and Divinity in Porphyry's *Life of Plotinus*' in Tomas Hägg and Philip Rousseau (eds), *Greek Biography and Panegyric in Late Antiquity* (Berkeley: University of California Press, 2000), pp. 52–71.

— 'Scenes from the Later Wanderings of Odysseus', in *Classical Quarterly* 38 (1988), pp. 509–21.

— 'A Portrait of Plotinus', in *Classical Quarterly* 43 (1993), pp. 480–90.

Ellis, Linda and Frank L. Kidner (eds), *Travel, Communication and Geography in Late Antiquity: Sacred and Profane* (Aldershot: Ashgate, 2004).

Efthymiadis, Stephanos, Claudia Rapp and Dimitris Tsougarakis (eds), *Bosphorus: Essays in Honour of Cyril Mango* (Amsterdam: Hakkert, 1995).

— 'Two Gregories and Three Genres: Autobiography, Autohagiography and Hagiography', in Jostein Børtnes and Tomas Hägg (eds), *Gregory of Nazianzus: Images and Reflections* (Copenhagen, Museum Tusculanum, 2006), pp. 246–56.

Ferguson, Margaret, 'St Augustine's Region of Unlikeness: The Crossing of Exile and Language', *The Georgia Review* 29 (1975), pp. 842–64.

Ferrari, Leo, 'The Pear-Theft in Augustine's *"Confessions"*', *Revue des études augustiniennes* 16 (1970), pp. 233–42.

— 'Saint Augustine's Conversion Scene: the End of a Modern Debate' in *Studia Patristica* 22 (1989), pp. 235–50.

— 'The Theme of the Prodigal Son in Augustine's *Confessions*', in *Recherches augustiniennes* 12 (1977), pp. 105–18.

— 'Truth and Augustine's Conversion Scene', in Joseph C. Schnaubelt and Frederick van Fleteren (eds), *Augustine 'Second Founder of the Faith'* (New York: Peter Lang, 1990), pp. 9–19.

Ferwerda, Rein, *La signification des images et des métaphores dans la pensée de Plotin* (Groningen: J.B. Wolters, 1965).

Festugière, André-Jean, 'Cadre de la mystique hellénistique', in Oscar Cullman and Philippe Ménoud (eds), *Aux sources de la tradition chrétienne: Mélanges Goguel* (Neuchâtel: Delachaux et Niestlé, 1950), pp. 74–85.

Fielder, John, H., '*Chorismos* and Emanation in the Philosophy of Plotinus' in R. Baine Harris (ed.) *The Significance of Neoplatonism* (Norfolk,Virginia: International Society for Neoplatonic Studies, 1976), pp. 101–20.

Fisher, Duncan, 'Liminality: the Vocation of the Church (I); the Desert Image in Early Christian Tradition', *Cistercian Studies* 24 (1989), pp. 181–205.

Flusin, Bernard, *Miracle et histoire dans l'oeuvre de Cyrille de Scythopolis* (Paris: Etudes augustiniennes, 1983).

Fontaine, Jacques, 'Valeurs antiques et valeurs chrétiennes dans la spiritualité des grands propriétaires terriens à la fin du Ive siècle occidental' in *Etudes sur la poésie latine tardive d'Ausone à Prudence: recueil du travail* (Paris: Belles-Lettres, 1980), pp. 241–65.

Fowden, Garth, 'The Pagan Holy Man in Late Antique Society', in *Journal of Hellenic Studies* 102 (1982), pp. 33–59.

Franzese, Sergio, 'Is Religious Experience the Experience of Something? "Truth", Belief, and "Overbelief" in The Varieties of Religious Experience' in Sergio Franzese and Felicitas Kraemer (eds), *Fringes of Religious Experience: Cross-perspectives on William James's* The Varieties of Religious Experience (Frankfurt: Ontos, 2007), pp. 139–55.

— and Felicitas Kraemer (eds), *Fringes of Religious Experience: Cross-perspectives on William James's* The Varieties of Religious Experience (Frankfurt: Ontos, 2007).

Frederiksen, Paula, 'Paul and Augustine Conversion Narratives, Orthodox Traditions and the Retrospective Self' in *Journal of Theological Studies* 37.1 (1986), pp. 3–34.

Fredouille, Jean-Claude, 'Les *Confessions* d'Augustin, Autobiographie au Présent', in Marie-Françoise Baslez, Philippe Hoffmann and Laurent Pernot (eds), *L'invention de l'autobiographie d'Hésiode à Saint Augustin* (Paris: Presses de l'Ecole normale supérieure, 1993), pp. 167–78.

Frow, John, *Genre* (London: Routledge, 2006).

Genette, Gérard, *Palimpsestes: La littérature au second degré* (Paris: Editions du Seuil, 1982).

Gibbon, Edward, *The History of the Decline and Fall of the Roman Empire*, ed. J.B. Bury (7 vols, London: Methuen and Co, 1897).

Gibson, Margaret (ed.), *Boethius: His Life, Thought and Influence* (Oxford: Oxford University Press, 1981)

Gill, Christopher and Wiseman, Timothy Peter (eds), *Lies and Fiction in the Ancient World* (Exeter: Exeter University Press, 1993).

Gleason, Maud W., 'Visiting and News: Gossip and Reputation Management in the Desert', *Journal of Early Christian Studies* 6.3 (1998), pp. 501–21.

Goehring, James E., 'The Dark Side of Landscape: Ideology and Power in the Christian Myth of the Desert' in *Journal of Medieval and Early Modern Studies* 33.3 (2003), pp. 437–52.

— 'The Encroaching Desert: Literary Production and Ascetic Space in Early Christian Egypt', *Journal of Early Christian Studies* 1 (1993), pp. 281–96. Reprinted in James E. Goehring, *Ascetics, Society and the Desert: Studies in Early Egyptian Monasticism* (Harrisburg PA: Trinity Press International, 1999), pp. 73–88.

Goddard Elliot, Alison, *Roads to Paradise: Reading the Lives of the Early Saints* (Hanover/London: University Press of New England for Brown University Press, 1987).

Goffart, Walter, 'Does the Vita. S. Severini have an Underside?' in Walter Pohl and Maximilian Diesenberger (eds), *Eugippius und Severin* (Vienna, 2001), pp. 34–9.

Goodman, Nelson, *Languages of Art* (Indianapolis: Hackett Pub. Co., 1976).

Goulet, Richard, *Etudes sur les vies de philosophes de l'antiquité tardive: Diogène Laërce, Porphyre de Tyr, Eunape de Sardes* (Paris: Vrin, 2001).

— 'Variations romanesques sur la mélancholie de Porphyre', in *Hermes* 110 (1982), pp. 443–57.

Goulet-Cazé, M-O, 'Kosmopolitismus', in Hubert Cancik and Helmut Schneider (eds), *Der Neue Pauly: Enzyklopädie der Antike* Band 6 (19 vols, Stuttgart: Metzler, 1996–2003), pp. 778–9.

Gould, Graham, *The Desert Fathers on Monastic Community* (Oxford, 1993).

Griffin, Jasper, 'Genre and Real Life in Latin Poetry' in *Journal of Roman Studies* 71 (1981), pp. 39–49.

Gruber, Joachim, *Kommentar zu Boethius* de Consolatione Philosophiae (Berlin/New York: Walter de Gruyter, 1978).

Gudeman, Alfred, 'Sind die Dialoge Augustins historisch?' in *Silvae Monacenses Festschrift zur 50 jährigen des philologischen-historisch Vereins an der Universität Münchens* (Munich, 1926), pp. 16–27.

Hadot, Pierre, *Exercises spirituels et philosophie antique* (Paris: Etudes augustiniennes, 1981).

Hägg, Tomas, Philip Rousseau (eds), *Greek Biography and Panegyric in Late Antiquity* (Berkeley: University of California Press, 2000).

Hargis, Jeffrey W., *Against the Christians: the Rise of Early Anti-Christian Polemic* (New York/Canterbury: Peter Lang, 2001).

Harrison, Carol, 'Augustine of Hippo's Cassiciacum *Confessions*: Towards a Reassessment of the 390's' in *Augustinian Studies* 31.2 (2000), pp. 219–24.

Hawkes, Terence, *Semiotics and Structuralism* (London: Routledge, 1977).

Heather, Peter, *The Fall of the Roman Empire: a New History* (London: Pan Macmillan, 2005).

Hinterberger, Martin, *Autobiographische Traditionen in Byzanz* (Vienna: Verlag der Österreichischen Akademie der Wissenschaften, 1999).

Hodgkin, Thomas, *Italy and Her Invaders* (8 vols, Oxford: Oxford University Press, 1880–89).

Howard-Johnston, James and Paul Anthony Hayward (eds), *The Cult of Saints in Late Antiquity and the Early Middle Ages: Essays on the Contribution of Peter Brown* (Oxford: Oxford University Press, 1999).

Hunt, E.D., 'The Itinerary of Egeria: Reliving the Bible in Fourth-Century Palestine', in R.N. Swanson (ed.), *The Holy Land, Holy Lands and Christian History* (Woodbridge: Published for the Ecclesiastical History Society by Boydell & Brewer 2000), pp. 34–54.

— *Holy Land Pilgrimage in the Later Roman Empire: AD 312–460* (Oxford, Oxford University Press, 1984).

Jerphagnon, Lucien, 'Les sous-entendus anti-chrétiens de la Vita Plotini ou l'évangile de Plotin selon Porphyre', in *Museum Helveticum* 47 (1990), pp. 41–52.

Kaegi, Walter Emil, 'The Emperor Julian's Assessment of the Significance and Function of History', *Proceedings of the American Philosophical Association* 108 (1964), pp. 29–38.

Kelly, John Norman Davidson, *Jerome: His Life, Writings and Controversies* (London: Duckworth, 1975).

Keyes, Charles F., 'Introduction: Charisma from Social Life to Sacred Biography' in Michael A. Williams (ed.), *Charisma and Sacred Biography, Journal of the American Academy of Religion Studies* 48 (1982), pp. 1–22.

Klaniczay, Gábor, 'Legends as Life Strategies for Aspirant Saints in the Later Middle Ages', *Journal of Folklore Research* 26 (1989), pp. 151–72.

König, Jason, 'The Cynic and Christian Lives of Lucian's *Peregrinus*' in Brian McGing and Judith Mossman (eds), *The Limits of Ancient Biography* (Swansea: Classical Press of Wales, 2006), pp. 227–54.

Konstan, David, 'How to Praise a Friend: St. Gregory of Nazianzus's Funeral Oration for St. Basil the Great' in Tomas Hägg and Philip Rousseau (eds), *Greek Biography and Panegyric in Late Antiquity* (Berkeley: University of California Press, 2000), pp. 160–79.

Kotzé, Annemaré, *Augustine's* Confessions: *Communicative Purpose and Audience* (Leiden: Brill, 2004).

Kris, Ernst, *Psychoanalytical Explorations in Art* (London: George Allen and Unwin Ltd., 1953).

Krueger, Derek, *Writing and Holiness: The Practice of Authorship in the Early Christian East* (Philadelphia: University of Pennsylvania Press, 2004).

Lamberton, Robert, *Homer the Theologian: Neoplatonist Allegorical Reading and the Growth of the Epic Tradition* (Berkeley: University of California Press, 1986).

Lampe, G.W.H., 'Miracles and Early Christian Apologetic' in C.F.D. Moule (ed.), *Miracles* (London: A.R. Mowbray, 1965), pp. 203–18.

Leclercq, Jean, '"Eremus" et "Eremita": Pour l'histoire du vocabulaire de la vie solitaire', in *Collecteana Ordinis Cistersiensium Reformatorum* 25.1 (1963), pp. 8–30.

Lejeune, Philippe, *Le Pacte Autobiographique* (Paris: Editions du Seuil, 1975).

Lerer, Seth, *Boethius and Dialogue: Literary Method in the* Consolation of Philosophy (Princeton: Princeton University Press, 1985).

Lévi-Strauss, Claude, *Structural Anthropology*, translated by Claire Jacobson and Brooke Grundfest Schoepf (Harmondsworth: Penguin, 1972).

Leyser, Conrad, *Authority and Asceticism from Augustine to Gregory the Great* (Oxford: Oxford University Press, 2000).

— 'Shoring Fragments against Ruin? Eugippius and the Sixth-Century Culture of the Florilegium', in Eugippius' *Vita Severini* in Walter Pohl and Maximilian Diesenberger (eds), *Eugippius und Severin* (Vienna: Verlag der Österreichischen Akademie der Wissenschaften, 2001), pp. 77–98.

— '"This Sainted Isle": Panegyric, Nostalgia and the Invention of Lerinian Monasticism' in William E. Klingshirn and Mark Vessey (eds), *The Limits of Ancient Christianity* (Michigan, 1999), pp. 188–206.

Liebeschuetz, J.H.W.G., *Continuity and Change in Roman Religion* (Oxford: Oxford University Press, 1979).

Lifshitz, Felice, 'Beyond Positivism and Genre: "Hagiographical" Texts as Historical Narrative' in *Viator* 25 (1994), pp. 95–114.

Ligota, Christopher R., '"This story is not true". Fact and Fiction in Antiquity', *Journal of the Warburg and Courtauld Institutes* 45 (1982), pp. 1–13.

Lindars, Barnabas, 'Elijah, Elisha and the Gospel Miracles', in C.F.D. Moule (ed.), *Miracles* (London, 1965): 63–79.

Lindemann, Uwe and Monika Schmitz-Emans (eds), *Was ist eine Wüste?: Interdisziplinäre Annäherungen an einen interkulturellen Topos* (Würzburg: Königshausen und Neumann, 2000).

Lindemann, Uwe, '"Passende Wüste für Fata Morgana gesucht". Zur Etymologie und Begriffsgeschichte der fünf lateinischen Wörter für *Wüste*', in Uwe Lindemann and Monika Schmitz-Emans (eds), *Was ist eine Wüste?:*

Interdisziplinäre Annäherungen an einen interkulturellen Topos (Würzburg: Königshausen und Neumann, 2000), pp. 87–100.

Lotter, Friedrich, *Severinus von Noricum: Legende und historische Wirklichkeit* (Stuttgart: Hiersemann: 1976), reviewed by Stancliffe, Claire, *Journal of Theological Studies* 29 (1978), pp. 576–7.

McGing, Brian and Judith Mossman (eds), *The Limits of Ancient Biography* (Swansea: Classical Press of Wales, 2006)

McLynn, Neil, 'A Self-Made Holy Man: The Case of Gregory Nazianzen', *Journal of Early Christian Studies* 6:3 (1998), pp. 463–83

McWilliam, Joanne (ed.), *Augustine: From Rhetor to Theologian* (Waterloo: Wilfrid Laurier University Press, 1992).

— 'The Cassiciacum Autobiography' in *Studia Patristica* 18.4 (1990), pp. 14–43.

MacCormack, Sabine, *The Shadow of Poetry: Vergil in the Mind of Augustine* (Berkeley: University of California Press, 1998).

MacDonald, Scott, 'Petit Larceny, the Beginning of all Sin: Augsutine's Theft of the Pears' in William E. Mann (ed.), *Augustine's* Confessions: *Critical Essays* (Oxford: Rowman and Littlefield, 2006), pp. 45–70.

MacIntyre, Alisdair, *After Virtue: a Study in Moral Theory* (London: Duckworth, 1981).

Mallarmé, Stéphane, 'Hérésies artistiques: l'art pour tous', in Henri Mondor and George Jean-Aubry (eds), *Oeuvres complètes* (Paris: Gallimard, 1945; repr. 1983).

Madec, Goulven, 'L'historicité des *Dialogues* de Cassiciacum' in *Revue des études augustiniennes* 32 (1986), pp. 207–31.

Malinowski, Bronislaw, *Magic, Science and Religion and Other Essays* (Garden City NY: Doubleday, 1948; repr. Bristol: Arrowsmith, 1982).

Mandouze, André, *Saint Augustin. L'aventure de la raison et de la grâce* (Paris: Etudes augustiniennes, 1968).

Mann, William E. (ed.), *Augustine's* Confessions: *Critical Essays* (Oxford: Rowman and Littlefield, 2006).

Mansfeld, Jaap, 'Plotinian Ancestry' in *Illinois Classical Studies* 20 (1995), pp. 149–56.

Marenbon, Jon, *Boethius* (Oxford: Oxford University Press, 2003).

Markus, Robert A., *The End of Ancient Christianity* (Cambridge: Cambridge University Press, 1990).

— *Signs and Meanings: World and Text in Ancient Christianity* (Liverpool: Liverpool University Press, 1996).

Mathisen, Ralph W., *Ecclesiastical Factionalism and Religious Controversy in Fifth-Century Gaul* (Washington: Catholic University of America Press, 1989).

Matthews, Gareth B. 'Augustine on the Teacher Within' in William E. Mann (ed.), *Augustine's* Confessions: *Critical Essays* (Oxford: Rowman and Littlefield 2006), pp. 31–44.

— (ed.), *The Augustinian Tradition* (Berkeley: University of California Press, 1999).

Matthews, John, 'Peter Valvomeres, Re-arrested' in Michael Whitby, Philip Hardie and Mary Whitby (eds), *Homo Viator: Classical Essays for John Bramble* (Bristol: Bristol Classical Press (and Bolchazy-Carducci), 1987), pp. 277–84.

— *The Roman Empire of Ammianus* (London: Duckworth, 1989).

Mayer, Cornelius Petrus, Feldmann, Erich, Chelius and Karl Heinz (eds), *Augustinus-Lexikon* (3 vols to date, Basel: Schwabe, 1986–).

Merino, P. and Torrecilla, J.M. (eds), *Augustinus: Charisteria Augustiniana. Iosepho Oroz Rota dicata* (Madrid: Editorial Augustinus, 1993).

Meulenbroek, B.L., 'The Historical Character of Augustine's Cassiciacum Dialogues' in *Mnemosyne* 13.3 (1947), pp. 203–29.

Moorhead, John, *Justinian* (London: Longman, 1994).

— *Theoderic in Italy* (Oxford: Oxford University Press, 1992).

Moreschini, Claudio, 'Il motivo dell'esilio dell'anima' in Fabio Rosa and Francesco Zambon (eds), *Pothos: Il viaggio, la nostalgia* (Trento: Dipartimento di Scienze Filologiche e Storiche, 1995), pp. 97–105.

Moule, C.F.D., *Miracles* (London: A.R. Mowbray, 1965).

Näsström, Britt-Mari, *O Mother of the Gods and Men: Some Aspects of the Religious Thoughts in Emperor Julian's Discourse on the Mother of the Gods* (Lund: Plus Ultra, 1990).

Newbold, Ron F., 'Power Motivation in Sidonius Apollinaris, Eugippius, and Nonnus', in *Florilegium* 7 (1985): 1–16.

Nouailhat, René, *Saints et Patrons: Les premiers moines de Lérins* (Paris: Belles Lettres, 1988).

Nürnberg, Rosemarie, *Askese als sozialer Impuls: monastisch-asketische Spiritualität als Wurzel und Triebfeder sozialer Ideen und Aktivitäten der Kirche in Südgallien im 5. Jahrhundert* (Bonn: Borengässer, 1988).

O'Connell, Robert, J., *St. Augustine's Confessions: the Odyssey of the Soul* (Cambridge MA: Belknap Press of Harvard University Press, 1969).

O'Meara, Dominic J., 'Patterns of Perfection in Damascius' *Life of Isidore*' in *Phronesis* 51.1 (2006), pp. 74–89.

— *An Introduction to the* Enneads (Oxford: Oxford University Press, 1993).

O'Meara, J. J., 'Augustine's *Confessions*: Elements of Fiction' in Joanne McWilliam (ed.), *Augustine: From Rhetor to Theologian* (Waterloo: Wilfrid Laurier University Press, 1992), pp. 77–96.

— 'The Historicity of Augustine's Early Dialogues', in *Vigiliae Christianae* 5 (1951), pp. 150–78, repr. in *Studies in Augustine and Eriugena* (Washington: Catholic University of America Press, 1992), pp. 11–23.

— (ed.), *Neoplatonism and Christian Thought* (New York: State University of New York Press, 1982).

— *The Young Augustine: An Introduction to the* Confessions *of Augustine* (London: Longmans Green, 1954, repr. 2001).

Opelt, Ilona, 'Zur literarischen Eigenart von Eucherius' Schrift *de laude eremi*', in *Vigiliae Christianae* 22 (1968), pp. 198–208.

Patlagean, Evelyne, 'Ancienne hagiographie byzantine et histoire sociale', *Annales: Economies, Sociétés, Civilisations* 23.1 (1968), pp. 106–26.

Pelling, Christopher, B.R., 'Truth and Fiction in Plutarch's *Lives*' in D.A. Russell (ed.), *Antonine Literature* (Oxford: Oxford University Press, 1990), pp. 19–51.

Penella, Robert J., *Greek Philosophers and Sophists in the Fourth Century A.D; Studies in Eunapius of Sardis* (Leeds: Francis Cairns, 1990).

Pépin, Jean, 'The Platonic and Christian Ulysses', in Dominic J. O'Meara (ed.), *Neoplatonism and Christian Thought* (New York: State University of New York Press, 1982), pp. 3–18.

Philippart, Guy (ed.), *Hagiographies: histoire internationale de la littérature hagiographique latine et vernaculaire en Occident des origines à 1550* (Turnhout: Brepols, 1994).

Pohl, Walter, 'Einleitung: Commemoratium – Vergegenwärtigungen des heiligen Severin' in Walter Pohl and Maximilian Diesenberger (eds), *Eugippius und Severin* (Vienna: Verlag der Österreichischen Akademie der Wissenschaften, 2001), pp. 9–24.

Popper, Karl, 'Science: Conjectures and Refutations' in Martin Curd and J.A. Cover (eds), *Philosophy of Science: the Central Issues* (New York/London: W.W. Norton, 1988), pp. 3–10.

Pratsch, Thomas, 'Exploring the Jungle: Hagiographical Literature between Fact and Fiction' in Averil Cameron (ed.), *Fifty Years of Prosopography: the Later Roman Empire, Byzantium and Beyond* (Oxford: Oxford University Press, 2003), pp. 59–72.

Pricoco, Salvatore, *L'isola dei Santi: il cenobio di Lerino e le origini del monachesimo gallico* (Rome: Edizione dell'Anteneo e Bizzarri, 1978).

— *Monaci, Filosofi, e Santi: Saggi di storia della cultura tardoantica* (Soveria Mannelli: Rubbettino, 1992).

Prinz, Friedrich, *Frühes Mönchtum in Frankenreich. Kultur und Gesellschaft in Gallien am Beispiel der monastischen Entwicklung (4–8 Jahrhundert)* (Vienna: Oldenbourg, 1965).

— 'Hagiographie und Welthaftigkeit: Überlegungen zur Vielfalt des hagiographischen Genus im Frühmittelalter' in Dorothea Walz (ed.), *Lateinische Biographie von der Antike bis in die Gegenwart: scripturus vitam: Festgabe für Walter Berschin zum 65. Geburtstag* (Heidelberg, 2002), pp. 49–58.

Rapp, Claudia, 'Byzantine Hagiographers as Antiquarians, Seventh to Tenth Centuries' in Stephanos Efthymiadis, Claudia Rapp and Dimitris Tsougarakis (eds), *Bosphorus: Essays in Honour of Cyril Mango* (Amsterdam: Hakkert, 1995), pp. 31–44.

— 'Desert, City, and Countryside in the early Christian Imagination' in *Church History and Religious Culture* 86 (2006), pp. 93–112.

— '"For next to God, you are my salvation": reflections on the rise of the holy man in late antiquity' in James Howard-Johnston and Paul Anthony Hayward (eds), *The Cult of Saints in Late Antiquity and the Early Middle Ages* (Oxford: Oxford University Press, 1999), pp. 63–81.

— 'Storytelling as Spiritual Communication in Early Greek Hagiography: the Use of *Diagesis*', *Journal of Early Christian Studies* 6 (1998), pp. 431–48.

— 'The Origins of Hagiography and the Literature of Early Monasticism: Purpose and Genre between Tradition and Innovation', Christopher Kelly, Richard Flower and Michael Stuart Williams (eds), *Unclassical Traditions: Alternatives to the Classical Past in Late Antiquity, Vol. 1* (Cambridge, 2010), pp. 119–38.

Rebenich, Stefan, 'Inventing an Ascetic Hero: Jerome's *Life of Paul the First Hermit*', in Andrew Cain and Josef Lössl (eds), *Jerome of Stridon: His Life, Writings and Legacy* (Farnham: Ashgate, 2009), pp. 13–28.

— *Jerome* (London: Routledge, 2002).

Régérat, Philippe, '*Vir Dei* als Leitbild in der Spätantike: Das Beispiel der *Vita Severini* des Eugippius' in Jürgen Dumner and Meinholf Vielberg (eds), *Zwischen Historiographie und Hagiographie* (Stuttgart: Steiner, 2005), pp. 61–78.

Ricoeur, Paul, *Time and Narrative*, translated by Kathleen McLaughlin and David Pellauer (3 vols, Chicago: University of Chicago Press, 1984–88).

Rollinson, Philip, *Classical Theories of Allegory and Christian Culture* (Pittsburg: Duquesne Univeristy Press, 1981).

Rombs, Ronnie J., *Saint Augustine and the Fall of the Soul: Beyond O'Connell and his Critics* (Washington: Catholic University Press, 2006).

Rosa, Fabio and Francesco Zambon (eds), *Pothos: Il viaggio, la nostalgia* (Trento: Dipartimento di Scienze Filologiche e Storiche, 1995).

Rothfield, Lawrence, 'Autobiography and Perspective in the *Confessions* of St. Augustine', *Comparative Literature*, 33.3 (1981), pp. 209–23.

Rousseau, Philip, *Ascetics, Authority and the Church in the Age of Jerome and Cassian* (Oxford: Oxford University Press, 1978).

— 'Retrospect: the "essential" Gregory' in Jostein Børtnes and Tomas Hägg (eds), *Gregory of Nazianzus: Images and Reflections* (Copenhagen, Museum Tusculanum, 2006), pp. 283–95.

Russell, D.A. (ed.), *Antonine Literature* (Oxford: Oxford University Press, 1990).

Said, Edward W., *Orientalism: Western Concepts of the Orient* (Harmondsworth: Penguin, 1971; repr. 1995).

Sartre, Jean-Paul, *Being and Nothingness*, translated by Mary Warnock (London: Methuen, 1989).

Scherliess, Carsten, *Literatur und Conversio: literarische Formen im monastichen Umkreis des Klosters von Lérins* (Frankfurt: Peter Lang, 2000).

Schnaubelt, Joseph C. and Frederick van Fleteren (eds), *Augustine 'Second Founder of the Faith'*, (New York: Peter Lang, 1990).

Schramm, Michael, 'Augustinus' *Confessiones* und die (Un)-Möglichkeit der Autobiographie', *Antike und Abendland* 54 (2008), pp. 173–92.

Schrift, Alan D. (ed.), *The Logic of the Gift: Towards an Ethic of Generosity* (London/New York: Routledge, 1997).

Schuol, Monika, Udo Hartmann and Andreas Luther (eds), *Grenzüberschreitungen: Formen des Kontakts zwischen Orient und Okzident im Altertum* (Stuttgart: Steiner, 2002).

Schwarz, Andreas, 'Severinus of Noricum between Fact and Fiction', in Walter Pohl and Maximilian Diesenberger (eds), *Eugippius und Severin* (Vienna: Verlag der Österreichischen Akademie der Wissenschaften, 2001), pp. 25–32.

Shakespeare, William, *The Tragedy of Richard III*, ed. Janis Lull (Cambridge: Cambridge University Press, 1999).

Shanzer, Danuta, 'Pears before Swine: Augustine, *Confessions* 2.4.9, in *Revue des études augustiniennes* 42 (1996), pp. 45–55.

Smith, Andrew (ed.), *The Philosopher and Society in Late Antiquity* (Swansea, 2005).

Smith, Rowland, *Julian's Gods: Religion and Philosophy in the Thought and Action of Julian the Apostate* (London/New York: Routledge, 1995).

Stancliffe, Clare, *Saint Martin and his Hagiographer* (Oxford: Oxford University Press, 1983).

Sterk, Andrea, *Renouncing the World yet Leading the Church: the Monk-Bishop in Late Antiquity* (Cambridge MA: Harvard University Press, 2004).

Strubel, Armand, '"Allegoria in factis" et "allegoria in verbis"' in *Poétique* 21 (1975), pp. 342–57.

Swanson, R.N. (ed.), *The Holy Land, Holy Lands and Christian History* (Woodbridge: Published for the Ecclesiastical History Society by Boydell & Brewer 2000).

Tardieu, Michel, *Les paysages reliques: routes et haltes syriennes d'Isidore à Simplicius* (Louvain/Paris: Peeters, 1990).

Taylor, Charles, *Varieties of Religion Today: William James Revisited* (Cambridge MA: Harvard University Press, 2002).

Thompson, E.A., *Romans and Barbarians: the Decline of the Western Empire* (Madison: University of Wisconsin Press, 1982).

Trout, Dennis E., 'Augustine at Cassiciacum: *Otium Honestum* and the Social Dimensions of Conversion' in *Vigiliae Christianae* 42 (1988), pp. 132–46.

Van Dam, Raymond, *Leadership and Community in Late Antique Gaul* (Berkeley: University of California Press, 1985).

— 'Self-Presentation in the Will of Gregory Nazianzus', *Journal of Theological Studies* 46 (1995), pp. 118–48.

Van den Berg, Robert '"Live unnoticed." The invisible Neoplatonic politician', in Andrew Smith (ed.), *The Philosopher and Society in Late Antiquity* (Swansea, 2005), pp. 101–16.

Van Uytfanghe, Marc, 'La Bible dans la *Vie de Saint Séverin* d'Eugippe' in *Latomus* 33.2 (1974), pp. 324–52.

Verdenius, W.J., *Mimesis: Plato's Doctrine of Artistic Imitation and its Meaning to Us* (Leiden: Brill, 1949).

Vessey, Mark, 'The Demise of the Christian Writer and the Remaking of "Late Antiquity": from H-I. Marrou's *Saint Augustin* (1938) to Peter Brown's Holy Man (1983)' in *Journal of Early Christian Studies* 6.1 (1998), pp. 377–411.

Villenueva, Darío, *Theories of Literary Realism* (Madrid, 1992), translated by Mihai I. Spariosu and Santiago García-Castanón (State University of New York Press, New York, 1997).

Von Albrecht, Michael (ed.), *Jamblich: Peri tou Pythagoreiou biou. Pythagoras: Legende – Lehre – Lebensgestaltung* (Darmstadt: Wissenschaftliche Buchgesellschaft, 2002).

Wallis, Richard T., *Neoplatonism* (London: Duckworth, 1972).

Walz, Dorothea (ed.), *Lateinische Biographie von der Antike bis in die Gegenwart: scripturus vitam: Festgabe für Walter Berschin zum 65. Geburtstag* (Heidelberg, 2002).

Ward, Benedicta, *Miracles and the Medieval Mind: Theory, Record and Event 1000–1215* (Philadelphia: University of Pennsylvania Press, 1982).

Watts, Edward J., 'Orality and Communal Identity in Eunapius' *Lives of the Sophists and Philosophers*', *Byzantion* 75 (2005), pp. 334–61.

— 'Student Travel to Intellectual Centers: what was the Attraction?' in Linda Ellis and Frank L. Kidner (eds), *Travel, Communication and Geography in Late Antiquity: Sacred and Profane* (Aldershot: Ashgate, 2004), pp. 13–24.

Weber, Max, *On Charisma and Institution Building: Selected Papers*, edited with an introduction by S.N. Eisenstadt (Chicago: University of Chicago Press, 1968).

Weiss, Jean-Pierre, 'Honorat héros antique et saint chrétien: étude du mot *gratia* dans la *Vie de Saint Honorat* d'Hilaire d'Arles', in *Augustinianum* 24 (1984), pp. 265–80.

Whitmarsh, Timothy, *Greek Literature and Roman Empire: The Politics of Imitation* (Oxford: Oxford University Press, 2001).

Whittaker, Helene, 'The purpose of Porphyry's letter to Marcella', in *Symbolae Osloenses* 76 (2001), pp. 150–68.

Williams, Bernard, *Truth and Truthfulness: an Essay in Genealogy* (Princeton: Princeton University Press, 2002).

Williams, Michael A. (ed.), *Charisma and Sacred Biography, Journal of the American Academy of Religion Studies* 48 (1982).

Williams, Michael Stuart, *Authorised Lives in Early Christian Biography* (Cambridge: Cambridge University Press, 2008).

Wiseman, Timothy Peter, 'Lying Historians: Seven Types of Mendacity', in Gill, Christopher and Wiseman, Timothy Peter (eds), *Lies and Fiction in the Ancient World* (Exeter: Exeter University Press, 1993), pp. 122–46.

Wolterstoff, Nicholas, 'God's Speaking and Augustine's Conversion' in Mann, William E. (ed.), *Augustine's* Confessions: *Critical Essays* (Oxford: Rowman and Littlefield, 2006), pp. 161–74.

Wood, Michael, 'Prologue', in Gill, Christopher and Wiseman, Timothy Peter (eds), *Lies and Fiction in the Ancient World* (Exeter: Exeter University Press, 1993), pp. xiii–xviii.

Woods, David, 'The Origin of Honoratus of Lérins' in *Mnemosyne* Series 4 46.1 (1993), pp. 78–86.

Unpublished Thesis

Buck, David Frederick, 'Eunapius of Sardis', Oxford D.Phil thesis (1977).

Index